W9-DFG-587

SIMONE DE BEAUVOIR:
A CRITICAL READER

Simone de Beauvoir: A Critical Reader is an invaluable collection of critical texts on Simone de Beauvoir's work, as a feminist, a novelist and an autobiographer. It includes key essays examining her fiction, her writings on her life and her most famous work, *The Second Sex*, by an outstanding list of contributors comprising: Toril Moi, Hazel Barnes, Elaine Marks, Alex Hughes, Judith Butler, Jane Heath, Anne Ophir, Eva Lundgren-Gothlin, Judith Okely, Sonia Kruks, Francis Jeanson.

In an informative and compelling introduction Elizabeth Fallaize contextualises the readings of Beauvoir within the evolution of feminism, and considers her changing role within contemporary culture and thought. She provides a timely reassessment of Beauvoir's significance over the decades and an understanding of why she continues to matter today.

This collection of critical writings on Simone de Beauvoir is an essential resource for students of twentieth-century culture, women's studies and modern literature.

Elizabeth Fallaize is a Fellow of St John's College, Oxford, and has written extensively on Simone de Beauvoir.

SIMONE DE BEAUVOIR: A CRITICAL READER

Edited by
Elizabeth Fallaize

London and New York

First published 1998
by Routledge
11 New Fetter Lane, London EC4P 4EE

Simultaneously published in the USA and Canada
by Routledge
29 West 35th Street, New York, NY 10001

Typeset in Galliard and Helvetica by
RefineCatch Limited, Bungay, Suffolk
Printed and bound in Great Britain by
TJ International Ltd, Padstow, Cornwall

British Library Cataloguing in Publication Data
A catalogue record for this book is available from the British Library

Library of Congress Cataloging in Publication Data
Simone de Beauvoir: a critical reader/[edited by] Elizabeth Fallaize.
Includes bibliographical references and index.
1. Beauvoir, Simone de, 1908–   —Criticism and interpretation.
I. Fallaize, Elizabeth.
PQ2603.E3627876   1998
848′.91409—dc21   97–44992
CIP

ISBN 0–415–14702–6 (hbk)
ISBN 0–415–14703–4 (pbk)

FOR MY SON, JACK DRISCOLL

CONTENTS

Readings of the fiction 155

ACKNOWLEDGEMENTS

I would like to thank Ursula Tidd for helpful comments on the introduction; Alice Driscoll for help with preparing the manuscript; and Alan Grafen for constant support.

The editor and publishers would like to thank the following sources for permission to reproduce material:

Judith Butler, 'Sex and Gender in Simone de Beauvoir's *Second Sex*' from *Yale French Studies* 72 (New Haven, Yale French Studies, 1986); reprinted by permission of Yale *French Studies*.

Jane Heath, '*She Came to Stay*: The Phallus Strikes Back' from Heath's *Simone de Beauvoir* (Brighton, Harvester, 1989); reprinted by permission of the author.

Alex Hughes, 'Murdering the Mother in *Memoirs of a Dutiful Daughter*' from *Yale French Studies* 48 (1994), reprinted by kind permission of The Society for French Studies.

Francis Jeanson, 'The Father in *Memoirs of a Dutiful Daughter*' from Jeanson's *Simone de Beauvoir ou l'enterprise de vivre* (Paris, Seuil, 1966); reprinted and translated by kind permission of Editions du Seuil.

Sonia Kruks, 'Beauvoir: The Weight of Situation' from *Signs* 18 (1992, pp. 89–110).

Eva Lundgren-Gothlin, 'The Master–Slave Dialectic in *The Second Sex*' from Lundgren-Gothlin's *Sex and Existence: Simone de Beauvoir's 'The Second Sex'*, translated by L. Schenck (London, Athlone, 1996, and Middleton, Wesleyan University Press, 1996); reprinted by kind permission of the Athlone Press and University Press of New England.

Elaine Marks, 'Encounters with Death in *A Very Easy Death*' from Marks' *Simone de Beauvoir: Encounters with Death* (New Brunswick, Rutgers University Press, 1973); reprinted by permission of Rutgers University Press; and 'The Body in Decline in *Adieux: A Farewell to Sartre*' from *Yale French Studies* 72 (New Haven, Yale French Studies, 1986); reprinted by permission of Yale French Studies.

Toril Moi, 'Independent Women' and 'Narratives of Liberation' from Moi's

Simone de Beauvoir: The Making of an Intellectual Woman (Oxford, Blackwell, 1994); reprinted by permission of Blackwell Publishers.

Judith Okely, 'Rereading *The Second Sex*' from Okely's *Simone de Beauvoir: A Re-Reading* (London, Virago, 1986); reprinted by permission of the author.

Anne Ophir, 'Mythical Discourse in "The Woman Destroyed"' from Ophir's *Regards féminins: Beauvoir, Etcherelli, Rochefort* (Paris, Denoël, 1976); reprinted and translated by permission of Editions Denoël.

INTRODUCTION

Elizabeth Fallaize

The name of Simone de Beauvoir has come to be synonymous with the feminist voice of the twentieth century. Signalling both the life of an exceptional woman, and her status as a towering figure in the history of women's emancipation, her name has attracted such a volatile mix of adulation and hostility, even within feminism itself, that her life and writing have continued to inspire passionate debate. The purpose of this collection of critical responses to a wide range of Beauvoir's writing is to explore the changing nature of that debate, to offer a sense of the differing cultural and theoretical assumptions which readers have brought to their engagement with Beauvoir's work, and to give a sense of why her writing continues to matter to readers today.

Beauvoir was deeply committed to writing: her published work spans more than four decades and takes a wide variety of forms, including the philosophical essay, the novel, drama, autobiography, travel writing, correspondence, newspaper articles and interviews. The first part of this introduction presents a chronological overview of her writing career, together with an indication of how her work was received by her contemporary readers; a second part examines the general issue of the reception of Beauvoir as a woman writer, and the final part turns to questions in the wider critical field, focusing on three main strands of Beauvoir's writing – the autobiographical, her seminal essay *The Second Sex*, and her fiction.

Beauvoir's writing career

Beauvoir's first published work, the novel *She Came to Stay*, appeared in the autumn of 1943, in occupied Paris. Her long held ambition to be a writer had at last been achieved: 'I had written a real book . . . – I had become, overnight, a real writer. I could not contain my joy,' she later recorded in her autobiography.[1] Born on 9 January 1908, into a conservative bourgeois milieu, Beauvoir was 35 when the novel was published and was well launched on a life of unusual independence which bore little resemblance to her parents' original ambitions for her. Benefiting from a crisis in her family's finances, she had taken and brilliantly succeeded in the prestigious *agrégation de philosophie* examination which had

1

enabled her to earn her own living from teaching posts that she had first at a lycée in Marseilles, then in Rouen and, from 1936, in Paris.[2] Occupying a series of cheap hotel rooms, she had a minimum of domestic obligations and devoted most of her waking hours to writing, teaching and leading an intense emotional life within a close group of intimate friends. Her immediate circle consisted of her former pupils Olga Kosakiewicz and Nathalie Sorokine, Jacques-Laurent Bost, a former pupil of Sartre's, and Jean-Paul Sartre himself, returned from a prisoner-of-war camp in Germany in 1941, and installed on a different floor of the same rather miserable hotel. Sartre had entered Beauvoir's life when they were both preparing for the *agrégation* examination and he was never to leave it, despite the complex web of relationships in which the couple involved themselves.

Until the outbreak of the Second World War, Beauvoir had taken little interest in politics. As a woman in France she was debarred from voting, but in any case she and Sartre were more directly concerned with metaphysical than political freedom. The Spring of 1939, and the subsequent outbreak of war, revolutionised her attitude and she discovered with a shock that historical forces were a reality.[3] However, her first novel had been conceived in the period of her refusal to countenance the idea of historical and social pressures and deals with the metaphysical and personal threat of another human being rather than with the threat of war itself. Both an exploration of the Hegelian dictum 'Each consciousness pursues the death of the other', and a fictionalised account of the trio which she and Sartre formed with Olga Kosakiewicz, the text plays out a highly charged set of psycho-sexual conflicts, expressed in a strongly philosophical vocabulary. Beauvoir was justifiably delighted by her first reviews which spoke warmly of the novel, although she was irritated to find herself criticised on the grounds of the immorality of her characters' behaviour: 'this finicky mock modesty took me by surprise: there is really so little bedroom stuff in *She Came to Stay!*'[4]

Within two years of this modest and much awaited success, Beauvoir had become a major intellectual figure in post-Liberation Paris. Her rapid rise was directly linked to the intellectual fashionability of existentialism. The long discussions on the subject of freedom which Sartre had held with her throughout the 1930s, and which he had continued to work on and correspond with Beauvoir about in the early years of the war, had culminated in 1943 in the publication of *Being and Nothingness*. Beauvoir had worked over every page of the manuscript with Sartre, and frequently restated her intellectual adherence to its general framework. The extent to which she actually disagreed with elements of the theory, and to which she was obliged to modify it when she wanted to use it for her own purposes, has give rise to considerable debate, but there can be little doubt that she was both intellectually and emotionally committed to the work. Existentialism became the dominant philosophy in French intellectual circles and was to remain so throughout the 1940s and into the 1950s. In the euphoria of post-Liberation Paris, Beauvoir and Sartre rapidly gained celebrity status, and their unconventional lifestyle was widely commented on.

After the war she did not return to teaching, devoting herself instead to *Les*

Temps modernes, the journal which she and Sartre set up as a forum for left-wing discussion, and to writing in quick succession two further novels, *The Blood of Others* (1945) and *All Men Are Mortal* (1946), and her only play, *Who Shall Die?* (1945). During the 1940s she also wrote a number of important philosophical essays, examining a series of ethical and ontological problems within the phenomenological and existential traditions. *Pyrrhus et Cinéas* (1944) addresses the ethical problem of the individual's relation to others, whilst *The Ethics of Ambiguity* (1947) examines the individual as situated and ambiguous subject. Both texts have recently been receiving renewed critical attention as part of a reassessment of Beauvoir as a philosopher.[5]

Despite the public attention which Beauvoir was receiving in the postwar period, the critical reception of her work was decidedly mixed. *The Blood of Others* focuses on the moral dilemmas of a Resistance leader; it sold well and was initially warmly received. Beauvoir was pleased when Camus described it as a 'fraternal book' and its uncompromising support for extreme action in the face of Occupation matched the mood of many of its readers. However, this response proved to be short-lived, and Beauvoir was further discomforted by the reception which met *All Men Are Mortal*, a long and demanding novel dealing with the philosophical and ethical questions raised by immortality within a dialectical view of history. It was little understood and almost universally declared to be a disappointment. Perhaps it was hardly possible for Beauvoir's published work to match the hubris of her presumed lifestyle.

In 1947 she spent five months in the United States on a lecture tour. On her return she published her impressions in *America Day by Day* (1948), a lively and favourably received account which voices her criticisms of incipient racism and Fascism in America, though it omits the fact that she had fallen in love. Her relationship with the American writer Nelson Algren, which lasted until 1951, created a major crisis in her life and provided some of the material for *The Mandarins* (1954). It also coincided with the greater part of the writing of *The Second Sex*, for by 1946 Beauvoir had become interested in the situation of women. Planning to write something autobiographical, she had begun to ask herself 'What has it meant to me to be a woman?'[6] Attempting to answer this crucial question became so deeply absorbing that Beauvoir dropped her autobiographical project and began work on an essay which was to become an onslaught on contemporary ideas about women and a founding text of the women's movement in the second half of the twentieth century. 'I began to look at women with new eyes and found surprise after surprise waiting for me. It is both strange and stimulating to discover suddenly, after forty, an aspect of the world that has been staring you in the face all the time which somehow you have never noticed.'[7] The discrepancy between Beauvoir's initial amazement at her discoveries, and the extent to which readers today find some of her arguments self-evident, is a measure both of how radical her theses were in the context of 1940s France and of the way in which those same ideas have forced themselves into received thinking. How was Beauvoir able to engage in such a radical and ambitious enterprise? Clearly her own exceptional status as an intellectual woman provides one element of the answer; the intellectual support which she received from Sartre and her general intellectual milieu is another. Toril Moi has pointed out that the subject of women allowed Beauvoir to pursue the question of freedom on her own terrain, whilst at the same time ostensibly employing Sartre's intellectual framework. And, as Moi persuasively adds, it also allowed for an extensive discussion of the very difficulties of uniting love and freedom with which Beauvoir was struggling in her personal life.[8]

The first volume of Beauvoir's ambitious, multidisciplinary essay containing sections on biology, psychoanalysis, Marxism, history and mythology appeared in June 1949. It was received with considerable interest and sold well over twenty thousand copies in the first week. However, in May, June and July, extracts from the second volume on 'The Sexual Initiation of Women', 'The Lesbian', and 'Maternity' appeared in *Les Temps modernes*, and the second volume itself was published in November. Both publications caused a storm in the press, although the volume sold as well as the first. The Catholic writer François Mauriac led a campaign lasting several months in *Le Figaro littéraire* to get young people to condemn pornography in general and *The Second Sex* in particular.[9] Beauvoir received sackfuls of letters from men offering to cure her of her frigidity or, alternatively, of her nymphomania. Even well-meaning commentators called it 'courageous', while many others suggested that Beauvoir suffered from an inferiority complex and had evident difficulties in dealing with her sexuality.

Beauvoir writes in her memoirs that though she had never before been conscious of having been attacked as a woman this was henceforth to become a recurrent pattern, and one she saw as being a direct result of her questioning of male superiority and her claim that many French women were unhappy with their sexual lives.[10] In fact, it seems that contemporary women readers as well as men were struck by the frank discussion of female sexuality which the book contained, despite the fact that the recently published Kinsey report had made serious public discussion of sexuality possible. French writer and critic Nicole Ward-Jouve writes that her grandmother enjoyed the book as a bawdy read; when *The Second Sex* was recommended to Blanche Knopf, part of the husband and wife team of publishers who eventually published an English translation of the book in the United States, she was led to understand that it was a 'modern-day sex manual, something between Kinsey and Havelock Ellis'.[11]

Beauvoir's name had thus become synonymous with public notoriety; the discussion of sexuality obscured the political thrust of the book which, even when it was understood, seems to have created limited contemporary impact. As a recent introductory text to feminism incisively remarks, the book 'lay ticking like a time-bomb, waiting for a new generation of rebellious women to discover when they burst upon the scene'.[12] Beauvoir, meanwhile, returned to fiction writing, and this time with considerable public success since *The Mandarins*, published in 1954, won the Prix Goncourt, France's most prestigious literary award. This long, rich and complex novel examining the political and moral dilemmas of a fictional group of left-wing French intellectuals in the postwar period struck a deep chord in a France conscious of having become a bit player on the world stage in the era of the Cold War, shocked by its defeat in Indo-China, and on the verge of a new conflict in Algeria.[13] Beauvoir was only the third woman ever to receive this annual prize, first awarded in 1902.

Although a Communist sympathiser during the 1940s, Beauvoir had not hitherto been a political activist. In the early 1950s she moved much closer to Marxism, partly as a result of her debates with Claude Lanzmann, who shared with her for several years the studio behind the Montparnasse cemetery which she bought with the proceeds of the Prix Goncourt. During the 1950s she visited China and the Soviet Union, and published *The Long March* (1957), an enthusiastic essay on Communist China, which was not well received, especially in the United States. She rejoiced at the defeat of the French in Vietnam and involved herself heavily in the campaign against French atrocities in Algeria. In 1962, in collaboration with Gisèle Halimi, she published a book entitled *Djamila Boupacha*, denouncing the systematic use of torture by the French in Algeria by focusing on the case of a young Algerian girl arrested and tortured by the French authorities. A year later she wrote in *Force of Circumstance* that 'the horror my class inspires in me has been brought to a white heat by the Algerian War'.[14]

A new phase opened up in Beauvoir's writing life in 1958 when she published *Memoirs of a Dutiful Daughter*, an account of her early life up to the late 1920s. It was so well received, and had such high sales, that Beauvoir was encouraged to go on to write two further bestselling volumes, *The Prime of Life* (1960) and *Force of Circumstance* (1963). The latter made a strong mark on the way in which Beauvoir was perceived by her reading public because of the famous last line in which she writes that she feels let down by life. Intended to convey the political point that she had been led to imagine as a child that the world was a place of happiness and opportunity when, in fact, it is a place of starving and warring humanity, her statement was widely understood as an admission of defeat and failure in the face of old age. *A Very Easy Death* (1964), an account of the death of her mother and a retrospective reflection on the nature of their relationship, again both proved extremely popular and created controversy as she was accused of using her own mother's death to demonstrate a point about wealth and privilege in French society. The seeds of the public image of an unfeeling Beauvoir, never parted from her notebook at the most emotional or delicate of moments, were planted here, ready to flourish nearly twenty years later when she came to publish an account of Sartre's last years.

However, in 1966 and 1967 she returned to fiction with first a short text, *Les Belles Images*, followed by the three short stories of *The Woman Destroyed*. Although they sold very well, and are clearly amongst the most sophisticated and literary of Beauvoir's fictional texts, they were dismissed as superficial by many critics who failed to grasp the radical new tack which Beauvoir's fictional writing had taken. Humour and irony are deployed in *Les Belles Images* to deconstruct the marvellous new world of the 1960s French bourgeoisie, smugly installed in its own certainties and technocratic values. The social and linguistic formation of a class is cruelly scrutinised. In *The Woman Destroyed* Beauvoir again places her narrative in the hands of characters who unwittingly condemn themselves as they speak; the focus on women goes bleakly hand in hand with a focus on self-deception. Beauvoir's change of focus and technique can be traced to a number of factors: the writing of her autobiographical volumes may have palliated her need to write about situations close to her own, as she had done in *The Mandarins*; her change of technique is also undoubtedly linked to the consciousness of inadequacies in the traditional novel form which the practitioners of the new novel had brought about during the 1950s, although Beauvoir was sharply critical of their refusal to deal with political realities. More generally, there had been a shift in the intellectual climate since the heyday of existentialism. In the 1960s the younger generation of structuralists and post-structuralists radically contested Beauvoir and Sartre's belief in human freedom and agency – Beauvoir parodies Foucault in *Les Belles Images*, underlining the political dangers of a philosophy of the 'death of man'.

The end of the 1960s and the beginning of the 1970s opened up an extremely active and involved period of Beauvoir's life. The events of May 1968 and the period of turmoil which followed gave her a new political role, supporting the students and lending her name to banned revolutionary newspapers. She researched and wrote an important new essay on the constructions of old age in western society, *Old Age* (1970), arguing that the treatment meted out to the old is the proof that our society requires completely recasting. In the early 1970s she found herself approached by members of the newly formed women's movement asking her to join them in their campaign to change the abortion laws. More than twenty years after *The Second Sex* Beauvoir publicly declared herself to be a feminist, affirming in an interview in 1972 in *Le Nouvel Observateur* that she no longer believed that a socialist revolution would be sufficient to bring about women's liberation. 'Women must take their destiny into their own hands,' she declared: campaigning on abortion, contraception and battered women, setting up a regular column in *Les Temps modernes* on sexism, launching with other Marxist feminists a journal, *Questions féministes*, she engaged in a feminist practice which would have been unthinkable at the time of writing *The Second Sex*.[15]

Despite all this activity, Beauvoir's writing life, and the controversy it had so often created, was far from over. In 1981, a year after Sartre's death, Beauvoir published an account of his last ten years, translated as *Adieux: A Farewell to Sartre*; it was received in the French press as a round in the battle between herself and Sartre's adopted daughter and literary executor, Arlette El Kaïm-Sartre, for control of Sartre's image. There was indignation at the details given of Sartre's physical diminution, seen less as evidence of Beauvoir's determination to record and be observant of all circumstances of life than as a desire to diminish the man. The publication of the *Lettres au Castor*, the letters Sartre had written to her (1983) and, after Beauvoir's own death, of her *Letters to Sartre* (1990) and her *Journal de guerre* (1990), written in the early years of the war, led to a torrent of

6

criticism, as the extent to which the two had plotted and discussed their sexual adventures at the expense of the emotions of others became clear.[16] However, in 1997 a deeply passionate Beauvoir re-emerged with the publication of three hundred and four letters written to Nelson Algren. Charting the progress of their relationship between 1947 and 1964, the letters are a heartfelt record of the sway which feelings and emotions always held over this most intellectual of women. Her death, on 14 April 1986, commanded worldwide attention and there was general recognition of the simple epitaph expressed in a newspaper headline on the day following her final disappearance: 'Women, you owe her everything'.[17]

The critical field: reading the woman writer

In what ways, and to what extent, has critical reaction to Simone de Beauvoir's work been marked by the fact that she is a woman writer, and one, moreover, whose name is synonymous with modern feminism? Little serious critical attention has been given to the development of a gendered reception theory; however, it is possible to identify some key issues in the reception of Beauvoir's work which can help us go some way towards a response. It is notable, first of all, that a substantial fraction of serious academic studies devoted to Beauvoir's work display a quite extraordinary antipathy to their subject. Toril Moi contends that 'Comparable French women writers are not treated in this way: nothing in the criticism of say, Simone Weil, Marguerite Yourcenar, Marguerite Duras or Nathalie Sarraute matches the frequency and intensity of virulence displayed by so many of Simone de Beauvoir's critics.'[18] In the introduction to a book written in French and published in 1976, Anne Ophir asks pointedly: 'Who's afraid of Simone de Beauvoir?'[19] Moi goes on to identify a number of recurrent stereotypes which are used to discredit Beauvoir as a speaker (in place of entering into an engagement with her work) and Moi's point is that Beauvoir is routinely subjected to this treatment because she claims to speak as an intellectual woman.[20] The claim by a woman to engage in serious intellectual activity, and in philosophy in particular, is thus posited as a central challenge to patriarchy.

Moi's case is a powerful one because it goes to the heart of the problem of the speaking position of the author of *The Second Sex*. There is also the question of the speaking position of the critic. The great majority of the critical pieces collected in this volume have been written by Anglo-American women, and this is arguably a fair representation of the critical field. As recently as 1987 Elaine Marks, a highly respected American academic and critic, drew attention to the academic risk involved in pursuing research on women writers; it is evident, both in the example of her own earlier work included in this volume and, to a lesser extent, in a 1961 piece by Hazel Barnes, that the critic is struggling with an anxiety about her choice of author.[21] The overall paucity of French criticism suggests that the French academic environment is even less hospitable to such a choice. The sharp rise in Beauvoir studies in the 1990s suggests, fortunately, that response to her work is unlikely to be hampered by this difficulty in the future.

A central issue which has clearly always been present in both the production and the reception of Beauvoir's work is the question of her identification with Sartre.[22] On the one hand he undoubtedly offered intellectual nurturance and made her access to male-dominated intellectual circles easier;[23] on the other, Beauvoir's critical reputation has both suffered with his and has been affected by her being always considered a disciple. The vivacity of the current critical debate about the extent to which Beauvoir and Sartre borrowed from each other's work is itself a demonstration of the impatience which the master–disciple scenario has created in Beauvoirean criticism.

A second issue, which has marked the reception of Beauvoir's work and which seems likely to be closely related to her as a woman writer, is the stress given to the sexual content of her writing. From *She Came to Stay* to *The Second Sex* her work is represented as being strongly sexual in nature, and not just in France. Kate Millett has described reading the translation of *The Second Sex* in Oxford: 'I read it shortly after it came out. It was a very disturbing book. In fact, early editions often had nude ladies on the cover and it almost had a sort of mischievous cachet. Apparently it was so subversive that it got mixed up with being a little sexy too.'[24] Another American critic described it as 'probably the best manual of instruction on making love now available in English'.[25] François Mauriac is famous for having said that the book had made him entirely familiar with Beauvoir's vagina.[26] Taking account of the different circumstances of these readers of Beauvoir's work, it is hard to imagine that such a universal stress on the sexual would have greeted the work had it been written by a man. Later, the English translation of *The Mandarins* was cut to leave out some sexual details. In the context of contemporary writing by Henry Miller or Jean Genet, a reading of Beauvoir's texts focusing on the sexual seems curiously skewed.

Two further issues are relevant. The first is the question of what subjects women write about. Beauvoir was so aware of the danger of being dismissed as a writer of 'ladies' books', as she put it, that she was determined to underline her own distance from such parochial pursuits and stressed the universal, philosophical aspects of her work rather than the personal ones.[27] It has often been remarked that the accounts of her work which Beauvoir gives in her autobiography are excessively self-critical; these can also be seen as an expression of her apprehensiveness about her reception. Connected to the question of subject matter is the question of singularity. Historically speaking, so few women writers have gained a critical standing in France that those who do may appear strangely anomalous. Beauvoir's work cannot be fitted into a tradition of French women's writing and has largely been read against works by her male contemporaries, as indeed she would have wished. This undoubtedly contributed to critical astonishment at, and rejection of, her switch to 'women's subjects' in her final two pieces of fiction. It may also be another partial explanation for the fact that critical reaction to her work is much more subdued in France than it is outside it.[28]

Beauvoir's switch of subjects raises a final question relating to gender and reception. Before the writing of *The Second Sex*, it is highly doubtful whether

Beauvoir ever considered the question of the gender of her readership. In so far as her immediate circle of intimates provided a model of her reader, that model was likely to be male. However, Beauvoir records in her memoirs her surprise and pleasure at the warmth of the post bag she received from women readers of *The Second Sex*. She writes:

> I should have been surprised and even irritated if, when I was thirty, someone had told me that I would be concerning myself with feminine problems, and that my most serious public would be made up of women. I don't regret that it has been so. Divided, lacerated in a world made to put them at a disadvantage, for women there are far more victories to be won, more prizes to be gained, more defeats to be suffered than there are for men. I have an interest in them; and I prefer having taken a limited but real hold upon the world through them to drifting in the universal.[29]

This is a radical declaration for Beauvoir; this new view of who her readers were and in what terms she could speak to them seems to have played a role both in her decision to begin her autobiography, in which she speaks of herself as a woman, and in her decision to write about and for women in her last two works of fiction.[30]

Readers of *The Second Sex*

At the time of its publication in France, *The Second Sex* appears to have had more of a personal effect on individual readers than a more general intellectual or political impact. Its status as a daringly sexy book may have blunted its political edge and the French climate was particularly inimical to the language of women's rights. However, after the publication of the English translation, in 1953, a generation of American and English women read the book and used Beauvoir's work as their inspiration, even when they did not always acknowledge it. Betty Friedan, whose *The Feminine Mystique* (1963) is usually credited with having launched the American women's movement, offered her readers a popularised and sanitised version of many of Beauvoir's analyses; more than a decade later she admitted that reading *The Second Sex* in the early 1950s, 'led me to whatever original analysis of women's existence I have been able to contribute to the Women's movement and to its unique politics. I looked to Simone de Beauvoir for a philosophical and intellectual authority.'[31] Kate Millett, Shulamith Firestone, Juliet Mitchell, Ann Oakley and Germaine Greer similarly read the translation and took up and developed some of Beauvoir's ideas, generally to more radical effect. They dedicated their work to her, visited Paris to meet Beauvoir and turned to her for help at times of crisis. In France, by contrast, the schism in French feminism which took place early in the history of the post-1968 women's movement had the effect that whilst French radical and Marxist feminists continued to work alongside Beauvoir, both they and *The Second Sex* were eclipsed by the influential group of theorists who rose to dominance in the 1970s. Hélène Cixous, Luce Irigaray and Julia Kristeva developed their theories of female difference in a philosophical tradition drawing on Derrida, Lacan and Foucault which was alien to Beauvoir's belief in individual agency and freedom.[32]

Despite the relative invisibility of *The Second Sex* in France, Beauvoir's multi-disciplinary work was elsewhere providing inspiration to a host of branches of feminist enquiry. Feminist theorists, literary critics, historians, philosophers, theologians, critics of scientific discourse and even psychotherapists have drawn and continue to draw on Beauvoir's seminal analyses.[33] As science historian Donna Haraway writes, 'despite important differences, all the modern feminist meanings of gender have roots in Simone de Beauvoir's claim that "one is not born a woman"'.[34] Beauvoir's famous distinction between sex and gender has also been developed in unexpected and radical directions. Monique Wittig, one of the French feminists of the strand of the movement with which Beauvoir worked in the 1970s, developed Beauvoir's postulate to lesbian political ends in a famous essay of 1981 entitled 'One Is Not Born a Woman'.[35] Wittig has no truck with any concept of sex based on biology, arguing that 'man' and 'woman' are political categories which should be abolished. Judith Butler has also given Beauvoir's distinction a startling tack, arguing that Beauvoir's use of the verb 'become' suggests that gender choice is a constantly renewed act, an interplay of individual choice and acculturation.[36]

There are undoubtedly problems for feminists in reading *The Second Sex* today. Beauvoir's unconsciously ethnocentric assumptions, her tendency to overestimate men and masculinity, the apparent distaste displayed by the text for some aspects of the female body, and her lack of interest in the maternal, appear at odds with contemporary preoccupations and sensitivities. Yet, as feminist theory finds itself at something of a crossroads, there is considerable evidence of a renewed interest in *The Second Sex* as a possible way forward. Thus Toril Moi writes in 1994:

> In an intellectual field dominated by identity politics, *The Second Sex* represents a real challenge to established dogmas: if we are to escape from current political and theoretical dead ends, feminism in the 1990s cannot afford to ignore Beauvoir's pioneering insights.[37]

Moi argues that Beauvoir develops a strikingly original theory of female subjectivity under patriarchy which offers an analysis of how patriarchal power structures are at work in the construction of female subjectivity. Beauvoir also offers, as Moi argues in the piece included in this volume, an extraordinary vision of freedom, a vision of an alternative to the status quo of the kind which every political movement requires. Sonia Kruks has argued along similar lines to Moi that Beauvoir can help with the impasse of choice between the 'unhappy alternatives' of a feminism based on an Enlightenment subject and the postmodern attempt to get rid of the subject itself. She shows in the piece included here how Beauvoir's account of situated subjectivity allows both for the responsibility and possibility of political action, and, simultaneously, for the constraints of oppression. A crucial element which *The Second Sex* offers us today is thus the hope of a way through between essentialism and the postmodern dissolution of the subject. On the one hand the growth of identity politics implies a theory and practice which is always embedded in an essentialist group identity and experience. On the other, the postmodern understanding of gender dissolves the individual subject and locates the feminine in discursive practices and institutional frameworks. Beauvoir's confidence in the possibility of action together with a freely constructed identity offers an attractive alternative.

In clearing the way for the return to Beauvoir, a number of recent readers of *The Second Sex* have been concerned to remove long-held misapprehensions about her work, to emphasise her philosophical approach and, in particular, to move her away from a total fidelity to Sartre's existentialist framework. Re-readings of Beauvoir's philosophical essays, as well of *The Second Sex* itself, have underlined her phenomenological method, her deployment of a materialist rather than a strictly ontological analysis of oppression, her recognition of the embodied nature of consciousness and her concern with establishing a basis for fruitful interaction between individual freedoms.[38] As Karen Vintges has recently written, *The Second Sex* suffered for many years from the fate of being at one and the same time 'one of the most criticised *and* one of the least read works in feminism'.[39] Its fate is rapidly changing.

Readers of the autobiography

In a stimulating essay entitled *What Does a Woman Want?* (1993) Shoshana Felman recasts and indirectly answers Freud's infamous question by strongly underlining women's need for 'a female sharing and exchange of stories'. 'Only women', she goes on, 'can *empower* women's story *to become a story*' and 'each woman's story can become a story only through women's collective perception of themselves'.[40] Simone de Beauvoir's narrative of her girlhood and adolescence, her escape from the traditional class and gender roles which awaited her, her fulfilment of her ambition to become a writer, the years spent at the centre of intellectual Parisian life, her friendships, her passions and love affairs, as well as the darker side of her sufferings, her emotions at the time of her mother's death, and the death of Sartre, her own experience of growing old – all this offers her reader a female story which is both emblematic, in its account of a twentieth-century woman's bid for freedom, and yet exceptional, since so few women have publicly chronicled their lives in this way. The volumes of her memoirs have always attracted her largest readership and they remain immensely popular today. It would indeed be difficult for the reader not to be seduced by the subject position of an elegant Beauvoir, sitting in the Café de Flore in Montparnasse, with Sartre or Olga, a cocktail in one hand and a pen in the other.

11

It is undeniable that there is a strong autobiographical current running through much of Beauvoir's writing – *The Second Sex* itself began life as an autobiographical project and even in its final form draws heavily on Beauvoir's own experiences and those of her friends and acquaintances. The early novels equally rework many of the emotional and political dramas through which their author lived. Yet the memoirs have a different status and create the possibility of a different kind of reading bond because Beauvoir speaks them in her own name and offers an explicit guarantee of their authenticity, if not of their completeness. For some readers she nevertheless spoke too frankly – Nelson Algren never forgave her for describing their relationship in vivid detail.[41] Like all autobiographers, Beauvoir does not offer us an impartial version of her life. Autobiography 'made as many demands on my powers of imagination and reflection as it did on my memory,' she writes in *Force of Circumstance*.[42] Critics have found suspect her insistence on her escape from her genteel background, her relentless construction of her couple with Sartre as superior to and untouched by the couple's other emotional entanglements, and her silence over the sexual nature of some of her friendships with women. Yet the self-creation of the memoirs is one of its most crucial aspects, permitting her to 'create a coherent identity for herself', as Karen Vintges puts it, and elaborate possibilities for her readers.[43]

The memoirs have also been read (too frequently) as an oblique biography of Sartre, and, more interestingly, as a testimonial narrative in which Beauvoir bears witness to the major events of her times, from the Occupation, the Holocaust and the Algerian War, to May '68 and the women's movement.[44] The critics represented in this collection have focused their attention above all on the construction of relationships within the narrative – with her father, Beauvoir's intellectual role model, with her mother, with her childhood friend Elisabeth Mabille (Zaza), whose death Beauvoir represents as the antithesis and in some ways the price of her own escape, and, finally, with Sartre.

Readers of the fiction

Beauvoir's childhood ambition to become a writer stemmed from her own early reading of fiction. At 15 she read, in English, George Eliot's *The Mill on the Floss*, which 'made an even deeper impression on me than *Little Women*'; identifying herself with Maggie Tulliver and, through the heroine, with the author, Beauvoir vowed that 'one day other adolescents would bathe with their tears a novel in which I would tell my own sad story'.[45] Novels seemed to her to be the 'dizzy summits' of writing, a genre in which 'the most celebrated women had distinguished themselves'.[46] Thirty years later she wrote in *The Prime of Life*: 'Perhaps the most profound desire I entertain today is that people should repeat in silence certain words that I have been the first to link together.'[47]

An acute consciousness of the relationship between reader and text is thus at the heart of Beauvoir's fictional enterprise. Her memoirs are peppered with references to letters received from readers, which she often answered, and she drew great satisfaction from the fact that most of her fictional texts were – and continue to be – bestsellers. Yet academic readers of Beauvoir's fiction have tended, by and large, to harness it to Beauvoir's other work: the first study to appear was in French, by Geneviève Gennari in 1958, examining the four novels Beauvoir had then published as an interlocking whole with her philosophical essays. In English Hazel Barnes, in 1961, published an excellent philosophical reading of Beauvoir's first novel, which has been highly influential. Later studies tended to be thematic, focusing on death, nature, politics; from the mid-1970s onwards, the first generation of feminist studies began to appear, reading the fiction in the light of *The Second Sex*, or in the context of new feminist debates. More recently, the novels and short stories have begun to receive a more diverse treatment within a variety of theoretical frameworks drawing on the work of Freud, Lacan, Bachelard, Barthes, Kristeva, Benveniste and Genette. Broadly speaking, a psychoanalytic approach (of varying schools) has proved extremely fruitful.

Critical readings have tended to cluster on two of Beauvoir's fictional works: her first novel, *She Came to Stay* (1943), and her last fictional work, the collection of three short stories entitled *The Woman Destroyed* (1967). The two present an interesting contrast; the first is a dense novel of four hundred pages, written before *The Second Sex*, narrated in the third person and presenting a small group of Parisian intellectuals caught up in an intense psycho-sexual conflict with strong Hegelian overtones. The principal woman emerges strong and victorious. The second text is a loosely constituted collection of three short stories, each narrated by a middle-aged woman struggling with a situation of her own making from which there appears to be little escape. Language, writing and identity are central concerns. The readings collected in the final section of this volume echo the critical clustering of focus on these two texts in order to give the reader a sense of the breadth and divergence of response to these engaging fictions.

'Women', wrote Beauvoir in *The Second Sex*, 'still dream through the dreams of men'.[48] Far from being utopian, Beauvoir's fictional writing is rooted in daily existence, yet it forges stories and dreams which continue to fascinate her readers. Annie Ernaux, one of France's best-known contemporary writers, wrote of her mother in the closing paragraphs of *Une Femme* (1987): 'She died a week before Simone de Beauvoir'.[49] This poignant homage to Beauvoir shows her legacy still unfolding.

Notes

1 S. de Beauvoir, *The Prime of Life*, translated by P. Green, Harmondsworth, Penguin, 1986, p.556.
2 Beauvoir's teaching career came to an abrupt end in 1943 when she was dismissed from her post after a complaint made by the parents of one of her pupils, Nathalie Sorokine, about Beauvoir's immoral influence over their daughter. After the war she was offered reinstatement but preferred to devote herself to writing.
3 See Beauvoir, *The Prime of Life*, p.359.
4 Ibid., p.557.

5 See for example D. Bergoffen, *The Philosophy of Simone de Beauvoir: Gendered Phenomenologies, Erotic Generosities*, Albany, SUNY Press, 1996; K. Vintges, *Philosophy as Passion. The Thinking of Simone de Beauvoir*, Bloomington, Indiana University Press, 1996; E. and K. Fullbrook, *Beauvoir: A Critical Introduction*, Cambridge, Polity Press, 1998.

6 See S. de Beauvoir, *Force of Circumstance*, translated by Richard Howard, Harmondsworth, Penguin, 1985, p.103.

7 Ibid., p.195.

8 T. Moi, *Simone de Beauvoir. The Making of an Intellectual Woman*, Oxford, Blackwell, 1994, pp.189–90.

9 On 18 June 1949 Mauriac addressed a public question to young writers and intellectuals through the columns of *Le Figaro*, formulated in the following terms: 'Do you believe that the systematic recourse to instinctual forces and to insanity in literature, and the exploitation of eroticism which it has encouraged, constitute a danger to the individual, to the nation, to literature itself, and that certain persons, certain doctrines, carry the responsibility for this?' *Le Figaro*, 18 June 1949, p.1. This scarcely veiled reference to Sartre and existentialism is followed up in an editorial of 25 June in which Mauriac writes: 'Is the subject treated by Madame Simone de Beauvoir, "The sexual initiation of women" in the right place in the contents list of a serious philosophical and literary review?' *Le Figaro littéraire* 25 June, p.1. Mauriac's campaign clearly disappointed him; he concludes sadly on 6 August that even eminent Catholics have defended Beauvoir's courage in treating lesbianism and sexual initiation.

10 Beauvoir, *Force of Circumstance*, pp.198–200.

11 N. Ward-Jouve, *White Woman Speaks with Forked Tongue. Criticism as Auto-biography*, London, Routledge, 1991, p.109. See D. Bair, *Simone de Beauvoir: A Biography*, London, Jonathan Cape, 1990, p.432.

12 S. Watkins, M. Rueda and M. Rodriguez, *Feminism for Beginners*, Cambridge, Icon Books, 1992, p.98.

13 The reception of *The Mandarins* has been studied in an interesting and useful book by Bjorn Larsson, *La Réception des Mandarins*, Lund, 1988.

14 Beauvoir, *Force of Circumstance*, p.665.

15 The article is reprinted in A. Schwartzer, *Simone de Beauvoir Today, Conversations 1972–1982*, London, Chatto, 1984.

16 The publication of the letters and diary in their turn unleashed a series of publications by people who had been part of the so-called 'family' at one time or another. The most damaging was Bianca Lamblin's *Memories of an Undutiful Daughter*.

17 *Libération*, 15 April 1986.

18 Moi, *Simone de Beauvoir*, p.75.

19 A. Ophir, *Regards féminins*, Paris, Denoël, 1976, p.9. See the excerpt from Ophir's book in this volume, and my introduction to it.

20 See Moi, *Simone de Beauvoir*, pp.73–92 for a striking analysis of the various topoi which can be identified. These include the 'personality topos' in which Beauvoir's looks, life and morality are discussed with the implication that whatever a woman says or thinks or writes is less important than what she is; the sexist personality topos which presents all Beauvoir's political choices as emotional reactions; the cliché of the cold, non-maternal woman, used to suggest a disregard for the human race; the bluestocking topos, the desexualised schoolmarm who has

worked hard to get on and please her father but who is not a real intellectual, and the naivety topos of the naive schoolgirl, the epistemological impostor.

21 See my introduction to the pieces by Elaine Marks which appear in the autobiography section. Hazel Barnes's piece appears in the fiction section.

22 In the following discussion I draw on Joanna Russ's *How to Suppress Women's Writing*, London, The Women's Press, 1984. I also discuss the issue of Beauvoir's reception as a woman writer in 'Reception Problems for Women Writers: The Case of Simone de Beauvoir', in *Women and Representation*, ed. D. Knight and J. Still, Nottingham, Nottingham WTF publications, 1995, pp.43–56.

23 See A. Jardine, 'Death Sentences: Writing Couples and Ideology', *Poetics Today*, 6, 1985, pp.119–31 for an interesting discussion of the notion that Beauvoir found in Sartre a fantasy of the phallic mother, crucial to her writing production.

24 K. Millett in *Daughters of de Beauvoir*, ed. P. Forster and I. Sutton, London, The Women's Press, 1989, p.20.

25 Bair, *Simone de Beauvoir*, p.439.

26 Beauvoir, *Force of Circumstance*, p.197.

27 See my discussion in the last critical piece of this volume of the ways in which Beauvoir deliberately sought to place her writing in a male tradition of writing.

28 By far the greatest number of critical works on Beauvoir are published in English. Between 1972 and 1992 only 14 completed theses with Beauvoir's name in the title were recorded at French universities, compared with 51 on Sartre, 31 on Duras and 80 on Camus in the same period. Only two of the critical pieces included in this volume were first published in French, although Moi's *Simone de Beauvoir* has itself been translated into French.

29 Beauvoir, *Force of Circumstance*, p.203.

30 Beauvoir nevertheless misjudged her female audience in asking them to read between the lines and denounce her female narrator in 'The Woman Destroyed'. She strikes out savagely at their response in her final volume of memoirs. See S. de Beauvoir, *All Said and Done*, translated by P. O'Brian, Harmondsworth, Penguin, 1987, p.142.

31 In 'Sex, Society and the Female Dilemma. A Dialogue between Simone de Beauvoir and Betty Friedan', *Saturday Review*, 14 June 1975, p.16. There is only one reference to Beauvoir in the index to *The Feminine Mystique*, and that is to a comment by a male American journalist that Beauvoir 'didn't know what life was all about'. B. Friedan, *The Feminine Mystique*, Harmondsworth, Penguin, 1963, p.16.

32 See Moi, *Simone de Beauvoir*, pp.179–85, for a more detailed discussion of responses to *The Second Sex* in France and America.

33 Beauvoir's influence has been so widespread that it is impossible to draw up an exhaustive list of feminists indebted to her work. A helpful starting point is Jo-Ann Pilardi's article 'Feminists Read *The Second Sex*' in M. Simons, ed., *Feminist Interpretations of Simone de Beauvoir*, University Park, PA, Penn State University Press, 1995, pp.29–43.

34 Donna J. Haraway, *Simians, Cyborgs and Women. The Reinvention of Nature*, London, Free Association Books, 1991, p.131.

35 See M. Wittig, *The Straight Mind*, Hemel Hempstead, Harvester Wheatsheaf, 1992, pp.9–20.

36 See Butler's essay in the section on *The Second Sex*.

37 Moi, *Simone de Beauvoir*, p.185.
38 See in particular the work of Margaret Simons, Sonia Kruks, Eva Lundgren-Gothlin, Edward and Kate Fullbrook, Debra Bergoffen and Karen Vintges.
39 K. Vintges, *Philosophy as Passion. The Thinking of Simone de Beauvoir*, Bloomington, Indiana University Press, 1996, pp.21–2.
40 S. Felman, *What Does a Woman Want? Reading and Sexual Difference*, Baltimore and London, Johns Hopkins University Press, 1993, p.126.
41 Algren's literary executors refused permission in consequence for the publication of Beauvoir's letters to Algren to be accompanied by his replies. See *Lettres à Nelson Algren. Un amour transatlantique. 1947–1964*, ed. Sylvie Le Bon de Beauvoir, Paris, Gallimard, 1997, p.9.
42 Beauvoir, *Force of Circumstance*, p.384.
43 See Vintges's interesting remarks on this subject in *Philosophy as Passion*, p.117 and p.119. She also draws attention to the last quotation from *Force of Circumstance* given above.
44 The testimonial function of the memoirs is explored in U. Tidd, *Simone de Beauvoir; Writing the Self, Writing the Life*, Cambridge, Cambridge University Press, forthcoming.
45 S. de Beauvoir, *Memoirs of a Dutiful Daughter*, translated by James Kirkup, Harmondsworth, Penguin, 1987, p.140.
46 Ibid., p.141.
47 Beauvoir, *The Prime of Life*, p.666.
48 Beauvoir, *The Second Sex*, p.174.
49 A. Ernaux, *Une Femme*, Paris, Gallimard, 1987, p.105.

READINGS OF
THE SECOND SEX

REREADING *THE SECOND SEX*

Judith Okely

Judith Okely brings to her reading of *The Second Sex* both an anthropological eye and a strong sense of the way in which both writer and reader are shaped by their history, class, age, race and culture. Her book *Simone de Beauvoir. A Re-Reading* (1986), from which the following extract is taken, is organised around a double reading: the one which she made as a young woman studying in Paris in 1961, and the one which she makes twenty years later as an academic working in Social Anthropology.[1] This double perspective allows her to take into account both the inspiration which *The Second Sex* offered to a generation of readers in the 1950s and early 1960s, and the problems Beauvoir's essay presented to a 1980s feminist generation.

The powerful nature of the inspiration which Beauvoir offered to her early readers is emphasised through the reproduction of underlined pages from Okely's 1961 copy of *The Second Sex*; from her 1980s perspective, she brings to bear her anthropological training to show how Beauvoir's claim to speak universally for all women is unsustainable. Drawing on her own experience, and that of her friends, pupils and acquaintances, Beauvoir in fact produces, in Okely's view, 'an anthropological village study', in which the village is that of mid-century Paris (or, one might even say, Montparnasse). Universalising on the basis of a local study, Beauvoir nevertheless succeeds for Okely in raising questions which go far beyond her immediate sources. Indeed, Okely sees Beauvoir's hidden use of herself as a case-study as a paradoxical strength, which partly accounts for the intimate relationship the text succeeds in setting up with its female readers.

In the following extract, Okely examines Beauvoir's discussion of myths and shows that although Beauvoir sharpens scepticism in her reader and achieves the dismantling of a variety of western myths of the feminine, she is unable to resist a strong tendency towards pan-cultural generalisation. Thus, for example, Beauvoir reads all rituals surrounding childbirth as evidence that gestation is naturally and universally found to be disgusting. In the extract

Okely refers in highly critical terms to Howard Parshley's translation into English of *The Second Sex*. Deirdre Bair's account of the tribulations suffered by Parshley may make Okely's view seem rather harsh in retrospect.[2] Okely also discusses Beauvoir's use of Hegel in terms which differ from the analysis offered by Eva Lundgren-Gothlin in a piece which appears later in this section.

The great strength of Okely's reading is her constant appreciation of the different reading positions which can be taken up towards the text. Although she concludes her book by emphasising that Beauvoir lived her life as an intellectual, isolated from the mass of women, she recognises that it was only possible for Beauvoir to speak about women from a position which entailed solitude among men and exile from women.

Notes

1 J. Okely, *Simone de Beauvoir. A Re-Reading*, London, Virago, 1986, pp.70–80.
2 See D. Bair, *Simone de Beauvoir: A Biography*, London, Jonathan Cape, 1990, pp.432–39. But see also M. Simons, 'The Silencing of Simone de Beauvoir: Guess What's Missing from *The Second Sex*', *Women's Studies International Forum*, 6, 1983, pp.559–64.

Though de Beauvoir's study now reads differently both for her past and her new readers, the earlier reading cannot be easily jettisoned. The book is part of some women's personal history and part of the history of feminism. This double reading, then and now, is the rationale for my selection of certain themes for a critical discussion.

De Beauvoir's central section on mythology proved startling and evocative to a young woman like myself in the early 1960s. Today, thanks partly to anthropology and to feminists' interrogation of the subject and greater awareness of race and class, it is easier to recognise that de Beauvoir's generalisations fit neither all cultures nor all women. Women readers whose experience in no way approximated that of de Beauvoir were undoubtedly sceptical long ago. From the myths, I have selected for critical discussion those concerned with the female body and sexuality: matters which women now feel freer to talk and write about. De Beauvoir's examination of five male authors stands better the test of time. She initiated a way of looking at 'great' literature from a woman's perspective and there is now a serious body of work in feminist literary criticism. I have also recreated some of my past enthusiasm and mixed response to her text.

In the last decade, a number of women have been concerned to consolidate a theoretical approach to feminism. While the attempt to find the 'origins' or 'first cause' of women's subordination has been largely abandoned, greater emphasis is now placed on explanations for women's continuing subordination and the conditions that could change it. As part of this enterprise, feminists have re-examined Marx and Freud. De Beauvoir's interpretation of these two theorists therefore requires comment. Her extensive debate with biological explanations is of continuing and crucial relevance since the resurgence of sociobiologism in the last decade. The implications of the biological difference between males and females have provoked debates both within feminism and outside it. Considerable space is therefore devoted to various biological explanations and a closer reading of de Beauvoir's text.

My general comments on Volume II of *The Second Sex* invite the reader to place her detailed ethnography of women's lives in a specific context. From this volume, I have selected de Beauvoir's discussion of early childhood which contrasts with her more generalised comments on psychoanalysis and social influences in Volume I. Inevitably the record here of a re-reading has to be selective and cannot do justice to de Beauvoir's enterprise of encyclopaedic proportions.[1]

In Volume II de Beauvoir does not make use of statistical or in-depth social science studies of women; the latter appeared in strength only from the late 1960s. Instead she draws on the representation of women's experience in psychoanalysts' case studies and literature, especially those written by women. Parshley [the American translator] has tended to retain the evidence from the former and cut the latter. The other major source is personal observation and experience. Insights into the young girl were drawn both from her own past and from many years of teaching in girls' lycées. De Beauvoir sometimes gives examples of friends and acquaintances to back up her argument, making use of the 'continual interest' which she and Sartre had had for many years in 'all sorts of people; my memory provided me with an abundance of material' (*FC*, p.196). Her autobiographies in fact reveal how restricted her acquaintance was with people outside café society and the bourgeoisie.

De Beauvoir has in part done an anthropological village study of specific women, but without the anthropological theory and focus. Her village is largely mid-century Paris and the women studied, including herself, are mainly middle class. There are almost no references to working-class urban women and only rare glimpses of the rural, peasant women who still made up the majority of French women at that time. There is just one striking discussion of the burden of the peasant woman in post-war France in the history section (*SS*, p.165). Despite this hidden subjectivity, her observations and her recourse to historical, literary and psychoanalytical documentation raise questions beyond the local study. A paradoxical strength is the hidden use of herself as a case study, and it was one to which many of her women readers intuitively responded. Although in the text she never uses the word 'I' in a personal example, we can, when we examine her autobiography written nearly ten years later, see the link between her own experience and some of her generalised statements about the girl and woman.

Myths and ideology

The discussion of the myths which surround 'woman' is the core to Volume I. As with her treatment of other aspects, its strength lies in its focused *description* rather than in any convincing *explanation* or first cause of women's subordination. Some later feminists have read the section only for an explanation of women's subordination and thus missed its cumulative impact.[2]

Whether or not she has been misread and simplified, ideas from this section are frequently referred to by feminists and others. De Beauvoir's words hold the imagination by pointing to powerful symbols of 'the feminine' and either explicitly or implicitly challenge their truth. Her description is not neutral, but accompanied by a mocking value judgement. Certain repetitive themes in different ideologies about women are systematically collected together, but de Beauvoir is most convincing in the treatment of western culture. Her description reminds the reader of a long tradition of the 'earth mother' and the 'eternal feminine' which, she argues, while purporting to be laudatory towards woman, is thoroughly dehumanising. The myths which present woman as a powerful symbol mask her effective powerlessness. De Beauvoir's women readers could learn that western myths which were so often said to be complimentary to themselves were only mystifications; that is, they served to mask the truth of women's objective subordination and oppression.

The opening pages try to link the myths of the feminine to existentialist concepts which de Beauvoir has refined by introducing a gender difference. 'Man' needs 'Others' to affirm his existence and to break away from immanence. He engages in projects to achieve transcendence. The female is used by the male as this 'Other' and she remains the object; she never becomes the subject. De Beauvoir does not convincingly explain why woman never becomes the subject, she merely asserts this, yet she described a painful truth of her time.

There are oblique references to Hegel's 'master–slave dialectic', although she does not always bother to name him. She develops Hegel's ideas by contrasting the position of the slave with that of woman. Whereas in Hegel's view the slave is able also to see himself as subject or 'essential' in his struggle with the master, de Beauvoir asserts that woman is in a worse position because she does not see herself as subject and cannot, like the slave, ever see the master (man) as inessential. Whereas the slave can supersede the master, apparently woman cannot supersede man by the same means. In de Beauvoir's view, woman cannot reach the necessary consciousness for emancipation. It is this use of Hegel which later feminist theorists have teased out of de Beauvoir's text in their analysis of her underlying theoretical position.[3] If woman is deprived even of the potential victory attained by a slave, then it seems that de Beauvoir's message is that woman can never win freedom for herself, except perhaps by some independent change in society and the 'master' male.

If indeed de Beauvoir's Hegelian theory is taken as the major if not sole message of *The Second Sex*, then it would seem that all she is saying is that woman's subordinate state is fixed. But few of de Beauvoir's readers were aware of such embedded theoretical implications. Today it is certainly important to make explicit de Beauvoir's theoretical underpinnings; however, it should not be concluded that these were the key contributions to a past feminist reading of *The Second Sex*.

In contrast to de Beauvoir's preceding examination of biology, psychology, economics and history, the section on myths explores a process whereby women's subordination is continually reaffirmed or 'overdetermined' through ideology. Whether or not de Beauvoir is offering these ideas about women as causes or consequences of women's subordination, she should be credited for pointing to recurrent aspects of the myth of woman, especially in European culture. De Beauvoir sharpened scepticism in her reader.

That woman is the 'Other' is devastatingly stated:

> Since women do not present themselves as subject, they have no virile myth in which their prospects are reflected; they have neither religion nor poetry which belongs to themselves in their own right. It is still through the dreams of men that they dream. It is the gods fabricated by males which they adore.
>
> (*DS* I, p.235)

The representation of the world, like the world itself, is the work of men; they describe it from the point of view which is theirs and which they confuse with the absolute truth (*DS* I, p.236).

Whereas de Beauvoir's comments on much of European Christian ideology are fairly systematic, her tendency towards generalisations is very misleading when she strays into cultures in another time and space. De Beauvoir selects from social anthropology cross-cultural examples which confirm her argument and avoids reference to the many available counter-examples. To be fair, she does attempt some broad distinctions between Islam, Graeco-Roman culture and Christianity. But otherwise, random cases are plucked from India, Egypt and Oceania, with only occasional counter-examples.

Indeed, the text oscillates between a defiant angry declaration that woman is always 'Other' and a subdued acknowledgement that this view of women may be eclipsed by the presence of some non-female idols in the course of history (*DS* I, p.234). For example, under dictatorships, woman may no longer be a privileged object, and in the 'authentic democratic society' advocated by Marx, de Beauvoir observes there is no place for 'the Other'. This recognition of broad differences is modified when she notes that Nazi soldiers held to the cult of female virginity and that communist writers like Aragon created a special place for woman. De Beauvoir hopes that the myth of woman will one day be extinguished: 'the more that women affirm themselves as human beings, the more the wondrous quality of the Other will die in them. But today it still exists in the heart of *all* men' (*DS* I, p.235; my emphasis). This last sentence reveals her continuing need to conclude with a pan-cultural generalisation.

While she is ambivalent as to whether woman as 'Other' is a universal, she states that 'the Other' is itself ambiguous. It is evil, but 'being necessary for good' it returns to good. Woman embodies 'no fixed concept' (*DS* I, p.236). In this way, de Beauvoir can explain the apparently conflicting fantasies which women are believed to embody for men. One of these myths is the association of woman with nature. There is a double aspect to this. Nature can be seen as mind, will and transcendence as well as matter, passivity and immanence. On the one hand nature is mind, on the other it is flesh. As evidence for the latter view of nature de Beauvoir looks back to the classical Greek scholars (for example Aristotle), who asserted that only the male is the true creator, while female fertility is merely passive; that is, that woman is the passive earth while man is the seed.

De Beauvoir's examination of classical European writers was helpful to both western and non-western women in exposing the mystification of 'woman' in a long-standing tradition. It was harder for de Beauvoir to look beyond the traditions of her own culture, especially when she had to rely on less accessible sources for a view of nature elsewhere. She offered some examples from India which compare the earth to a mother, but random selections do not prove the universality of any such principle; moreover, her example from Islamic texts where woman is called a field or grapevine (*DS* I, p.238) is an image from *agriculture* not wild nature. The two are certainly not the same.

Despite these errors, de Beauvoir systematically outlines a dominant European tradition which, since the eighteenth-century Enlightenment, sees nature as inferior to culture.[4] Her suggestions about women and nature have stimulated anthropologists to think about the association.[5] De Beauvoir's link between women and nature is not as absolute as some of her successors have tried to make it.[6] More recently, anthropologists have given examples from other cultures which challenge any pan-cultural generalisation.[7] For example, Olivia Harris has argued that Indians of the Bolivian Highlands equate the married couple with 'culture' and unmarried persons with 'nature'; the nature–culture opposition is thus not linked simplistically to a gender opposition.[8]

As elsewhere, de Beauvoir proceeds through the stages of a woman's life. Here, they are examined in the light of external ideology rather than of a woman's concrete experience. Women as a group may comply with and internalise these beliefs as if they were 'natural'. Whereas de Beauvoir tries to suggest that much of the ideology is universal, it was in fact her revelation that this was mere belief, mere myth, which was so powerful to her early readers. Insofar as western women were indoctrinated to believe that they might represent 'mother earth', the 'eternal feminine', erotic temptress or virgin purity, de Beauvoir dismantled these images. Some of us could recognise apparently individual fantasies about ourselves as part of an overarching tradition made outside us, not born with us; the fantasies were historical, not fixed. The problem for us was how to throw them off. Non-western women, by contrast, gained a novel critical perspective on western ideology which was seen even more as one to reject.

In searching for the basis for certain ideas and myths of woman, de Beauvoir seizes upon woman's capacity to gestate. Her approach is rooted in the European Cartesian tradition which separates mind from body. Man apparently would like to be a pure Idea, absolute Spirit, but his fate is to be trapped in the 'chaotic shadows of the maternal belly . . . it is woman who imprisons him in the mud of the earth' (*DS* I, p.239). De Beauvoir compares the womb to 'quivering jelly which evokes the soft viscosity of carrion' (*DS* I, p.239). 'Wherever life is in the making – germination, fermentation – it arouses disgust . . . the slimy embryo begins the cycle that is completed in the putrefaction of death' (*SS*, p.178). These extraordinary references to viscosity and slime echo Sartre's extensive discussion of viscous substance both in *Nausea* (1938) and in *Being and Nothingness* (1943) and some of his own personal disgust with aspects of the sexual body (see *Adieux*, 1981).

In aiming to deconstruct the myth of the feminine, de Beauvoir thus naively reproduces her male partner's and lover's ideas about the female body, while possibly deceiving herself that these are objective and fixed philosophical truths. As in her discussion of biology, she is on dubious ground in suggesting that bodily parts inevitably arouse the same feelings (of disgust) in all individuals and all cultures. She is implying it is 'natural' to look at 'nature' in a specific way. In fact she reveals the extent to which she has internalised both the views of her own culture and the extreme reactions of Sartre.

Her problematic assertions are compounded when she makes unsubstantiated generalisations about primitive people's attitudes to childbirth. In her text such people are an undifferentiated lump and she repeats a clichéd belief that their attitudes to childbirth are always surrounded by the most severe taboos. It is interesting to be informed that childbirth in a number of different societies is subject to elaborate ritual; the danger comes when de Beauvoir implies either that taboos vary according to an evolutionary 'progress' or that attitudes to birth are unvaried. De Beauvoir asserts that all the ancient codes demand purification rites from women in confinement, and that gestation always inspires a 'spontaneous repulsion' (*DS* I, p.240).

De Beauvoir thus falls into the trap of suggesting that gestation is *naturally* and universally disgusting. Her evidence about so-called primitives is suspect, first because even 'taboos' do not necessarily reflect disgust, and second because a people's cultural treatment of childbirth is linked to differences in descent, marriage and kinship systems and control over offspring. De Beauvoir's assertion that disgust at gestation is spontaneous speaks more of herself and her own time. Today I can criticise de Beauvoir for her suspect generalisation about humanity's spontaneous psychological reactions to the physicality of childbirth, but some twenty years ago I underlined it.

De Beauvoir makes similar sweeping statements about menstruation. She maintains that in all civilisations woman inspires in man the horror of his own carnal 'contingence' – she reminds him of his mortality. This, according to de Beauvoir, is confirmed by an assertion that everywhere before puberty the young girl is without taboo. It is only after her first menstruation that she becomes impure and is then surrounded by taboos. De Beauvoir then offers a random collection of menstrual 'taboos' from Leviticus, Egypt, India, nineteenth-century Britain and France to support this suspect generalisation.

In the 1950s and 1960s this made interesting reading, but it is perilously close to an old-fashioned type of anthropology, exemplified in Frazer's *The Golden Bough*, in which customs are lumped together for their superficial similarity, although in fact they are meaningless when torn from their different contexts. By contrast, a few detailed examples of menstrual taboos in specific cultures are more informative for placing them in context. De Beauvoir does indeed give three such extended examples, but these are excluded by Parshley (*DS* I, pp.243–6).

In de Beauvoir's view, the taboos associated with menstruation 'express the horror which man feels for feminine fertility' (*DS* I, p.247). This emphasis on 'horror' is little different from the now discredited view that primitive people's rituals are merely a response to 'fear'. Today, after a wider anthropological reading on these menstrual 'issues' across cultures, I can criticise de Beauvoir's explanation, but I have also to recognise that in 1961 I underlined that single sentence above. Both female writer and reader identified with a myth that woman's body and blood inspired horror and believed it as fact, not fiction. Thus neither de Beauvoir nor the female reader escaped the myths of her own culture.

The myths associated with virginity and the drama of defloration are also discussed by de Beauvoir in terms of psychological fear. Sometimes, de Beauvoir vaguely suggests that customs surrounding decoration have 'mystical' causes, as if this were sufficient explanation. De Beauvoir is at the mercy of outdated European explanations for ritual, partly because any systematic study of rituals associated with women had to await a feminist anthropology.

In recent decades, anthropologists have looked at rituals associated with menstruation, virginity, defloration, pregnancy and childbirth and the connections between a group's specific control over women's sexuality or fertility and the material context. In some societies menstruation will be merely a private event and without ritual taboo. In some cases childbirth and the arrival of a new member to the group will be publicly significant and so marked by ritual elaboration or specific taboos.[9]

De Beauvoir's discussion of the control of women's sexuality and reproduction cross-culturally is in places thoroughly misleading, but in its time it told us about some of the strongest taboos in a specific Judaeo-Christian culture, if not class. In 1961 I underlined in painful recognition her psychological explanation as to the relative importance of virginity:

> Depending whether man feels crushed by the forces which encircle him or whether he proudly believes himself capable of annexing them, he either refuses or demands that his wife be handed over as a virgin.
>
> (*DS* I, p.250)

In the 1980s the western bourgeois demand for a virgin wife has all but disinte-grated, and *not* because the male has miraculously overcome some innate mys-tical fear. Changes in attitudes towards female virginity coincide with changes in attitudes to sexuality and marriage and even advances in the technology of birth control. In the early 1960s, as a virgin, I could not see that the bourgeois cult of virginity depended only on the social and historical context. In those days, de Beauvoir's critical discussion of virginity had maximum impact precisely because she mistakenly argued that it was widely valued in a variety of cultures. Today, we may be more concerned to point to the many counter-examples in order to argue, as she intended, for alternative freedoms. There is a demand for specific case studies rather than broad and inaccurate generalisations.

Inevitably the author's own culture was the most closely observed. It is there-fore not surprising that de Beauvoir should suggest that the most disturbing image of woman as 'the Other' is found in Christianity: 'It is in her that are embodied the temptations of the earth, sex and the devil' (*DS* I, p.270). In the margin I exclaimed 'et on m'a fait Chrétienne!' ('And they made me a Christian woman!'). De Beauvoir, the former Catholic, suggests that all Christian literature intensifies 'the disgust which man can feel for woman' (*DS* I, p.270), and her examples from modern male writers show the continuing tradition. Again, as elsewhere, she presumed this disgust to be universal and innate. Thus she had not fully freed herself of her own indoctrination into Christianity when she asserted that its ingredients were general to all societies. But for the reader of the 1950s and early 1960s, de Beauvoir's selection of western traditions, when juxtaposed with a splatter of historical and cross-cultural examples, had a powerful effect. Dominant western beliefs were exposed as of no greater truth than other beliefs and customs.

References and notes

FC   *Force of Circumstance*, Harmondsworth, Penguin, 1965.
SS   *The Second Sex*, Harmondsworth, Penguin, 1972.
DS I/DS II   *Le Deuxième Sexe*, vol.I/vol.II, Paris, Gallimard, 1949 (Okely's trans-lations).

1   See also Okely, 'Sexuality and Biology in *The Second Sex*', paper given to the Social Anthropology Inter-Collegiate Seminar, London University, 1984.
2   See for example M. Barrett, *Women's Oppression Today*, London, Verso, 1980.
3   For example C. Craig, 'Simone de Beauvoir's *The Second Sex* in the light of the Hegelian Master–Slave Dialectic and Sartrean Existentialism', PhD, University of Edinburgh, 1979.
4   See J. and M. Bloch, 'Women and the Dialectics of Nature in Eighteenth-century Thought' in C. McCormack and M. Strathern (eds), *Nature, Culture and Gender*, Cambridge, Cambridge University Press, 1980.
5   See E. Ardener, 'Belief and the Problem of Women', in E. Ardener (ed.), *Perceiving Women*, London, Dent, 1975.

6 For example S. Ortener, 'Is Female to Male as Nature is to Culture?', in M. Rosaldo and L. Lamphere (eds), *Woman, Culture and Society*, Stanford, Stanford University Press, 1974.
7 McCormack and Strathern, *Nature, Culture and Gender*.
8 O. Harris, 'Complementarity and Conflict: An Andean View of Women and Men', in J. La Fontaine (ed.), *Sex and Age as Principles of Social Differentiation*, London, Academic Press, 1978; and 'The Power of Signs: Gender, Culture and the Wild in the Bolivian Andes', in McCormack and Strathern, *Nature, Culture and Gender*.
9 See J. La Fontaine, 'Ritualisation of Women's Life Crises in Bugisu', in *The Interpretation of Ritual*, London, Tavistock, 1972. See also J. Okely, *The Traveller Gypsies*, Cambridge, Cambridge University Press, 1983.

SEX AND GENDER IN SIMONE DE BEAUVOIR'S *SECOND SEX*

Judith Butler

This stimulating essay, published in 1986, argues that Beauvoir's famous for-mulation 'One is not born, but rather becomes, a woman' can be read as a radical programme for the role of the body in interpreting gender norms.[1] Gen-der choice becomes a daily act of which the 'styles of the flesh' are a constitu-tive part. The point of departure of Butler's reading is the distinction between sex and gender which Beauvoir's formulation offers: it suggests, for Butler, that whereas being female may be only a more or less fixed set of biological facts, being a woman is an active process of negotiation between the individual and the cultural norms with which we have to deal. Butler argues that it is Beauvoir's use of the verb 'become' which allows for the process of gender acquisition to be seen as an interplay of individual choice and acculturation, and which emphasises the constantly ongoing nature of this process.

But does the verb 'become' imply that there is a moment at which we are outside gender? It cannot do so, Butler replies, because we cannot know our-selves simply as body, simply as female; our experience of our sex is always gendered. Thus we begin the process of becoming our genders from an already embodied, already culturally assigned place. Culture, body and choice combine in a manoeuvre which Butler appealingly describes as putting 'the Cartesian ghost to rest' – in other words a manoeuvre which succeeds in stepping outside the dualism of mind and body posited by Descartes. Further-more, it represents, in Butler's view, an example of the ways in which Beauvoir was prepared to go beyond Sartre, when it suited her purpose.

Butler goes on to raise the question of whether, if gender is choice, women could conceivably be blamed for choosing their situation; her conclusion is that although Beauvoir is well aware of the complex material origins of oppression, which prevent it from being simply generated by choice, her emphasis on choice is empowering because it reminds us that oppression is contingent and that oppressive gender norms only persist to the extent that individuals take them up repeatedly. She also argues that despite Beauvoir's emphasis on the need for women to seek transcendence, she does not intend women to imitate the masculine project of disembodiment. Finally, Butler indicates the ways in which Beauvoir's view of the body anticipates the radical challenge to the notion of natural sex subsequently developed by Michel Foucault and Monique Wittig.

This important article on *The Second Sex* prepares the way in a number of respects for the influential theoretical texts which Butler has gone on to write in the 1990s. *Gender Trouble* (1990) analyses the rule-bound discourses which generate gender and sexual identity and proposes a performative theory of gender. Both here, and in *Bodies That Matter* (1993), she argues that far from being 'natural', gender is acquired through the repetition of a multiplicity of injunctions and performances which can be subverted and parodied to expose the illusion of fixed gender identity.[2] Butler's work is a striking example of the way in which Beauvoir's insights in *The Second Sex* continue to inspire feminist theorists.

Notes

1 J. Butler, 'Sex and Gender in Simone de Beauvoir's *The Second Sex*', *Yale French Studies* 72, 1986, pp.35–49.
2 J. Butler, *Gender Trouble. Feminism and the Subversion of Identity*, London, Routledge, 1990. *Bodies That Matter. On the Discursive Limits of 'Sex'*, London, Routledge, 1993.

'One is not born, but rather becomes, a woman' – Simone de Beauvoir's formulation distinguishes sex from gender and suggests that gender is an aspect of identity gradually acquired.[1] The distinction between sex and gender has been crucial to the long-standing feminist effort to debunk the claim that anatomy is destiny; sex is understood to be the invariant, anatomically distinct, and factic aspect of the female body, whereas *gender* is the cultural meaning and form that that body acquires, the variable modes of that body's acculturation. With the distinction intact, it is no longer possible to attribute the values or social functions of women to biological necessity, and neither can we refer meaningfully to natural or unnatural gendered behaviour: all gender is, by definition, unnatural. Moreover, if the distinction is consistently applied, it becomes unclear whether being a given sex has any necessary consequence for becoming a given gender. The presumption of a causal or mimetic relation between sex and gender is undermined. If being a woman is one cultural interpretation of being female, and if that interpretation is in no way necessitated by being female, then it appears that the female body is the arbitrary locus of the gender 'woman', and there is no reason to preclude the possibility of that body becoming the locus of other constructions of gender. At its limit, then, the sex/gender distinction implies a radical heteronomy of natural bodies and constructed genders with the consequence that 'being' female and 'being' a woman are two very different sorts of being. This last insight, I would suggest, is the distinguished contribution of Simone de Beauvoir's formulation, 'one is not born, but rather becomes, a woman'.

According to the above framework, the term 'female' designates a fixed and self-identical set of natural corporeal facts (a presumption, by the way, which is seriously challenged by the continuum of chromosomal variations), and the term 'woman' designates a variety of modes through which those facts acquire cultural meaning. One *is* female, then, to the extent that the copula asserts a fixed and self-identical relation, i.e. one is female and therefore not some other sex. Immeasurably more difficult, however, is the claim that one *is* a woman in the same sense. If gender is the variable cultural interpretation of sex, then it lacks the fixity and closure characteristic of simple identity. To be a gender, whether man, woman or otherwise, is to be engaged in an ongoing cultural interpretation of bodies and, hence, to be dynamically positioned within a field of cultural possibilities. Gender must be understood as a modality of taking on or realizing possibilities, a process of interpreting the body, giving it cultural form. In other words, to be a woman is to become a woman; it is not a matter of acquiescing to a fixed ontological status, in which case one could be born a woman, but, rather, an active process of appropriating, interpreting, and re-interpreting received cultural possibilities.

For Simone de Beauvoir, it seems, the verb 'become' contains a consequential ambiguity. Gender is not only a cultural construction imposed upon identity, but in some sense gender is a process of constructing ourselves. To *become* a woman is a purposive and appropriative set of acts, the acquisition of a skill, a 'project', to use Sartrean terms, to assume a certain corporeal style and significance. When 'become' is taken to mean 'purposefully assume or embody', it seems that Simone de Beauvoir is appealing to a voluntaristic account of gender. If genders are in some sense chosen, then what do we make of gender as a received cultural construction? It is usual these days to conceive of gender as passively determined, construct*ed* by a personified system of patriarchy or phallogocentric language which precedes and determines the subject itself. Even if gender is rightly understood to be constructed by such systems, it remains necessary to ask after the specific mechanism of this construction. Does this system unilaterally inscribe gender upon the body, in which case the body would be a purely passive medium and the subject utterly subjected? How, then, would we account for the various ways in which gender is individually reproduced and reconstituted? What is the role of personal agency in the reproduction of gender? In this context, Simone de Beauvoir's formulation might be understood to contain the following set of challenges to gender theory: to what extent is the 'construction' of gender a self-reflexive process? In what sense do we construct ourselves and, in that process, *become* our genders?

In the following, I would like to show how Simone de Beauvoir's account of 'becoming' a gender reconciles the internal ambiguity of gender as both 'project' and 'construct'. When 'becoming' a gender is understood to be both choice and acculturation, then the usually oppositional relation between these terms is undermined. In keeping 'become' ambiguous, Beauvoir formulates gender as a corporeal locus of cultural possibilities both received and innovated. Her theory of gender, then, entails a reinterpretation of the existential doctrine of choice whereby 'choosing' a gender is understood as the embodiment of possibilities within a network of deeply entrenched cultural norms.

Sartrean bodies and Cartesian ghosts

The notion that we somehow choose our genders poses an ontological puzzle. It might at first seem impossible that we can occupy a position outside of gender from which to stand back and choose our genders. If we are always already gendered, immersed in gender, then what sense does it make to say that we choose what we already are? Not only does the thesis appear tautological, but insofar as it postulates a choosing agent prior to its chosen gender, it seems to adopt a Cartesian view of the self, an egological structure which lives and thrives prior to language and cultural life. This view of the self runs contrary to contemporary findings on the linguistic construction of personal agency and, as is the problem with all Cartesian views of the ego, its ontological distance from language and cultural life seems to preclude the possibility of its eventual verification. If Simone de Beauvoir's claim is to have cogency, if it is true that we become our genders through some kind of volitional and appropriative sets of acts, then she must mean something other than an unsituated Cartesian act. That personal agency is a logical prerequisite for *taking on* a gender does not imply that this agency itself is disembodied; indeed, it is our genders which we become, and not our bodies. If Simone de Beauvoir's theory is to be understood as freed of the Cartesian ghost, we must first turn to her view of bodies and to her musings on the possibilities of disembodied souls.

Whether consciousness can be said to precede the body, or whether it has any ontological status apart from the body – these are claims alternately affirmed and denied in Sartre's *Being and Nothingness*, and this ambivalence toward a Cartesian mind/body dualism reemerges, although less seriously, in Simone de Beauvoir's *The Second Sex*. In fact, we can see in *The Second Sex* an effort to radicalize the Sartrean programme to establish an embodied notion of freedom. Sartre's chapter, 'The Body', in *Being and Nothingness* echoes Cartesianism which haunts his thinking as well as his own efforts to free himself from this Cartesian ghost. Although Sartre argues that the body is coextensive with personal identity ('I am my body'), he also suggests that consciousness is in some sense beyond the body ('My body is a *point of departure* which I *am* and which at the same time I surpass . . . ').[2] Rather than refute Cartesianism, Sartre's theory seeks to understand the disembodied or transcendent feature of personal identity as paradoxically, yet essentially, related to embodiment. The duality of consciousness (as transcendence) and the body is intrinsic to human reality, and the effort to locate personal identity exclusively in one or the other is, according to Sartre, a project in bad faith.

Although Sartre's references to 'surpassing' the body may be read as presupposing a mind/body dualism, we need only conceive of this self-transcendence as itself a corporeal movement to refute that assumption. The body is not a static phenomenon, but a mode of intentionality, a directional force and mode of desire. As a condition of access to the world, the body is a being comported beyond itself, sustaining a necessary reference to the world and, thus, never a self-identical natural entity. The body is lived and experienced as the context and medium for all human strivings. Because for Sartre all human beings strive after possibilities not yet realized or in principle unrealizable, humans are to that extent 'beyond' themselves. This *ek-static* reality of human beings is, however, a corporeal experience; the body is not a lifeless fact of existence, but a mode of becoming. Indeed, for Sartre the natural body only exists in the mode of being surpassed, for the body is always involved in the human quest to realize possibilities: 'we can never apprehend this contingency as such insofar as our body is for us; for we are a choice, and for us, to be is to choose ourselves ... this inapprehensible body is precisely the necessity that *there be a choice*, that I do not exist *all at once*' (p.328).

Simone de Beauvoir does not so much refute Sartre as take him at his non-Cartesian best.[3] Sartre writes in *Being and Nothingness* that 'it would be best to say, using "exist" as a transitive verb, that consciousness *exists* its body ...' (p.329). The transitive form of 'exist' is not far removed from her disarming use of 'become', and Simone de Beauvoir's becoming a gender seems both an extension and a concretization of the Sartrean formulation. In transposing the identification of corporeal existence and 'becoming' onto the scene of sex and gender, she appropriates the ontological necessity of paradox, but the tension in her theory does not reside between being 'in' and 'beyond' the body, but in the move from the natural to the acculturated body. That one is not born, but becomes, a woman does not imply that this 'becoming' traverses a path from disembodied freedom to cultural embodiment. Indeed, one is one's body from the start, and only thereafter becomes one's gender. The movement from sex to gender is internal to embodied life, i.e. a move from one kind of embodiment to another. To mix Sartrean phraseology with Simone de Beauvoir's, we might say that to 'exist' one's body in culturally concrete terms means, at least partially, to become one's gender.

Sartre's comments on the natural body as 'inapprehensible' find transcription in Simone de Beauvoir's refusal to consider gender as natural. We never experience or know ourselves as a body pure and simple, i.e. as our 'sex', because we never know our sex outside of its expression as gender. Lived or experienced 'sex' is always already gendered. We become our genders, but we become them from a place which cannot be found and which, strictly speaking, cannot be said to exist.

For Sartre, the natural body is an 'inapprehensible' and, hence, a fictional starting point for an explanation of the body as lived. Similarly, for Simone de Beauvoir, the postulation of 'sex' as fictional heuristic allows us merely to see that gender is non-natural, i.e. a culturally contingent aspect of existence. Hence, we do not become our genders from a place prior to culture or to embodied life, but essentially within their terms. For Simone de Beauvoir at least, the Cartesian ghost is put to rest.

Although we 'become' our genders, the temporal movement of this becoming does not follow a linear progression. The origin of gender is not temporally discrete because gender is not originated at some point in time after which it is fixed in form. In an important sense gender is not traceable to a definable origin precisely because it is itself an originating activity incessantly taking place. No longer understood as a product of cultural and psychic relations long past, gender is a contemporary way of organizing past and future cultural norms, a way of situating oneself with respect to those norms, an active style of living one's body in the world.

Gender as choice

One chooses one's gender, but one does not choose it from a distance which signals an ontological juncture between the choosing agent and the chosen gender. The Cartesian space of the deliberate 'chooser' is fictional, but the question persists: if we are mired in gender from the start, what sense can we make of gender as a kind of choice? Simone de Beauvoir's view of gender as an incessant project, a daily act of reconstitution and interpretation, draws upon Sartre's doctrine of prereflective choice and gives that difficult epistemological structure a concrete cultural meaning. Prereflective choice is a tacit and spontaneous act which Sartre terms 'quasi knowledge'. Not wholly conscious, but nevertheless accessible to consciousness, it is the kind of choice we make and only later realize we have made. Simone de Beauvoir seems to rely on this notion of choice in referring to the kind of volitional act through which gender is assumed. Taking on a gender is not possible at a moment's notice, but is a subtle and strategic project which only rarely becomes manifest to a reflective understanding. Becoming a gender is an impulsive yet mindful process of interpreting a cultural reality laden with sanctions, taboos, and prescriptions. The choice to assume a certain kind of body, to live or wear one's body a certain way, implies a world of already established corporeal styles. To choose a gender is to interpret received gender norms in a way that organizes them anew. Rather than a radical act of creation, gender is a tacit project to renew one's cultural history in one's own terms. This is not a prescriptive task we must endeavour to do, but one in which we have been endeavouring all along.

The predominance of an existential framework has been criticized by Michèle Le Doeuff and others for resurrecting 'a classical form of voluntarism' which insidiously blames the victims of oppression for 'choosing' their situation.[4] When the doctrine of existential choice is used in this context, it is assuredly insidious, but this usage is itself a misusage which diverts attention from the empowering possibilities of the position. The phenomenology of victimization that Simone de Beauvoir elaborates throughout *The Second Sex* reveals that oppression, despite the appearance and weight of inevitability, is essentially contingent. Moreover, it takes out of the sphere of reification the discourse of oppressor and oppressed, reminding us that oppressive gender norms persist only to the extent that human beings take them up and give them life again and again. Simone de Beauvoir is not saying, however, that oppression is generated through a series of human choices. Her own efforts in anthropology and history underscore her awareness that oppressive systems have complicated material origins. The point is rather that these systems persist only to the extent that gender norms are tacitly yet insistently taken up in the present through individual strategies which remain more or less disguised. Over and against a less sophisticated view of 'socialization', she is using the existential apparatus to understand the moment of appropriation through which socialization occurs. Through this emphasis on appropriation, she is providing an alternative to paternalistic explanatory models of acculturation which treat human beings only as products of prior causes, culturally determined in a strict sense, and which, consequently, leave no room for the transformative possibilities of personal agency.

By scrutinizing the mechanism of agency and appropriation, Beauvoir is attempting, I believe, to infuse the analysis with emancipatory potential. Oppression is not a self-contained system which either confronts individuals as a theoretical object or generates them as its cultural pawns. It is a dialectical force which requires individual participation on a large scale in order to maintain its malignant life.

Simone de Beauvoir does not directly address the burden of freedom[5] that gender presents, but we can extrapolate from her view how constraining norms work to subdue the exercise of gender freedom. The social constraints upon gender compliance and deviation are so great that most people feel deeply wounded if they are told that they are not really manly or womanly, that they have failed to execute their manhood or womanhood properly. Indeed, insofar as social existence requires an unambiguous gender affinity, it is not possible to exist in a socially meaningful sense outside of established gender norms. The fall from established gender boundaries initiates a sense of radical dislocation which can assume a metaphysical significance. If existence is always gendered existence, then to stray outside of established gender is in some sense to put one's very existence into question. In these moments of gender dislocation in which we realize that it is hardly necessary that we be the genders we have become, we confront the burden of choice intrinsic to living as a man or a woman or as some other gender identity, a freedom made burdensome through social constraint.

The anguish and terror of leaving a prescribed gender or of trespassing upon another gender territory testifies to the social constraints upon gender interpretation as well as to the necessity that there be an interpretation, i.e. to the essential freedom at the origin of gender. Similarly, the widespread difficulty in accepting motherhood, for instance, as an institutional rather than an instinctual reality expresses this same interplay of constraint and freedom. Simone de Beauvoir's view of the maternal instinct as a cultural fiction often meets with the argument that a desire so commonly and so compellingly felt ought for that very reason to be considered organic and universal. This response seeks to universalize a cultural option, to claim that it is not one's choice but the result of an organic necessity to which one is subject. In the effort to naturalize and universalize the institution of motherhood, it seems that the optional character of motherhood is being denied; in effect, motherhood is actually being promoted as the *only* option, i.e. as a compulsory social institution. The desire to interpret maternal feelings as organic necessities discloses a deeper desire to disguise the choice one is making. If motherhood becomes a choice, then what else is possible? This kind of questioning often engenders vertigo and terror over the possibility of losing social sanctions, of leaving a solid social station and place. That this terror is so well known gives perhaps the most credence to the notion that gender identity rests on the unstable bedrock of human invention.

Autonomy and alienation

That one becomes one gender is a descriptive claim; it asserts only that gender is taken on, but does not say whether it ought to be taken on a certain way. Simone de Beauvoir's prescriptive programme in *The Second Sex* is less clear than her descriptive one, but her prescriptive intentions are nevertheless discernible. In revealing that women have become 'Other', she seems also to be pointing to a path of self-recovery. In criticizing psychoanalysis, she remarks that

> Woman is enticed by two modes of alienation. Evidently to play at being a man will be for her a source of frustration; but to play at being a woman is also a delusion: to be a woman would mean to be the object, the Other – and the Other nevertheless remains subject in the midst of her resignation. . . . The true problem for woman is to reject these flights from reality and seek self-fulfilment in transcendence.
>
> (p.57)

The language of 'transcendence' suggests, on the one hand, that Simone de Beauvoir accepts a gender-free model of freedom as the normative ideal for women's aspirations. It seems that Beauvoir prescribes the overcoming of gender altogether, especially for women, for whom becoming one's gender implies the sacrifice of autonomy and the capacity for transcendence. On the other hand, insofar as transcendence appears a particularly masculine project, her prescription seems to urge women to assume the model of freedom currently embodied by the masculine gender. In other words, because women have been identified with their anatomy, and this identification has served the purposes of their oppression, they ought now to identify with 'consciousness', that transcending activity unrestrained by the body. If this were her view, she would be offering women a chance to be men, and promoting the prescription that the model of freedom currently regulating masculine behaviour ought to become the model after which women fashion themselves.

And yet, Simone de Beauvoir seems to be saying much more than either of the above alternatives suggests. Not only is it questionable whether she accepts a view of consciousness or freedom which is in any sense beyond the body (she applauds psychoanalysis for showing finally that 'the existent is a body': (pp.10, 38) but her discussion of the Other permits a reading which is highly critical of the masculine project of disembodiment. In the following analysis, I would like to read her discussion of Self and Other as a reworking of Hegel's dialectic of master and slave in order to show that, for Simone de Beauvoir, the masculine project of disembodiment is self-deluding and, finally, unsatisfactory.

The self-asserting 'man' whose self-definition requires a hierarchical contrast with an 'Other' does not provide a model of true autonomy, for she points out the bad faith of his designs, i.e. that the 'Other' is, in every case, his own alienated self. This Hegelian truth, which she appropriates through a Sartrean filter, establishes the essential interdependence of the disembodied 'man' and the corporeally determined 'woman'. His disembodiment is only possible on the condition that women occupy their bodies as their essential and enslaving identities. If women are their bodies (which is not the same as 'existing' their bodies which implies living one's body as a project and bearer of created meanings), if women are only their bodies, if their consciousness and freedom are only so many disguised permutations of bodily need and necessity, then women have, in effect, exclusively monopolized the bodily sphere. By defining women as 'Other', 'men' are able through the shortcut of definition to dispose of their bodies, to make themselves other than their bodies, and to make their bodies other than themselves. This Cartesian 'man' is not the same as the man with distinct anatomical traits, and insofar as a 'man' is his anatomical traits, he seems to be participating in a distinctively feminine sphere. The embodied aspect of his existence is not really his own, and hence he is not really a sex, but beyond sex. This sex which is beyond sex must initiate a splitting and social projection in order not to know his own contradictory identity.

The projection of the body as 'Other' proceeds according to a peculiar rationality which relies more on associative beliefs and conclusions which defy the laws of commutativity than on sound reasoning. The disembodied 'I' identifies himself with a noncorporeal reality (the soul, consciousness, transcendence), and from this point on his body becomes Other. Insofar as he inhabits that body, convinced all the while that he is not the body which he inhabits, his body must appear to him as strange, as alien, as an alienated body, a body that is *not* his. From this belief that the body is Other, it is not a far leap to the conclusion that others *are* their bodies, while the masculine 'I' is a noncorporeal phenomenon. The body rendered as Other – the body repressed or denied and, then, projected

– reemerges for this 'I' as the view of Others as essentially body. Hence, women become the Other; they come to embody corporeality itself. This redundancy becomes their essence, and existence as a woman becomes what Hegel termed 'a motionless tautology'.

Simone de Beauvoir's use of the Hegelian dialectic of Self and Other argues the limits of a Cartesian version of disembodied freedom and implicitly criticizes the model of autonomy upheld by masculine gender norms. The masculine pursuit of disembodiment is necessarily deceived because the body can never really be denied; its denial becomes the condition for its reemergence in alien form. Disembodiment becomes a way of living or 'existing' the body in the mode of denial. And the denial of the body, as in Hegel's dialectic of master and slave, reveals itself as nothing other than the embodiment of denial.

The body as situation

Despite Simone de Beauvoir's occasional references to anatomy as transcendence, her comments on the body as an unsurpassable 'perspective' and 'situation' (p.38) indicate that, as for Sartre, transcendence must be understood within corporeal terms. In clarifying the notion of the body as 'situation', she suggests an alternative to the gender polarity of masculine disembodiment and feminine enslavement to the body.

The body as situation has at least a twofold meaning. As a locus of cultural interpretations, the body is a material reality which has already been located and defined within a social context. The body is also the situation of having to take up and interpret that set of received interpretations. No longer understood in its traditional philosophical senses of 'limit' or 'essence', the body is a *field of interpretive possibilities,* the locus of a dialectical process of interpreting anew a historical set of interpretations which have become imprinted in the flesh. The body becomes a peculiar nexus of culture and choice, and 'existing' one's body becomes a personal way of taking up and reinterpreting received gender norms. To the extent that gender norms function under the aegis of social constraints, the reinterpretation of those norms through the proliferation and variation of corporeal styles becomes a very concrete and accessible way of politicizing personal life.

If we understand the body as a cultural situation, then the notion of a natural body and, indeed, a natural 'sex' seems increasingly suspect. The limits to gender, the range of possibilities for a lived interpretation of a sexually differentiated anatomy, seem less restricted by anatomy itself than by the weight of the cultural institutions which have conventionally interpreted anatomy. Indeed, it becomes unclear when one takes Simone de Beauvoir's formulation to its unstated consequences, whether gender need be in any way linked with sex, or whether this conventional linkage is itself culturally bound. If gender is a way of 'existing' one's body, and one's body is a 'situation', a field of cultural possibilities both received and reinterpreted, then gender seems to be a thoroughly cultural affair. That one becomes one's gender seems now to imply more than the distinction between sex and gender. Not only is gender no longer dictated by anatomy, but anatomy does not seem to pose any necessary limits to the possibilities of gender.

Although Simone de Beauvoir occasionally ascribes ontological meanings to anatomical sexual differentiation, her comments just as often suggest that anatomy alone has no inherent significance. In 'The Data of Biology' she distinguishes between natural facts and their significance, and argues that natural facts gain significance only through their subjection to non-natural systems of interpretation. She writes: 'As Merleau-Ponty very justly puts it, man is not a natural species; he is a historical idea. Woman is not a completed reality, but rather a becoming, and it is in her becoming that she should be compared with men; that is to say, her *possibilities* should be defined' (p.40).

The body as a natural fact never really exists within human experience, but only has meaning as a state which has been overcome. The body is an *occasion* for meaning, a constant and significant *absence* which is only known through its significations: 'in truth a society is not a species, for it is in a society that the species attains the status of existence – transcending itself toward the world and toward the future. Individuals . . . are subject rather to that second nature which is custom and in which are reflected the desires and fears that express their essential nature' (p.40).

The body is never a self-identical phenomenon (except in death, in the mythic transfiguration of women as Other, and in other forms of epistemic prejudice). Any effort to ascertain the 'natural' body before its entrance into culture is definitionally impossible, not only because the observer who seeks this phenomenon is him/herself entrenched in a specific cultural language, but because the body is as well. The body is, in effect, never a natural phenomenon: 'it is not merely as a body, but rather as a body subject to taboos, to laws, that the subject is conscious of himself and attains fulfilment – it is with reference to certain values that he evaluates himself. And, once again, it is not upon physiology that values can be based; rather, the facts of biology take on the values that the existent bestows upon them' (p.40).

The conceptualization of the body as non-natural not only asserts the absolute difference between sex and gender, but implicitly questions whether gender ought to be linked with sex at all. Gender seems less a function of anatomy than one of its possible uses: 'the body of woman is one of the essential elements of her situation in the world. But that body is not enough to define her as woman; there is no true living reality except as manifested by the conscious individual through activities and in the bosom of a society' (p.41).

The body politic

If the pure body cannot be found, if what *can* be found is the situated body, a locus of cultural interpretations, then Simone de Beauvoir's theory seems implicitly to ask whether sex was not gender all along. Simone de Beauvoir herself does not follow through with the consequences of this view of the body, but we can see the radicalization of her view in the work of Monique Wittig and Michel Foucault: the former self-consciously extends Simone de Beauvoir's doctrine in 'One is Not Born a Woman'; the latter is not indebted to Simone de Beauvoir (although he was a student of Merleau-Ponty) and yet promotes in fuller terms the historicity of the body and the mythic status of natural 'sex'.[6] Although writing in very different discursive contexts, Wittig and Foucault both challenge the notion of natural sex and expose the political uses of biological discriminations in establishing a compulsory binary gender system. For both theorists, the very discrimination of 'sex' takes place within a cultural context which requires that 'sex' remain dyadic. The demarcation of anatomical difference does not precede the cultural interpretation of that difference, but is itself an interpretive act laden with normative assumptions. That infants are divided into sexes at birth, Wittig points out, serves the social ends of reproduction, but they might just as well be differentiated on the basis of earlobe formation or, better still, not be differentiated on the basis of anatomy at all. In demarcating 'sex' as sex, we construct certain norms of differentiation. And in the interest which fuels this demarcation resides already a political programme. In questioning the binary restrictions on gender definition, Wittig and Foucault release gender from sex in ways which Simone de Beauvoir probably did not imagine. And yet, her view of the body as a 'situation' certainly lays the groundwork for such theories.

If 'existing' one's gender means that one is tacitly accepting or reworking cultural norms governing the interpretation of one's body, then gender can also be a place in which the binary system restricting gender is itself subverted. Through new formulations of gender, new ways of amalgamating and subverting the oppositions of 'masculine' and 'feminine', the established ways of polarizing genders becomes increasingly confused, and binary opposition comes to oppose itself. Through the purposeful embodiment of ambiguity binary oppositions lose clarity and force, and 'masculine' and 'feminine' as descriptive terms lose their usefulness. Inasmuch as gender ambiguity can take many forms, gender itself thus promises to proliferate into a multiple phenomenon for which new terms must be found.

Simone de Beauvoir does not suggest the possibility of other genders besides 'man' and 'woman', yet her insistence that these are historical constructs which must in every case be appropriated by individuals suggests that a binary gender system has no ontological necessity. One could respond that there are merely various ways of being a 'man' or a 'woman', but this view ascribes an ontology of substance to gender which misses her point: 'man' and 'woman' are *already* ways of being, modalities of corporeal existence, and only emerge as substantial entities to a mystified perspective. One might wonder as well whether there is something about the dimorphic structure of human anatomy that necessitates binary gender arrangements cross-culturally. Anthropological findings of third genders and multiple gender systems suggest, however, that dimorphism itself becomes significant only when cultural interests require, and that gender is more often based upon kinship requirements than on anatomical exigencies.

Simone de Beauvoir's own existential framework may seem anthropologically naïve, relevant only to a postmodern few who essay to trespass the boundaries of sanctioned sex. But the strength of her vision lies less in its appeal to common sense than in the radical challenge she delivers to the cultural status quo. The possibilities of gender transformation are not for that reason accessible only to those initiated into the more abstruse regions of existential Hegelianism, but reside in the daily rituals of corporeal life. Her conceptualization of the body as a nexus of interpretations, as both 'perspective' and 'situation', reveals gender as a scene of culturally sedimented meanings and a modality of inventiveness. To become a gender means both to submit to a cultural situation and to create one, and this view of gender as a dialectic of recovery and invention grants the possibility of autonomy within corporeal life that has few if any parallels in gender theory.

In making the body into an interpretive modality, Beauvoir has extended the doctrines of embodiment and prereflective choice that characterized Sartre's work from *Being and Nothingness*, through *Saint Genet: Actor and Martyr* and his final biographical study of Flaubert. Just as Sartre in that last major work revised his existential assumptions to take account of the material realities constitutive of identity, so Simone de Beauvoir, much earlier on and with greater consequence, sought to exorcize Sartre's doctrine of its Cartesian ghost. She gives Sartrean choice an embodied form and places it in a world thick with tradition. To 'choose' a gender in this context is not to move in upon gender from a disembodied locale, but to reinterpret the cultural history which the body already wears. The body becomes a choice, a mode of enacting and reenacting received gender norms which surface as so many styles of the flesh.

The incorporation of the cultural world is a task performed incessantly and actively, a project enacted so easily and constantly it seems a natural fact. Revealing the natural body as already clothed, and nature's surface as cultural invention, Simone de Beauvoir gives us a potentially radical understanding of gender. Her vision of the body as a field of cultural possibilities makes some of the work of refashioning culture as mundane as our bodily selves.

Notes

1   S. de Beauvoir, *The Second Sex*, New York, Vintage Books, 1973, p.301. Henceforth, page references to this will be given in the text.

2   J.-P. Sartre, *Being and Nothingness: An Essay in Phenomenological Ontology*, trans. Hazel E. Barnes, New York, Philosophical Library, 1947, p.329.

3   Simone de Beauvoir's defence of the non-Cartesian character of Sartre's account of the body can be found in 'Merleau-Ponty et le Pseudo-Sartrisme', *Les Temps modernes*, 10, 1955. For a general article tracing Sartre's gradual overcoming of

Cartesianism, see T. Busch, 'Beyond the Cogito: The Question of the Continuity of Sartre's Thought', *The Modern Schoolman*, 60, 1983.

4   Michèle Le Doeuff, 'Simone de Beauvoir and Existentialism', *Feminist Studies*, 6, 1980, p.278.

5   A term commonly used by Sartre to describe the experience of having to make choices in a world devoid of objective moral truths.

6   M. Wittig, 'One is Not Born a Woman', *Feminist Issues*, 1, 1981 and M. Wittig, 'The Category of Sex', *Feminist Issues*, 2, 1982. And see Foucault's introduction to the volume he edited, *Herculine Barbin, Being Recently Discovered Memoirs of a Nineteenth Century Hermaphrodite*, trans. Richard McDougall, New York, Pantheon, 1980. Also, Foucault, *The History of Sexuality, vol. 1*, New York, Bantam, 1979.

BEAUVOIR: THE WEIGHT OF SITUATION

Sonia Kruks

Sonia Kruks's work on Beauvoir is a significant contribution to recent re-evaluations of Beauvoir's status as a philosopher. In this piece, taken from her *Situation and Human Existence* (1990), she examines how Beauvoir, starting out from the philosophical framework set out by Sartre in *Being and Nothingness*, gradually develops a notion of the subject which ultimately permits her to offer an analysis of women's oppression.[1] Whereas the Sartrean view of the absolute autonomy and freedom of the subject leads Sartre to argue that the slave is as free as his master, always able to constitute his own situation and choose what attitude he takes up to his enslavement, Beauvoir develops a notion of the subject which allows her to theorise women's oppression as a general condition, historically constituted by external and institutional forces which operate with such power that women may in extreme cases lose all possibility of choice. Thus, though Beauvoir undoubtedly tried to work within the framework of *Being and Nothingness*, and certainly claimed to have done so, Kruks concludes that she is of necessity an unfaithful disciple who comes to some very un-Sartrean conclusions.

Kruks traces through Beauvoir's philosophical essays the development of three aspects of subjectivity which she draws on in *The Second Sex*. The first aspect is the notion of the interdependence of free subjects, which Beauvoir begins to tackle in *Pyrrhus et Cinéas* (1944). Kruks shows how Beauvoir sets off from the Sartrean position that when we act on each other, we do not impinge on the other's fundamental freedom. However, instead of taking up Sartre's view of the inherently conflictual relationship between individuals, she goes on to explore the ways in which we depend on others and to argue that it is in every individual's interest to try to secure an equal balance of power between themselves and others. Kruks identifies this argument as Beauvoir's first step towards the crucial linking of Sartre's philosophy of existence to the ethical and political domain.

She then goes on to show how Beauvoir elaborates her account of the interdependence of freedoms in *The Ethics of Ambiguity* (1947), and at the same time develops a second aspect of subjectivity, that is to say the notion of subjectivity as socially embedded. In *The Ethics of Ambiguity* Beauvoir presents a world of multiple projects with complex relations between them. Within this perspective, collective projects become possible and collective oppression of particular social groups can also be described. Kruks draws our attention to two important points: firstly, oppression now involves not only the Sartrean conflict of all consciousnesses, but also allows for a systematic attempt to maintain a particular group in a socially unequal role. Secondly, Beauvoir begins to argue that although it is the responsibility of the oppressed to rebel and exert their fundamental freedom, there are circumstances in which oppression can permeate subjectivity to such a point that the freedom of the oppressed is reduced to a suppressed potentiality.

When Beauvoir comes, in *The Second Sex*, to examine the situation of a particular oppressed group, that of women, she thus has at her disposal a notion of the subject as both intersubjective and socially embedded. She is able to analyse how a group of free individuals have been subjected to what Kruks calls a 'man-made destiny', functioning through a set of social institutions which, at the limit, the individual is not in a position to challenge. In a third development of the notion of the subject, Beauvoir now also presents the subject as embodied. Although Kruks concedes the difficulties inherent in Beauvoir's view of women's role in the perpetuation of the species as a misfortune, she points to the fact that in partially locating her account of the origins of women's oppression in the body, Beauvoir thereby reformulates the Sartrean view of the body and extends her notion of the ambiguity of the human condition to include the ambiguous mix of consciousness and materiality which embodied existence involves.

An important dimension of Kruks's discussion is the way in which she situates Beauvoir's notion of subjectivity as poised between on the one hand the concept of the free and responsible individual, always able to act in every situation, and on the other, the post-structuralist dissolution of the human subject. As she points out, much of Beauvoir's detailed account of the social conditioning to which women have historically been subjected could be retold to make of woman a historically constituted as opposed to constituting subject. It is the strength of Beauvoir's position, Kruks argues, that she is able to produce a theory of oppression which gives full weight to institutional structures without ever abandoning the notion of individual freedom, however repressed.

Note

1 Excerpt from S. Kruks, *Situation and Human Existence. Freedom, Subjectivity and Society*, London, Unwin Hyman, 1990, pp.83–112. Further work by Kruks is signalled in the 'Further reading' list.

In her autobiography, Simone de Beauvoir describes a damp, dreary evening in the Spring of 1940, when she and Sartre wandered around the streets of Paris discussing philosophy. Sartre, briefly in Paris on leave from the army, sketched out for her the main lines of the argument of what was to become *Being and Nothingness*. It was an argument which he had been working out in his notebooks during the several months of enforced idleness thrust upon him by life as a conscript during the 'phoney war'; but it was, of course, the culmination of many years of prior study and reflection.[1] Their discussions over the next few days, Beauvoir tells us, centred above all on the problem of 'the relation of situation to freedom'. On this point they disagreed. Since this disagreement was one that continued for several years – and was, I will argue, only resolved by Sartre gradually abandoning his own views of situation and subjectivity for ones much closer to Beauvoir's – it is worth quoting Beauvoir's account of their conversation in full:

> I maintained that, from the point of view of freedom, as Sartre defined it – not as a stoical resignation but as an active transcendence of the given – not every situation is equal: what transcendence is possible for a woman locked up in a harem? Even such a cloistered existence could be lived in several different ways, Sartre said. I clung to my opinion for a long time and then made only a token submission. Basically, I was right. But to have been able to defend my position, I would have had to abandon the terrain of individualist, thus idealist, morality, where we stood.[2]

Sartre continued in *Being and Nothingness* to maintain the view he had pushed Beauvoir to accept in 1940: torture victims, he insisted, can objectify the torturer and the slave is as free as his master. Since each individual subject constitutes his situation as the unique field of his own project, no comparison between two situations, from which we could judge one to be more free than the other, is possible. These views are the eminently consistent conclusions that must follow from Sartre's ontology, in which the for-itself, as pure nothingness, is unfounded and uncaused. In so far as Beauvoir questioned such conclusions, there was in her questioning at least an implicit challenge to Sartre's ontology.

The issue of Beauvoir's intellectual relation to Sartre is complex. She is best known (from her volumes of autobiography) as the chronicler of their interlinked lives; she is known as a novelist and, particularly in the anglophone world, for her treatise on women, *The Second Sex* (1949). The latter was acclaimed as a work of origin by the women's liberation movement of the late 1960s, especially in the USA. However, most commentators, even feminist ones, have generally treated Beauvoir as a derivative thinker, a kind of footnote to Sartre: her novels exemplify this philosophy, her essays offer marginal clarifications or, in the case of *The Second Sex,* at best a creative application of his main ideas. There is some truth in such an interpretation: Beauvoir did consciously work within Sartre's framework and she made no claim to be a philosopher of Sartre's stature.[3] Even so, their intellectual relationship was clearly very much a two-way process. As both of them have pointed out, Sartre modified ideas and even rewrote works at Beauvoir's instigation.[4] When, in the postwar period, Sartre began seriously to confront Marxism and to consider the question of social existence more fully, Beauvoir had preceded him. Although she engaged in a more muted and less direct conversation with Marxism than Sartre, Beauvoir was the one who first pointed the way beyond Sartre's dyadic account of human relations, sketching in its stead an account of socially mediated subjectivity.

Although Beauvoir said she worked within Sartre's framework, she did so rather unfaithfully. While beginning from Sartrean premises, by which I mean those of *Being and Nothingness,* her tenacious pursuit of her own questions led her at times to some most un-Sartrean conclusions. This is particularly the case with her treatment of the question of the situated nature of subjectivity. In *The Second Sex* especially, she came to conclusions – already presaged in the 1940 conversation cited above – which were clearly opposed to Sartre's account, in *Being and Nothingness,* of the autonomy of the subject.

Where, however, she stopped short was at the point of formulating the alternative ontology which her concrete analyses called for. If, as she argues, situations do indeed fundamentally modify the freedom of the individualized for-itself, then Sartre's radical disjuncture between being-for-itself and being-in-itself is put into question. In many ways Merleau-Ponty's ontology offers a better foundation than does Sartre's for Beauvoir's account of the subject and of the modification it undergoes in certain kinds of situation.

I will focus here on three works by Beauvoir, written over the period 1943–49. These are: two essays on ethics, *Pyrrhus et Cinéas* (written in 1943) and *The Ethics of Ambiguity* (written in 1946),[5] and *The Second Sex* (begun in 1946, but written mainly in 1948 and 1949). As a clear line of intellectual development links these three works, I will treat them chronologically. Over much the same period, of course, Sartre himself was beginning to encounter the inadequacies of *Being and Nothingness* as a foundation for social philosophy and ethics and gradually to attempt to modify some of his arguments. But, starting in 1943, Beauvoir was the one who first deepened and fleshed out Sartre's notion of *situation,* beginning to develop it into a tool for analysing social as well as individual existence; social as well as ontological aspects of freedom.[6]

Pyrrhus et Cinéas

Early in 1943, when *Being and Nothingness* had been completed but was not yet published, Beauvoir was invited to contribute to a series of books on existentialism. Her first reaction, she tells us, was that Sartre had already said all there was to say in *Being and Nothingness*.[7] Then she decided that there was a set of issues about which she had something fresh to say: issues she had already touched upon in her recently completed novel about the Resistance.[8] They concerned the interdependence of freedoms and the problem of violence. Working consciously within Sartre's framework, she produced *Pyrrhus et Cinéas*.[9]

Beauvoir begins her argument from two Sartrean propositions. Firstly, her doubts of 1940 notwithstanding, she still contends, with Sartre, that freedom, that is, subjectivity, is indestructible: whatever our condition we are free to choose. When we act on each other, we can act only on each other's exteriority: on each other's *situation*. Thus, with Sartre, she concludes that ultimately I can neither help nor harm another in his freedom. If we try to be generous, our action 'only reaches the exterior *[les dehors]* of the other' (*PC*, p.83). Violence too acts only on another's facticity (*PC*, p.86), and not on his freedom. 'In one sense', she tells us, 'violence is not an evil, since one can do nothing either for or against a man' (*PC*, p.116). Beauvoir secondly follows Sartre in initially asserting the radical separateness of freedom: each individual is for her a free subject, a unique transcendence, a Sartrean for-itself:

> Men do not to begin with depend on each other, because to begin with they *are* not: they must become. Freedoms are neither united nor opposed: they are separated. It is in projecting himself into the world that a man situates himself in situating other men around him.
>
> (*PC*, p.48)

This far Beauvoir's argument is familiar. However, from the indestructibility of individual freedom and the separate constitution by each subject of its unique situation, Sartre had proceeded to argue that relations between freedoms are inherently conflictual: each freedom encounters the other as a threat. The other is the constitutor of an alternative situation which is not mine, and in which I am now merely an object for him. While Beauvoir does not challenge Sartre head-on, she does not proceed to replicate this last part of Sartre's argument. Instead, she explores some startlingly different alternatives, involving such un-Sartrean notions as generosity and equality.

I have already suggested that Sartre was faced with a difficulty in the 1940s. The social philosophy implicit in *Being and Nothingness* was one in which society was conceived as a quasi-Hobbesian state of nature – as not only conflictual but also contingent and structureless; as an anarchic aggregate of freedoms in random conflict. Thus Sartre's philosophy was not able to provide a theoretical foundation for his growing commitment to the project of socialist revolution. Sartre was, of course, aware of the problem – it was implied in the questions concerning ethics with which he ended the book and which he explored in his abandoned *Cahiers*. But apart from the vague notion of an individual 'radical conversion', he did not address the problem in *Being and Nothingness*. In *Pyrrhus et Cinéas*, Beauvoir attempted to show that there is a connection between Sartre's account of ontological freedom and the commitment which they both shared to bringing about a different social order. To make this case, however, she had to modify Sartre's account of interpersonal relations, demonstrating that they need not be relations solely of conflict.

For Sartre, Heidegger's idea of *Mitsein,* that man is 'a being which in its own being implies the Other's being', must be rejected (*BN*, 247 ff.).[10] For Beauvoir also, 'men' are radically separate freedoms. Yet, she goes on to point out, paradoxically, they are also interdependent. If I try to imagine a world in which I am the only person in existence, the image is truly horrifying, for nothing I did would have any point to it. 'A man alone in the world would be paralysed by the self-evident vanity of all his goals; he undoubtedly could not bear to live' (*PC*, p.65; also p.110). Although I freely create my own project, its meaning *for me* depends on the existence of other people and their willingness and ability to confirm its significance. Above all, they must be willing and able to take up my creation and give it a future that goes beyond my present. Thus, Beauvoir insists, it is only from others that we can obtain an affirmation of our existence. For although others do indeed annihilate or objectify me, it is they alone who also can give my being the necessity I seek. I can to some degree escape the contingency which threatens to devour my actions through the recognition of others.

'Man' for Beauvoir, as for Sartre, is a useless passion, a nothingness which seeks in vain to be.[11] Man wishes to be a self-cause, a for-itself-in-itself, and he experiences his inevitable failure as an anguish which he generally attempts to avoid in 'bad faith'. What Beauvoir now suggests is that a certain partial escape from nothingness, a certain degree of being, can be achieved through the recognition of my project by others.

> Only the other can create a need for what we give him; all appeal, all demand comes from his freedom; in order for what I have established to appear as a good, the other must make it his good: then I am justified in having created it. Only the freedom of the other is able to give necessity to my being.
>
> (*PC*, pp.95–6)

Above all what I am able to obtain through others is a future: my project remains open beyond the end of my act, even beyond my death, if others take it up and use what I have created as the starting-point for their projects. It is important to point out that it would not be sufficient if only one other person were to take up my project. I require it to be taken up by a *multiplicity* of others. One other freedom could not give sufficient necessity to my project, since in isolation each individual freedom remains finite. It is only a multiplicity of freedoms, each supporting the others, that can overcome individual finitude (*PC*, p.120).

But not all relations with others involve such mutual affirmation. There has to be a *choice* of such relations – what Beauvoir calls a choice of 'generosity' on the part of the persons concerned.[12] Moreover, for such a choice to be possible, a certain objective condition also has to be met: there must be *equality* between them. By equality Beauvoir means, above all, social equality: equal power and equal access to those material means which are necessary for the projects we choose to undertake. In relations of generosity, the Sartrean conflict of consciousnesses is not abolished, but it is transcended by the willingness of each freedom also to recognize the subjectivity of the other. Instead of each attempting to make an object of the other, each recognizes that the other, even though apprehended in exteriority, as an object, is *also* a subject; and each agrees to respect the subjectivity of the other:

> In lucid, agreed recognition, these two freedoms which seem to exclude each other must be able to hold themselves face to face: mine and that of the other; I must grasp myself as at the same time object and freedom; I must recognise my situation as founded by the other, even while affirming my being beyond the situation.
>
> (*PC*, pp.83–4)

Even though Beauvoir herself is more concerned with the social preconditions for such relations of generosity than with analysing the relations themselves, this account implies a fundamental reworking of Sartre's account of relations with others. In arguing that the main precondition is *social* equality, Beauvoir attempts for the first time to create a link – however inadequately still – between Sartrean ontology and the ethical and political domain.

If I am to have relations of reciprocal generosity with others, and if my existence is to be given meaning through others taking up what I create, they must be my equals (*mes pairs*). This is to say, in the first instance, they cannot be *less free* than I am. For if I experience myself as transcendent over the other, then I simply cannot avoid objectifying him (*PC*, p.113) and he will not then be able to take up and give transcendence to my creation for me.

> The other's freedom can do nothing for me unless my own goals can serve as his point of departure; it is by using the tool which I have invented that the other prolongs its existence; the scholar can only talk with men who have arrived at the same level of knowledge as himself; only then can he suggest his theory as a basis for further work. The other cannot accompany my transcendence unless he is at the same point on the road as me.
>
> (*PC*, p.114)

Thus, in order to extend my own freedom, I need others to be able to attain my own level of creation. This in turn, Beauvoir next argues, requires me, for the sake of my own freedom, to struggle to make all men my equals with regard to their material well-being. For otherwise they will not be able to accompany my skills, my intellectual endeavours, etc. In other words, the social situation of my fellows has an effect upon my freedom, upon the meaning I am able to give my own project, and thus it is my concern.

> I must therefore endeavour to create for all men situations which will enable them to accompany and surpass my transcendence. I need their freedom to be available to make use of me, to preserve me in surpassing me. I require for men health, knowledge, well being, leisure, so that their freedom does not consume itself in fighting sickness, ignorance, misery.
>
> (*PC*, p.115)

Beauvoir emphasizes that her argument must apply to all human beings; in either perpetrating violence or failing to oppose its perpetration against anybody, I work against my own need to be surrounded by subjects who will be able to recognize me and be capable of taking up my projects: 'Even if I oppress only one man, all humanity appears to me as a pure thing in him' (*PC*, p.116).[13] The insoluble nature of political problems arises, however, from the fact that, given also the separateness of human projects and the conflicting interests that must arise, I cannot avoid doing violence to others. Violence is always a scandal and always self-defeating; yet we cannot avoid it. In struggling to create situations in which my fellow men no longer consume their freedom in a fight for mere physical survival, I may have to do violence to their oppressors; it is justified violence but is no less self-defeating for that. Beauvoir was to explore this paradox further in *The Ethics of Ambiguity*, written three years later. But before turning to that work, let me examine what the argument for the interdependence of freedoms in *Pyrrhus et Cinéas* implies for Sartre's account of individual subjectivity.

In *Being and Nothingness*, it will be recalled, freedom refers not to efficacy in completing our projects, but to a free choice of project: 'by oneself to determine oneself to wish' (*BN*, p.483). Furthermore, while subjectivity is always situated, situations are constituted by the subject. Situations are not only individual but incommensurable, and we could not – except by assuming the role of an objectifying Third – judge that a master is more free than his slave, or the torturer more free than his victim. From the point of view of freedom, all situations are equal.

Already in 1940, as we saw, Beauvoir was doubtful about this view. Reflecting on *Pyrrhus et Cinéas* in 1960, Beauvoir described the work as one in which she attempted to 'reconcile' her own conviction that situations are 'graded' (*hierarchisées*) with the Sartrean notion of freedom as the indestructible upsurge of the for-itself, or transcendence.[14] In order to attempt this, she adopted the Cartesian distinction between *freedom* (*liberté*) which has no external limits, and *power* (*puissance*), which can be restricted.[15]

Power is finite, and one can augment or limit it from without; one can
throw a man in prison, take him out of it, cut off an arm, lend him wings;
but in all cases his freedom remains infinite.

(*PC*, p.86)

However, as we will see, this is not a distinction which she was able consistently
to sustain. Since anything that I do affects only the 'exteriority' (*les dehors*) of
another, Beauvoir's argument concerning the interdependence of freedoms must
initially refer to what in this distinction she calls *power*. It is my *power* (what we
might call my *effective freedom*, as distinct from my *ontological freedom*) which
depends on the power of others. If others do not take up the tool I have
invented, or the theory I have developed, it would seem at first consideration that
the limit involved must be a limit only on my effective freedom and not on my
ontological freedom, or transcendence; for the latter is untouchable and infinite.
However, as Beauvoir's argument concerning the interdependence of freedoms
qua transcendences proceeds, the distinction between the two kinds of freedom
begins to break down.

Transcendence is the upsurge of the for-itself in the world, but it becomes
concrete; it particularizes itself in the specific projects of individuals. When it
does this, it of course encounters the limits of the situation of the individual. The
slave has transcendence and a project, like any other person, but the specific
content of the projects open to him is circumscribed by his situation as a slave, a
situation which is not of his own making. Thus his effective freedom is more
limited than that of his master. His choices can be made only within narrow
confines, not of his choosing. We might say that he cannot choose his situation,
although he remains free to choose *within* it. Moreover, his *future* is more closed
than that of his master. It is this lack of an 'open' future which begins, in
Beauvoir's account, to imply that there is a qualitative modification of tran
scendence itself. This is to say also that the lack of an open future implies a
modification of the for-itself, of ontological freedom.

If poverty, sickness, ignorance, as well as slavery, are to be opposed, it is
because they preclude projects that open on to the future. They condemn human
beings to 'consume' their freedom in a dreary cycle of repetition. A transcen
dence which so consumes itself lacks a project which enables it to appeal to other
men to accompany it into the future: it is qualitatively different from a transcen
dence which appeals to others and can open into a future that extends beyond
itself. It has, in comparison, a circular quality. Beauvoir was later to develop the
notion of *immanence* to describe such an entrapped transcendence. In *Pyrrhus et
Cinéas* we are simply left with the still undeveloped idea that although all men
have freedom, in the sense of transcendence or ontological freedom, it has a
different quality depending on the situation – the field of effective freedom – of
the person concerned. A consistent Sartrean position would not, of course, per
mit one to speak of such qualitative differences; as a pure upsurge of nothingness,
the for-itself could not in any way be qualified for Sartre. Thus the ideas which

Beauvoir begins to develop in *Pyrrhus et Cinéas* involve a radical, though only implicit, modification of Sartre's account of the autonomous subject.

The Ethics of Ambiguity

In *The Ethics of Ambiguity*, written some three years later, Beauvoir returned to the questions she had treated in *Pyrrhus et Cinéas*. Her use of the word 'ambiguity' in the title of the work is of considerable significance. Ambiguity for her refers to a paradoxical reality, in which each of two contradictory aspects of a single existent carries equal weight. For Sartre, the for-itself precedes and constitutes the meaning of its own facticity. My body, others, relations with others, are merely facticities of the for-itself. For Beauvoir, however, human existence is ambiguous because these facticities appear in her account to be of equal weight with consciousness: man *is* thing, body, as well as consciousness. He is object as well as subject; and he lives a continual tension between these equal and contradictory aspects of his existence. Life, she begins by saying, is the building of death. And it is only man who 'knows and thinks this tragic ambivalence which the animal and the plant merely undergo'. Thus, man is both 'a pure internality against which no external power can take hold' and, at the same time, 'he also experiences himself as a thing crushed by the dark weight of other things' (*EA*, p.7).[16]

Body and consciousness, object and subject – man's relations with other men must include this paradoxical dual reality. Separate, yet interdependent, men both threaten and empower each other; they both negate and extend each other's freedom. Taking these ambiguities as her starting-point, Beauvoir sets out to address the problem of ethics: what precepts, if any, can we develop that should govern our conduct towards each other, given who and what we are? My concern here, however, is not directly with the precepts she develops, but with the account of freedom-in-situation and its limits which she elaborates *en route* to the ethical precepts.

As in *Pyrrhus et Cinéas* Beauvoir refrains from directly criticizing the account of conflictual relations with others of *Being and Nothingness*, but she argues that we can in some conditions transcend them. An 'ethics of ambiguity', she tells us, 'will be an ethics which will refuse to deny *a priori* that separate existents can at the same time be bound to each other' (*EA*, p.18). She reiterates the argument from *Pyrrhus et Cinéas*: freedom needs an 'open future' and only others can give it to me (*EA*, p.72). Thus, Hegel's description of the struggle between consciousnesses in which 'each seeks the death of the other'[17] – a description which was closely paralleled by Sartre – is incomplete. While my first response to the arrival of the other is indeed to feel that he is stealing the world from me and to hate him accordingly, this hatred is 'naive' (*EA*, p.70 ff.). For '[i]f I were really everything there would be nothing beside me; the world would be empty'. The other in fact steals the world from me for Beauvoir only to give it back again enriched, and I would be foolish not to realize this and to overcome my initial hatred: 'One can reveal the world only against a background of the world revealed by other men. No project can be defined except by its interference with other projects.' Subjectivity, in short, cannot exist without intersubjectivity.

Projects in this account are separate, yet they also require each other. From this paradoxical insight Beauvoir develops both an initial notion of society, not to be found in *Being and Nothingness*, and an account of violence and oppression which introduces a *social* dimension. Violence and oppression are not only dyadic relations of self and other for her. They are embedded in the logic of a world of *multiple* projects and their complex 'interferences' (*EA*, p.71). This is a logic which Sartre had not attempted to examine, at least in *Being and Nothingness*.

Society

Beauvoir's notion of society in *The Ethics of Ambiguity* is sketchy and under-developed. However, it still offers a considerable advance in overcoming the atomistic notion implicit in *Being and Nothingness*. Beauvoir begins from a critique of Hegelian and Marxist notions which, in her view, erroneously attribute more substance to the state or to society than to individuals. 'If the individual is nothing, society cannot be anything,' she insists (*EA*, p.106). Yet she is also anxious to avoid the random and structureless conception of society which, she realizes, could be the result of such a radical individualism – and which I have argued was the outcome in Sartre's case. 'Separation does not exclude relation,' she insists; on the contrary, it implies it. And since I need not one but many others to take up my project and give it necessity, there is the possibility that multiple relations can cohere into intelligible forms with a degree of temporal permanency:

> Society exists only by means of the existence of particular individuals; likewise, human adventures stand out against the background of time, each finite to each, although they are all open to the infinity of the future and, thereby, their individual forms imply each other without destroying each other. A conception of this kind does not contradict that of a histori-cal intelligibility; for it is not true that the mind has to choose between the contingent absurdity of the discontinuous and the rationalistic necessity of the continuous; on the contrary, it is part of its function to make a multiplicity of coherent ensembles stand out against the single background of the world and, inversely, to comprehend these ensembles in the perspective of the ideal unity of the world. Without raising the question of historical comprehension and causality, it is enough to recognize the presence of intelligible sequences within temporal forms so that anticipations and consequently action may be possible.
>
> (*EA*, p.12a)

In this passage, Beauvoir raises the questions which Sartre did not, and could not, raise in *Being and Nothingness*. Although, with Sartre, she begins from the separateness of freedoms, she realizes that unless we can also demonstrate some coherence emerging from them, some social forms with a temporal continuity, we are condemned to a kind of solipsism in which comprehension of and reasoned action in relation to a multiplicity of men would be impossible. We would, as she puts it, be locked into 'the contingent absurdity of the discontinuous'. But since projects can be shown to be interdependent as well as separate we can, at least to some extent, escape such absurdity. There are 'coherent ensembles' which can be distinguished.[18] Beauvoir implies that such ensembles are not mere intellectual constructs, although she does not explain how they are objectively constituted. Nor does she discuss how such ensembles are connected to each other.

In another passage, however, Beauvoir raises the startling possibility that a *common situation* can give rise to a *common project* – in other words that a joint action is what creates ensembles. A social class, she claims, has a comparable freedom to an individual and, like an individual, can evade it in a collective 'bad faith'. Like an individual, a class chooses the meaning of its situation through its project:

> The proletariat, taken as a whole, as a class, can become conscious of its situation in more than one way. It can want the revolution to be brought about by one party or another. It can let itself be deluded, as happened to the German proletariat, or can sleep in the dull comfort which capitalism grants it, as does the American proletariat. It may be said that in all these cases it is betraying; still, it must be free to betray.
>
> (*EA*, p.20)

Unfortunately, Beauvoir does not go on to explain or develop this idea; nor does she explore its philosophical implications. But once again, what she is saying implies a non-Sartrean account of social existence. For Sartre, the nearest the proletariat could come to a collective choice of the meaning of its situation would be through experiencing itself as an Us-object, collectively objectified by the capitalist as Third. But what Beauvoir says in this passage would imply that a collective freedom is possible which is its *own* source, and which is not constituted from outside by a Third.

Oppression and violence

Although Beauvoir mentions such instances of collective freedom and talks more generally of the interdependence of freedoms, these are intimately linked in her analysis with oppression and violence. The ambiguity of freedoms, interdependent yet separate, makes possible not only generosity and collective freedom, but also the possibility of attacking another's freedom by denying it the recognition it needs: 'It is interdependence which explains why oppression is possible and why it is hateful' (*EA*, p.82). Beauvoir distinguishes two levels of violence in human relations. The first simply is given in the ambiguity of freedom and is ineradicable. The Sartrean conflict of consciousnesses might at times be transcended, but it is not thereby eliminated. As transcendences, men 'concretely compete with others for being . . . The truth is that if division and violence define war, the world has always been at war and always will be' (*EA*, pp.118–19). Conflict, resulting in violence, can arise even when our projects aim to increase the field of human freedom. It can happen 'that one finds oneself obliged to oppress and kill men who are pursuing goals whose validity one acknowledges oneself' (*EA*, p.99). For example, she says, anti-Fascists in Europe during the Second World War rightly opposed liberation movements in the British colonies even though the goals of these movements were valid. For their effect at the time was to weaken Britain in its yet more important struggle against Fascism. Political judgements have always to be made in situations of complexity, where conflicting goals, even legitimate ones, make violence unavoidable.

While Marxism and revolutionary politics are not explicitly the focus of *The Ethics of Ambiguity*, Beauvoir's meditations on violence clearly arise from her preoccupation with the question of revolutionary violence and the Marxist debate over ends and means. No 'science of history' can resolve these dilemmas, she points out, for 'at each particular moment we must in any case manoeuvre in a state of doubt' (*EA*, p.123). But, however imperfect our knowledge, we still must act; and we must try to do so in such ways that the means we choose do not contradict and undermine the ends we aim at. 'The means, it is said, will be justified by the end; but it is the means which define the end, and if it is contradicted in the moment that set it up, the whole enterprise sinks into absurdity' (*EA*, p.124). Thus, in the name of a mythical future liberation of the international proletariat, Stalinism has erroneously elevated the triumph of the Soviet Union from a means to an 'absolute end' – an end in whose name it in fact undermines international revolution and carries out what have become unjustifiable acts of violence. The best that can be done in politics is to be honest with ourselves and others about what we are doing, and to consider whether the violence we do in the name of a specific goal is likely to further or to undermine it. Violence 'must be legitimised concretely' (*EA*, p.148).[19]

Violence, then, is inherent in social existence and it cannot be avoided in even the most liberatory politics. However, over and above this fundamental level of violence, Beauvoir describes relations of violence of a second degree: oppression. Oppression, for Beauvoir, can include dyadic relationships, but it is generally a wider social relation. Oppression is usually practised against particular social groups – workers, but also women, blacks, colonial peoples, Jews. It involves not merely the attempted objectification described in the Hegelian struggle of consciousnesses or Sartre's conflictual looks, but a systematic attempt to modify the social situation of a group of people so as to prohibit them from developing a free transcendence which will compete with that of the oppressors. As such, oppression involves the establishment and maintenance of relations of social inequality.

Oppression divides humankind into two 'clans': those capable of free transcendence, and the oppressed, 'who are condemned to mark time hopelessly in order merely to support the collectivity'. They pay for the freedom of the elite and 'the oppressor feeds himself on their transcendence' (*EA*, p.83). The 'consumption' of the transcendence of the oppressed is, however, a concrete and material process in Beauvoir's analysis. Her use of the idea of consumption is clearly associated with Marx's account of the consumption of labour power in the capitalist labour process, and the concomitant reduction of human beings to abstract labour. Life, she says, involves two kinds of action: basic, material reproduction – what she calls life 'perpetuating itself' – *and* the movement of free transcendence towards an open future. It is of course the latter kind of action which distinguishes the uniquely human. As Marx had written, 'the realm of freedom actually begins only where labour which is determined by necessity and mundane considerations ceases; thus in the very nature of things it lies beyond the sphere of actual material production'.[20] If a life can do nothing but maintain itself at the material level, says Beauvoir, 'living is only not dying, and human existence is indistinguishable from an absurd vegetation' (*EA*, pp.82–3). Oppression, then, involves shutting off a group from transcendence and condemning it to a life of vegetation so as to increase the field of freedom of the oppressors.

Of course, oppression is in the final analysis self-defeating. For the oppressor undermines his own freedom in so far as he needs it to be supported by a world of free men. But the self-defeating nature of his project is not acknowledged by the oppressor, who always evades responsibility for his actions in 'bad faith' (*EA*, p.96). Since, for this reason, we cannot count on a 'collective conversion' (*EA*, p.97) of the oppressors, the only way forward towards a society of equal freedoms has to be through resistance and revolt on the part of the oppressed.

Turning, however, to the experiences of the oppressed, Beauvoir points out that many of them are not, in practice, capable of revolt. For their transcendence is not merely cut off from its future; it ceases even to be able to project a future. Yet more sharply than in *Pyrrhus et Cinéas,* Beauvoir's analysis diverges at this point from the Sartrean view of freedom. Some of the oppressed are complicitous in their oppression and, in bad faith, evade the revolt that alone could open the way to freedom for them. But others simply do not have that choice. Their situation has so penetrated even their ontological freedom, so modified it, that not even commencement of a transcendent project is possible. The very withdrawal of consciousness which, for Sartre, is the origin of transcendence and which enables freedom to choose its way of taking up its situation (for example, whether or not to give in to the torturer) has ceased to be possible.

The most severely oppressed live in what Beauvoir, following Sartre, calls the condition of 'seriousness'; their lot appears to them so natural, so immovable, that no choice of how to live their situation appears possible. For example, the present distribution of wealth is made to appear so natural that it is unquestionable. Yet far from being a moral fault of the oppressed, or an evasion of freedom in bad faith, seriousness is inflicted upon them. 'One of the ruses of oppression is to camouflage itself behind a natural situation since, after all, one cannot revolt against nature' (*EA*, p.83). This is the condition which Sartre had briefly described in passing in *Being and Nothingness* in the example of the workers of Lyon. For Beauvoir, however, such a condition is central to the issues of ethics and politics. The oppressed man 'can fulfill his human freedom only in revolt' (*EA*, p.87), yet his situation may have been made such that he is unable even to recognize that he is oppressed. The oppressed live in an 'infantile world', immediate, with no sense of future, or any alternative. They have 'no instrument, be it in thought or by astonishment or anger, which permits them to attack the civilization which oppresses them' (*EA*, p.38). Since they are human beings, they still retain an ontological freedom, but it is made 'immanent', irrealizable, by the situation others have imposed upon them (*EA*, pp.102–3). For Beauvoir, unlike Sartre, oppression can permeate subjectivity to the point where consciousness *itself* becomes no more than a passive registering of the oppressive situation. Although it cannot be definitively eliminated – and can always re-erupt should oppression start to weaken – freedom can be reduced to no more than a suppressed potentiality.

Social inequality is, above all, what brings about this condition: 'The less economic and social circumstances allow an individual to act upon the world, the more this world appears to him as given' (*EA*, p.48). Mystification and ignorance, deliberately perpetuated by those who have power, compound the grip of seriousness on the freedom of the oppressed (*EA*, p.98). Thus the struggle for a world of free and mutually confirming transcendences must aim to alter the situation of the oppressed. For those of us who already have freedom, yet whose transcendence is still limited by the oppression of others, the struggle must be to change the situation of the oppressed; we must intervene, not to help them directly, but to enable them to become themselves, capable of choosing to resist their situation. Beauvoir sharply distinguishes such support from charity. For charity is always 'practiced from the outside' and is a form of objectification (*EA*, p.86). Similarly, of course, an overly objectivist vanguardism must be rejected as a form of objectification. We cannot liberate other people. All that we can hope to do is to act on their situation, to reshape their exteriority, so that their freedom ceases to be closed in on itself and can assume its own transformative project.

In the course of her analysis Beauvoir frequently criticizes contemporary, 'orthodox', Marxism for its objectivism, for claiming that there are autonomous laws of historical development which act independently of individual human action. For Beauvoir, Marxism at its best is a 'radical humanism' which 'rejects the idea of an inhuman objectivity' (*EA*, p.18). But orthodox Marxists have frequently attempted to deny freedom and suppress subjectivity.

Neither *Pyrrhus et Cinéas* nor *The Ethics of Ambiguity* is a work explicitly about Marxism or socialism. But the call for a 'radical humanism' which is the unifying theme of both works provides the standpoint from which Beauvoir elaborates important elements of an existential critique of orthodox Marxism. Even more significantly, she also develops an argument concerning the interdependence of freedoms and the necessarily intersubjective character of subjectivity which supplies the missing link between Sartre's philosophy and Marxism. In *Materialism and Revolution* (1946), Sartre made some similar objections to orthodox Marxism to those Beauvoir made in *The Ethics of Ambiguity*. But it was she alone, starting in *Pyrrhus et Cinéas*, who began to make the case for that interdependence of freedoms which a synthesis of existentialism and Marxism must be able to demonstrate. She indicated the most crucial transformations that the philosophy of *Being and Nothingness* would have to undergo before it could be linked not only with ethics or political and social philosophy but, also and above all, with humanistic Marxism. Beauvoir's work must thus be seen as a prolegomenon to Sartre's later 'Marxist existentialism'.

The Second Sex

The Second Sex, published, in 1949, offers us a painstaking case-study of oppression – that of women by men.[21] Once again, Beauvoir begins from within Sartre's framework, but ends by offering us an analysis which bursts out of the confines of Sartreanism. Most evaluations of *The Second Sex*, even feminist ones, have uncritically accepted Beauvoir's claim that her work was philosophically derivative. Most assume that, as one author has recently put it, Beauvoir simply used Sartre's concepts as 'coat-hangers' on which to hang her own material, even to the point where it can be said that 'Sartre's intellectual history becomes her own'.[22] However, such a view is grossly misleading. For although Beauvoir doubtless tried to work within a Sartrean framework, she did not wholly succeed. Indeed, many of the inconsistencies in *The Second Sex* reflect the tension between her formal adherence to Sartrean categories and the fact that the philosophical implications of the work are in large measure incompatible with Sartreanism. It is, once again, on her divergences from Sartre that my discussion will focus.

The book begins on firmly Sartrean ground. 'What is a woman?' asks Beauvoir, and answers initially that woman is defined as that which is not man – as other:

> She is determined and differentiated with reference to man and not he with reference to her; she is the unessential as opposed to the essential. He is the Subject, he is the Absolute: she is the Other.
>
> (*SS*, p.16; xvi)

In the Sartrean struggle between consciousnesses, man consistently attempts to confirm his own subjectivity through the objectification of woman. Much of Volume I is taken up with describing the various facets of this objectification – from the reduction of woman to male property in marriage, to the way man conceives her as Other in myth and literature.

However, very early in the book Beauvoir introduces a distinction into the notion of otherness which is not found in *Being and Nothingness*. Extending the argument of her 'ethical essays', she points out that there can be relations of otherness between equals in which conflict, though not eliminated, is relativized by 'reciprocity': the recognition by each of the Other's freedom as equal to his or her own (SS, p.17; xvii).[23] If, however, the situation of the protagonists is, to begin with, *unequal*, then instead of a reciprocal relation of tension being created, otherness will be of a second kind, involving oppression. Where there is a conflict of equals, 'there is created between them a reciprocal relation, be it in enmity, be it in amity, always in tension'. However, 'if one of the two [groups] is in some way privileged, has some advantage, this one prevails over the other and undertakes to keep it in subjection' (SS, p.93; 61). The notion of otherness alone cannot explain woman's oppression for us. The problem is to explain why woman's otherness has not resulted in 'reciprocity', but has enabled man to objectify her. Why have men been able effectively to deny women their subjectivity, and to impose upon them conditions in which free transcendence is not possible?

Woman's man-made 'destiny'

Today it is unexceptionable to argue that women are not 'naturally' destined for marriage and motherhood above all else. In the France of the 1940s it was, as Beauvoir describes in her autobiography, a view which provoked widespread hostility.[24] Woman's condition, she argued, has been humanly created; it cannot be explained as a biological 'destiny'. We must look rather to human relations for an explanation. With Sartre, Beauvoir holds that only things, the in-itself, are subject to causality. Man, on the other hand, makes himself as a free project; the for-itself is *uncaused*. Thus we can never describe any human condition as inevitable. To claim that a condition is unchangeable is to commit the error of seriousness and it is in general a form of bad faith. We cannot then explain woman's condition as inevitable, however universal it appears. What is called the 'eternal feminine', the behaviour and character which seem to distinguish women from men, is humanly created and thus alterable. Woman could have a different future, her biological constitution notwithstanding.

However, this point having been made at some length, Beauvoir goes on to diverge even more widely from Sartre than she had done in the ethical essays. Although the eternal feminine is humanly created and not natural, it is created by *man* (the male), through the situation which he imposes on woman. From woman's perspective, this situation is generally experienced as a destiny, as inevitable and not alterable. Moreover, such an experience of her situation is not necessarily a choice of bad faith on the part of woman. For although her situation is indeed humanly created, *she* is not the one who has made or chosen it: 'the whole of feminine history has been man made' (SS, p.159; 128). If woman is oppressed to the point where transcendence is no longer possible, then her situation is effectively her destiny; it acts upon her like a natural force. Beauvoir had already described such a condition in her ethical essays. Now she elaborates the notion of *immanence* (introduced only in passing in *The Ethics of Ambiguity*) as a philosophical grounding for her description.

Extending from her earlier argument that freedoms, because they are inter-dependent, need to maintain an open future for each other, she writes as follows:

> Every subject continually affirms himself through his projects as a tran-scendence; he realises his freedom only through his continual transcen-dence towards other freedoms; there is no other justification for present existence than its expansion towards an endlessly open future. Each time that transcendence falls back into immanence there is a degradation of existence into the 'in-itself' of freedom into facticity; this fall is a moral fault if the subject agrees to it; it takes the form of a frustration and an oppression if it is inflicted upon him.
>
> (*SS*, pp.28–9; xxviii–ix)

Woman is locked in immanence by the situation *man* imposes upon her – and she is not necessarily responsible. As has been pointed out, a consistent Sartrean position would make woman responsible for herself, no matter how constrained her situation.[25] But for Beauvoir, women's acceptance of this imposition runs along a continuum. Some do choose to accept it in bad faith, because of the security and privilege it brings. Others, unable to conceive of real alternatives, accept it while engaging in forms of passive resistance and 'resentment'. But for yet others, as for the oppressed whom Beauvoir had described in *The Ethics of Ambiguity,* freedom is suppressed to the point where they cease to be capable of choice or resistance. Beauvoir shifts, sometimes rather arbitrarily, between these alternative accounts of women's relation to their oppression. But what is of inter-est is that, at the most oppressed end of the continuum, Beauvoir breaks even more sharply from the Sartrean notion of the subject than in her earlier essays. For many there is no 'moral fault' because there is no possibility of choice. In the notion that freedom can 'fall back into the "in-itself"', that the for-itself can be turned, through the action of other (i.e. male) freedoms, into its very opposite, Beauvoir has finally and definitively broken from the Sartrean notion of the abso-lute subject. Indeed, one might even formulate her position, albeit only at this extreme end of the spectrum, in the terms Foucault used: woman is a historically constituted, not a constitut*ing*, subject. Not only does woman fail to *constitute* her situation in any way, she is in fact its *product*: 'when an individual, or a group of individuals, is kept in a situation of inferiority, the fact is that he *is* inferior . . . yes, women on the whole *are* today inferior to men, which is to say that their situation gives them less possibilities' (*SS*, p.24; xxiv).

Although it is of human origin, the condition imposed on woman by man is analogous in its power over her to the rule of natural forces over other kinds of objects. As the young girl grows up she discovers that she *already* has been given inferiority as 'a fixed and preordained essence' (*SS*, p.324; 297). A girl is twelve – 'and already her story is written in the heavens. She will discover it day after day without ever making it' (*SS*, p.325; 298). Woman, says Beauvoir repeatedly, is 'doomed', 'destined', through the action of male freedom, to her condition. Beauvoir's notion of the falling back of freedom into the in-itself is not to be dismissed as a mere metaphor. It describes the real condition of a human life that lacks the freedom which normally characterizes human existence. Yet, from a Sartrean perspective, one cannot take the statement as wholly literal either. Strictly speaking, within Sartre's usage of the terms, the degradation of an existence into the in-itself would have to mean that oppressed woman has actually ceased to be human. For Sartre, either the for-itself, the uncaused upsurge of freedom, exists whatever the facticities of its situation, or else it does not exist. In the latter case one is dealing with the realm of inert being. In so far as Beauvoir's account of woman's situation as one of immanence involves the claim that the for-itself can be penetrated and modified by the action of others, it implies another notion of the subject than Sartre's. Beauvoir is trying to describe human existence as a synthesis of freedom and constraint, of consciousness and materiality which, finally, is incompatible with Sartre's notion of the subject.

However, Beauvoir also refuses to go as far as Sartre's structuralist and post-structuralist critics were later to go in wholly discarding the notion of free subjectivity; even when it is suppressed, reduced to immanence, subjectivity remains as a distinctly human potentiality. Thus while, for example, much of her detailed account of the young girl's 'formation' could well be retold in the Foucauldian mode of 'the political technology of the body', of 'discipline' and 'dressage', Beauvoir would never have agreed to abandon the notion of a *repression* of freedom.[26] However suppressed, however disciplined, it is still freedom-made-immanent which distinguishes even the most constituted human subject from a well-trained animal.

Immanence is a condition which must be continuously inflicted on woman. As long as it is inflicted it is, for her, her destiny. There is no way she can choose to live the condition of immanence as a free choice. Unlike Sartre's example of the oppressed Jew, who can choose how he lives the otherness imposed on him by the anti-Semite (*BN*, p.523 ff.), Beauvoir's most oppressed woman has no way of living her otherness as a free choice. Those women who try – through narcissism, all-consuming love, or mysticism – to assume their immanence as a choice can never succeed. Theirs is 'this ultimate effort – sometimes ridiculous, often pathetic – of imprisoned woman to transform her prison into a heaven of glory, her servitude into sovereign liberty' (*SS*, p.639; 628). But such choices are no more than fantasy. They involve relations with an 'unreality' (her own double in narcissism, God in mysticism), or else (in all-consuming love), 'an unreal relation with a real being' (*SS*, p.687; 678). These fantasies never permit woman to gain the 'grasp on the world' which freedom requires.

If woman is to escape from immanence she cannot then do so by an act of individual choice alone. Given her condition of immanence, any 'choice' she might make could be only a choice of immanence. Thus, Beauvoir argues, the liberation of woman must come, in the first instance, from the outside. As in the case of the slave who must be put 'in the presence of his freedom' (*EA*, p.87) before he can choose it, woman's *situation* must be altered before she can effectively struggle for her own freedom. Thus, we must now examine in more detail Beauvoir's account of woman's situation.

Woman's situation: institutions

Volume II of *The Second Sex*, 'Lived Experience', begins with the following statement: 'One is not born a woman: one becomes one'(*SS*, p.295; 267). From cradle to grave the female will be treated differently. Man creates for her a *situation* of otherness. Living her life in this situation, she experiences herself as other, and indeed she is other. There is a broad male consensus on the female 'character'. Across the ages woman has been described as emotional, irrational, amoral, devious, vain; as weak, helpless and passive. Beauvoir admits, perhaps far too readily, that all these qualities are generally to be observed in women.[27] However, she insists, they are not to be explained as an 'essence'. They are manifestations of woman's immanence, the product of her situation.

In painstaking detail, beginning with the different treatment received by young children according to sex, Beauvoir shows us how young girls and women are made to feel and to be non-agents; how horizons are cut off, the experiences of choice and responsibility denied to them. She traces, at least for her own era, society and class, woman's experience through all ages – childhood, puberty, sexual initiation, adulthood and old age – and she explores the interlinked aspects of the adult woman's situation; from marriage to childbirth and social life. The latter barely extends beyond the home: economic activity, politics, the high arts – all realms of significant action beyond the home – are barred to her. Prepared from birth only to catch a man – that is, to make herself his 'prey' (*SS*, p.361; 337) – and to bear children, dependent on man, confined as his property in his house, it is not surprising that woman has no 'grasp on the world'. The 'eternal feminine' is to be explained then not as an essence, but as a synthesis of 'economic, social, historical conditioning'(*SS*, p.608; 597).

If we compare Beauvoir's account of woman's situation with Sartre's discussion of situation in *Being and Nothingness*, we are struck by several divergences. Most obviously, situation has become in Beauvoir's analysis above all *condition*, external force. We are no longer in the realm of the free constitution of the meaning of its situation by an autonomous subject. But there are also other important, though related, divergences. These concern, above all, the greater emphasis on various social aspects of situation in Beauvoir's analysis and her claim that we can talk of a situation as *general*, as being an objective reality which is experienced in similar ways by the members of a certain category of human beings.

In Sartre's discussion of the structures of my situation (*BN*, p.489 ff.), other people are present (unless they attempt to annihilate me) indirectly, via the humanly produced instruments I use and the general techniques such as language which I have in common with them. They are also present as my being-outside-for-others but this too is an indirect presence. For Beauvoir, however, others are *directly* involved in my constitution of the meaning of my freedom-in-situation. In contrast to Sartre's solitary rock climber Beauvoir had described, in *Pyrrhus et Cinéas* a solitary walker experiencing his relation to nature – but as soon as the walk is over needing to tell his experience to a friend in order to confirm it (*PC*, pp.68–9). For Beauvoir, we have seen, my situation is always mediated for me by others – hence her argument that I need freedoms equal to mine in the world. However, for women (and other oppressed groups), such a confirmation through others is impossible. The social constitution of her situation entails the suppression of woman's freedom, not its confirmation.

To begin with, woman lacks relations of equality with man. To the significant figures in her world – father and husband especially, but also priest, doctor, etc. – she is an inferior, not an equal. Subtending these direct, personal relations in which she experiences her objectification, woman also encounters as a major structure of her situation what we might call a set of social institutions. It is these institutions which function analogously to natural forces in perpetuating her immanence. If all that took place between man and woman was a Hegelian (or Sartrean) struggle of consciousnesses between two human beings, one of whom happened to be male and the other female, we could not anticipate which one of them would win and remain a subject, making the other an object. However, if we examine the relations of a *husband* and a *wife*, then it is very different. For the institution of marriage in all its aspects – legal, economic, cultural, etc. – has formed in advance for the protagonists their own relation of inequality. As Beauvoir points out in a strikingly un-Sartrean passage,

> it is not as single individuals that human beings are to be defined in the first place; men and women have never stood opposed to each other in single combat; the couple is an original *Mitsein*; and as such it always appears as a permanent or temporary element in a larger collectivity.
>
> (*SS*, pp.67–8; 35)

The relations of any particular couple are embedded in the relations of the larger collectivity, and they are delimited by it. Thus, as Beauvoir also points out, although woman's situation and history are 'man made', *individual* men may be as much the victims of what has become an impersonal system of forces as are women:

> A colonial administrator has no possibility of behaving well towards the natives, nor a general towards his soldiers; the only solution is to be neither a colonist nor a military chief; but a man could not stop himself from being a man. So there he is, guilty in spite of himself and oppressed by this fault which he himself has not committed . . . The evil does not originate from individual perversity . . . it arises from *a situation against which all individual action is powerless*.
>
> (*SS*, pp.732–3; 723–4; my emphasis)

In other words, the result of multiple, free (male) human action throughout history has been to create a set of institutions which function as a real limit on freedom, of either men or women. The process of change will thus have to commence from the radical modification of the institutional aspects of women's situation. Marriage, motherhood, her exclusion from economic and other kinds of activity, all will have to be extensively transformed. What the Soviet Union once promised still offers a vision of such a world of equality (*SS*, pp.733–4; 724–5), and Beauvoir is optimistic that, should women attain economic and social equality, in time an 'inner metamorphosis' will also take place (*SS*, p.738; 729). Liberation is not a matter of individual choice to begin with, but of complex social processes which modify woman's situation until the point is reached where a free – but not wholly autonomous – subjectivity can come into play.

Towards the end of the book, Beauvoir examines the 'independent woman' (*SS*, pp.689–724; 679–715). She is the new professional woman, who has no need of a man to support her. In some ways she is the harbinger of the free woman of the future. But in fact she experiences her life as a series of irresolvable conflicts between her 'human' freedom and her 'feminine' destiny. For finally, Beauvoir concludes, woman's oppression cannot be overcome except within the framework of the fuller abolition of human oppression. Thus, although she criticizes the orthodox Marxist account for its overly economistic explanation of woman's oppression (*SS*, pp.84–91; 53–60),[28] Beauvoir concludes *The Second Sex* with an extended quotation from Marx's 'Economic and Philosophical Manuscripts'[29] concerning the relations between the sexes, followed by an appeal 'to establish the reign of liberty in the midst of the world of the given' (*SS*, p.741; 732).

In so far as woman's oppressive situation is not simply individual but is an impersonal complex of social institutions, we can talk of woman's situation as a *general* one. From a Sartrean perspective this raises certain difficulties. For Sartre, since situations are uniquely constituted, we could not talk of a general situation; nor could we judge one situation to be more free or to be preferable to another. Like Sartre, Beauvoir also wishes to start from individual experience. The 'lived experience' of woman's situation, examined in Volume II, is, of course, *individually* lived. Extensive citations from women's memoirs, novels, etc., give her account an intensely personal and subjective foundation. Yet, at the same time, Beauvoir also wants to be able to evaluate that experience as a whole. The very isolation to which women are condemned precludes each from seeing the generality of her situation. But, Beauvoir insists, not only can we generalize about woman's situation, we can also *judge* between her situation and that of man:

> all comparisons are idle which purport to show that woman is superior, inferior, or equal to man: their situations are profoundly different. If we compare these actual situations, we see clearly that the man's is far preferable; that is to say, he has many more concrete opportunities to project his freedom in the world.
>
> (*SS*, p.638; 627)

In *The Ethics of Ambiguity* Beauvoir had already posed more clearly than Sartre the problem of the intelligibility of social existence and the same problem is posed, yet again, by the position she now takes in *The Second Sex*. Human experience is individual experience but it also has *generality* – as becomes especially clear in the experience of immanence. We thus need a theory which can encompass both subjectivity and the objective givens of human existence – a theory of socially mediated subjectivity such as is precluded by Sartre's disjunction of being-in-itself and being-for-itself and the autonomy he grants to consciousness. In so far as Beauvoir's account of woman's situation as one of immanence involves the admission that free consciousness, the for-itself, can be penetrated by the objectivity of the in-itself, it implies a notion of the subject as socially embedded and intersubjective, and not as autonomous. It implies also a notion of embodied subjectivity which is significantly different from Sartre's account of embodiment in *Being and Nothingness*, and which puts into question Sartre's division of being into two different and incommunicable regions.

Woman's situation: the body

Beauvoir's description of the institutions which constitute woman's situation is impressively thorough. But by itself it does not answer the question she had posed at the beginning of the book: *why* has man been able to impose such an oppressive situation on woman? She has shown us how woman's inequality and otherness are sustained, but this does not explain why they are possible in the first place. To explain why, she argues, we need also to look at the biological differences between the sexes, even though these differences do not in themselves constitute a 'destiny'.

Mortality, as Sartre had pointed out, is one of the necessary structures of human existence. 'Were he immortal,' Beauvoir paraphrases, 'an existent would no longer be what we call a man' (*SS*, p.39; 7). Yet, she again adds, each individual man, though mortal, requires an infinite future – a future which only other free men can give him. Concretely what this means is that each individual freedom requires 'the perpetuation of the species'. Thus, she concludes, 'we can regard the phenomenon of reproduction as ontologically founded'. Human existence is no more possible without reproduction than it is without death, and a society which ceased to reproduce itself would be a society in which individual projects would be meaningless.

Individual women, especially today, may have the choice not to reproduce; and reproduction is as much a social as a biological process. But even so, it is an inescapable fact, a basic 'given' of any woman's situation, that she has a different physiology from a man's, a physiology geared to the role of her sex in the perpetuation of the species. Beauvoir repeatedly stresses that biological facts have no significance beyond the values which man chooses to give them. For example, although woman is physically weaker than man, having 'less muscular strength', her weakness only has a meaning in a humanly created context (*SS*, pp.66–7;

34). Yet this is not to deny that woman's biology does perhaps predispose her for immanence: her physical powers are less than those of man and, Beauvoir concludes, woman consequently tends to have a less firm 'grasp on the world'. Furthermore, through her reproductive function itself, she is the victim of natural forces over which she has no control. Although woman's body is not by itself sufficient to 'define' her as woman, it is 'an essential element of the situation she occupies in the world' (*SS*, p.69; 37). Biological givens do not necessarily condemn woman to subordination, but they 'play a part of the first rank' in woman's history and 'are one of the keys to the understanding of woman' (*SS*, p.65; 32).

Through her body, Beauvoir argues, woman is condemned to experience a conflict which man does not experience, 'the conflict between species and individual' (*SS*, p.63; 30). Woman, a human existence capable of transcendence, is condemned to consume a significant amount of time and energy in 'natural functions'.[30] These are necessary for the perpetuation of the species and for there to be freedoms which open to an infinite future, but according to Beauvoir they involve no *project*. Menstruation, pregnancy, childbirth and lactation are not *activities*, she insists; woman cannot affirm her existence through them. 'Her misfortune is to have been biologically destined for the repetition of Life' (*SS*, p.96; 64), while man's role in perpetuating the species as a producer and a defender has always involved more than 'vital process', and has required of him 'actions which transcend his animal condition' (*SS*, p.95 ff.; 63 ff.). Here, claims Beauvoir, is the 'key' to the mystery of woman's otherness. Production and risking one's life in warfare are free affirmations of existence, but the animal function of reproducing the species is not.

There is often, according to Beauvoir, a biological differentiation which provides a basis for the social construction of inequality between the sexes. Women, of course, are not only wombs. They are capable of free existence. But the fact that they must affirm their freedom beyond or in spite of their reproductive function puts them at a disadvantage – a disadvantage upon which men have capitalized. Man has taken advantage of woman's partial immanence to impose upon her a condition of greater immanence. Woman, having submitted passively to her 'biological fate', has found herself also condemned to incarceration in the endless cycle of domestic labour, which is the kind of activity most compatible with maternity. Across the centuries she has been condemned to the cycle of household tasks, effectively unchanging, which have excluded her from creative and transcendent activity. Thus, in Beauvoir's account of woman's situation, the female body is seen as a real and general obstacle to freedom, an objective 'given', upon which man has been able to construct the institutions that constitute her oppression.

As an explanation of the origin of woman's oppression, Beauvoir's analysis is not wholly compelling. For, as later feminists have pointed out,[31] she repeatedly undervalues that element of freedom which can be present in parenthood and the activities associated with it. In so doing, she also tends to valorize the male-biased dualisms in Western thought which identify the masculine with the active and the rational, and the female with the passive and the corporeal. However, the importance of Beauvoir's account lies less in its adequacy as an explanation of woman's oppression *per se* than in what it implies more generally about the relation of freedom and subjectivity to embodiment. For while much of her discussion focuses on the female body, it also implies a more general reformulation of the account of the body which Sartre had offered.

For Sartre, it will be recalled, there are two primary 'aspects' to the body, involving two different and 'incommunicable' levels of being. These are my body-for-others (my body as object), and my body-for-me (my body as consciousness). In so far as my body has objectivity, for Sartre, its objectivity comes to me through other freedoms. It is only through the mediation of the Other – prototypically through the look – that I grasp my body as an objective structure of my being. Without such mediation I simply live my body-for-me as my point of view, as integral to my project. Although Beauvoir describes the body which concretely exists as 'the body lived by the subject' (*SS*, p.69; 38), this is not identical with Sartre's body-for-me. Woman's relation to her body cannot be subsumed under Sartre's two aspects. For woman encounters her lived body as having an objectivity which is not mediated by another consciousness. She discovers her body as 'an obscure alien thing', from which biological processes obtrude without her consent:

> She is of all mammalian females at once the one who is most profoundly alienated and the one who most violently resists this alienation; in no other is the enslavement of the organism to reproduction more imperious, or more unwillingly accepted.
>
> (*SS*, p.64; 32)

Although shame, modesty, etc., arise from woman's relation to her body in the presence of others, what Beauvoir is describing is an objectivity that the body has irrespective of such interpersonal or social experiences. Woman's body is nature, the demands of the species; it is, in short, Sartre's in-itself, as well as a body-for-others. Furthermore, woman's body cannot have the non-reflective quality of Sartre's body-for-me. Woman cannot simply live her body as her point of view, for she continually encounters it as other than herself 'Woman, like man, *is* her body: but her body is something other than herself' (*SS*, p.61; 29). If woman says, 'I am my body',[32] the statement is complex. For she would surely have to say also, 'I am partly other than myself'. Beauvoir's woman is not a Sartrean freedom, a for-itself for whom the particularities of the body are merely facticities. She is a real compound of materiality and consciousness. At various points in the text Beauvoir states this very clearly, although she does not attempt to elucidate the ontological implications of such a view. For example, she writes 'To be present in the world implies strictly that there exists a body which is *at the same time* a thing in the world and a point of view on this world' (*SS*, p.39; 7, my emphasis).

Although woman experiences the thinghood of the body more profoundly than man, much of Beauvoir's account of woman's body describes more generally the 'ambiguity' of all human existence as materiality and consciousness, necessity and freedom. As she puts it in one passage,

> man is, like woman, flesh, therefore a passivity, the plaything of his hormones and the species, the restless prey of his desires. And she is, like him, in the midst of carnal fever, consent, voluntary giving, activity; they live out, each in their own manner, the strange ambiguity of existence made body.
>
> (*SS*, p.737; 728)

Woman's greater predisposition to immanence lies in her more pervasive subordination to the exigencies of the body – a subordination which man has built upon in constructing her oppression. Yet men also are not free of such ambiguity.

Beauvoir does not, unfortunately, work out the broader philosophical implications of such a notion of ambiguous existence. It is to Merleau-Ponty's philosophy (itself frequently described as a philosophy of ambiguity), that we must turn for an ontology which will support her descriptions. Beauvoir herself perhaps recognized as much. For citing Merleau-Ponty's view that 'the body is generality' at one point, she expands on it in the following un-Sartrean manner:

> Across the separation of existents, existence is all one: it makes itself manifest in analogous organisms; therefore there will be constants in the relation of the ontological to the sexual. At a given epoch, the techniques, the economic and social structure, of a collectivity will reveal an identical world to all its members: there will also be a constant relation of sexuality to social forms; analogous individuals, placed in analogous conditions, will take from what is given analogous significations. This analogy does not establish a rigorous universality, but it does enable us to rediscover general types within individual histories.
>
> (*SS*, p.78; 46–7)

Through the notion of the generality of the body, not only the question of woman's oppression but the philosophical difficulties which Sartreanism had raised for Beauvoir can be addressed. The problem of the radical separation of situations and the concomitant problem of social and historical intelligibility – problems with which we have also seen Beauvoir struggling in her ethical essays – become less acute if, through the generality of the body, we each encounter an 'analogous' condition. Moreover, it becomes possible to address more fully the question of the simultaneous separateness and interdependence of freedoms. It becomes possible to rethink the notion of the subject in full recognition of what 'encumbers' it, and yet to do so without reducing it to a mere 'effect'.

Notes

1 See *The War Diaries of Jean-Paul Sartre*, translated by Q. Hoare, New York, Pantheon Books, 1984. Published posthumously, these notebooks were written between September 1939 and March 1940. They contain a mixture of personal introspection, descriptions of army life, and extended discussion of the philosophical issues most central to *Being and Nothingness*.

2 *The Prime of Life*, translated by P. Green, Cleveland, World Publishing Co., 1962, p.346.

3 'In philosophical terms, he was creative and I am not . . . I always recognized his superiority in that area. So where Sartre's philosophy is concerned, it is fair to say that I took my cue from him because I also embraced existentialism myself': Beauvoir, in A. Schwarzer, *Conversations with Simone de Beauvoir*, translated by M. Howarth, New York, Pantheon Books, 1984, p.109.

4 Ibid. See also Sartre, 'Self-Portrait at Seventy', in *Life/Situations*, translated by P. Auster and L. Davis, New York, Pantheon Books, 1977, pp.58–9; M. Sicard, interview with Sartre and Beauvoir, entitled 'Interférences', *Obliques*, nos. 18/19, pp.325–9.

5 Beauvoir later described these essays as the works which she had most self-consciously written within Sartre's framework, see Sicard, op. cit., p.328.

6 Not much has yet been written on Beauvoir's role in Sartre's intellectual development, but see M. Simons, 'Beauvoir and Sartre: The Philosophical Relationship', *Yale French Studies* 72, 1986, pp.165–79; see also my article, 'Simone de Beauvoir: Between Sartre and Merleau-Ponty', in R. Aronson and A. Vandenhoven (eds), *Sartre Alive*, Detroit, Wayne State University Press, 1990.

7 *The Prime of Life*, p.433.

8 *The Blood of Others*, translated by Y. Moyse and R. Senhouse, London, Secker and Warburg, 1948.

9 The book takes its title from the imaginary conversation with which it opens between Pyrrhus (King of Epirus born *ca.* 318 BC) and his adviser Cinéas, concerning whether or not there is any point in setting out to conquer the world. References [*PC*] are to *Pyrrhus et Cinéas*, Paris, Gallimard, 1944.

10 References [*BN*] are to *Being and Nothingness*, translated by H. Barnes, New York, Philosophical Library, 1956.

11 Beauvoir, like Sartre, unfortunately uses 'man' to denote all human beings, irrespective of gender. In *The Second Sex* she additionally uses 'man' to refer to specifically male human beings, and one has to determine from the context which she means.

12 It is interesting to note that Sartre, some years later, elaborated extensively on the notion of 'generosity' in the *Cahiers pour une morale* (Paris, Gallimard, 1983); see esp. p.514 ff.

13 T. Anderson argues in *The Foundation and Structure of Sartrean Ethics*, Lawrence, The Regent's Press of Kansas, 1979, p.94 ff., that Beauvoir fails to make the case that I need the recognition of all men to be free: if my plumber does not recognize my project as a philosopher, his lack of recognition does not matter to me. In response, it has rightly been pointed out that the issue is not one of *actual* recognition for Beauvoir, but of the equality of conditions which would *enable* all others freely to recognize me. See R. Stone, 'Simone de Beauvoir and the Existential

Basis of Socialism', *Social Text*, no.17, 1987, pp.123–33. Sartre used a similar universalizing argument to Beauvoir in *Existentialism and Humanism*.

14 *The Prime of Life*, pp.434–5.

15 See Descartes's 'Meditations' in *The Philosophical Writings*, translated by J. Cottingham and D. Murdoch, Cambridge, Cambridge University Press, 1985.

16 References to *EA* are to *The Ethics of Ambiguity*, translated by B. Frechtman, New York, Citadel Press, 1967.

17 Hegel, *The Phenomenology of Mind* [1807], translated by J. Baillie, London, George Allen and Unwin, 1966, pp.228–40.

18 Sartre later uses the term 'ensemble' in the *Critique* to denote the various kinds of social groupings he examines. This passage is, as far as I can establish, the first published use of the term by either thinker.

19 Beauvoir also dwells on this theme in the essay 'Idéalisme morale et réalisme politique' in *L'Existentialisme et la sagesse des nations*, Paris, Nagel, 1948, pp.55–101. Merleau-Ponty was exploring the same theme at much the same time, in the essays published in 1947 as *Humanism and Terror*.

20 K. Marx, *Capital*, Vol. 3, New York, International Publishing Co., 1967, p.820.

21 The work appeared in two volumes which, together, ran to over 900 pages of text. The one-volume English translation by H.M. Parshley is considerably abridged and is also very weak. I have frequently retranslated passages but still give page references to the British and US editions of the Parshley translation, New York, Knopf, 1953 and Harmondsworth, Penguin, 1972. The first set of page references [*SS*] is to the British edition, the second to the American. See M. Simons, 'The Silencing of Simone de Beauvoir: Guess What's Missing from *The Second Sex*', *Women's Studies International Forum*, vol.6, 1983, pp.559–64.

22 J. Okely, *Simone de Beauvoir*, London, Virago, 1986, p.122. See also M. Le Doeuff, 'Simone de Beauvoir and Existentialism', *Feminist Studies*, vol.6, 1980, pp.277–89; M. Evans, *Simone de Beauvoir: A Feminist Mandarin*, London, Tavistock, 1985; D. McCall, 'Simone de Beauvoir, *The Second Sex*, and Jean-Paul Sartre', *Signs*, vol.5, 1979, pp.209–23.

23 This use of the notion of 'reciprocity' strikingly anticipates Sartre's use of it in the *Critique*.

24 *Force of Circumstance*, translated by R. Howe, New York, G.P. Putnam's Sons, 1964, pp.185–93.

25 See M. Le Doeuff, 'Simone de Beauvoir and Existentialism'.

26 For a very different reading of Beauvoir, one which emphasizes woman's own role in the constitution of her situation, see J. Butler, 'Variations on Sex and Gender: Beauvoir, Wittig and Foucault', *Praxis International*, vol.5, 1986, pp.506–16. My own view, however, is that a careful reading of the text cannot sustain Butler's interpretation.

27 One might well reply to Beauvoir that such qualities are also to be found in most men. Identifying man and his situation with freedom, Beauvoir has a tendency to idealize the male world and male qualities.

28 In the 1940s Engels's analysis of 'the woman question' still formed the unquestioned basis for the PCF (French Communist Party) position on women.

29 See *Karl Marx, Early Writings*, translated by T. Bottomore, New York, McGraw Hill, 1964, p.154.

30 Just how much time this involves is, of course, largely socially specified. Some

women choose not to reproduce at all. But they still live the conflict, according to Beauvoir, for (unlike men) they have to decide to deny their 'natural functions'. In any case, such women are the exceptions: woman in general remains and will remain the perpetuator of the species.

31 Several commentators have argued, I think correctly, that Beauvoir under-estimates the degree of freedom that can be involved in such activities. See Evans, op. cit., Suzanne Lilar, *Le Malentendu du Deuxième Sexe*, Paris, PUF, 1969. Beauvoir has also been attacked by the Lacanian feminists in France. For a brief overview see D. McCall, 'S. de Beauvoir: Questions of Difference and Genera-tion', *Yale French Studies* 72, 1986, pp.121–31.

32 The phrase is Merleau-Ponty's, cited in a note [*SS*, p.61; 29]. Marcel had of course used the same phrase, but with a somewhat different meaning.

'INDEPENDENT WOMEN' AND 'NARRATIVES OF LIBERATION'

Toril Moi

Toril Moi's groundbreaking work on Beauvoir is without doubt one of the most significant developments in the critical field in the 1990s. *Feminist Theory and Simone de Beauvoir* (1990) contains two important essays, one addressing the problem of Beauvoir's speaking position as an intellectual woman in France, and the second offering a persuasive reading of Beauvoir's short story, 'The Woman Destroyed'.[1] In *Simone de Beauvoir. The Making of an Intellectual Woman* (1994), Moi goes on to undertake what she terms a 'personal genealogy' of Beauvoir, combining a wide range of discourses and theoretical tools in order to lay bare the structures that produced Simone de Beauvoir as an intellectual woman in the first third of the twentieth century in France.[2] By the time of the publication of *The Second Sex*, Moi considers Beauvoir to have 'truly become Simone de Beauvoir' (1994, p.6). The two chapters on *The Second Sex* thus focus on the question which Beauvoir asked of herself when she first started work on her essay: what did it mean to Beauvoir to be a woman at that particular moment? How, in other words, does Beauvoir represent the conflicts of an intellectual woman in mid-century France?

The first chapter reads *The Second Sex* as an essay in feminist philosophy, focusing particularly on its rhetorical strategies, its theory of female subjectivity under patriarchy and its account of sexuality. The second chapter, from which the following piece is taken, reads Beauvoir's essay as a political project. Reviewing feminist critiques of *The Second Sex*, Moi points out that they frequently fail to grasp that Beauvoir's political project is radically different from the identity politics which presupposes a theory of female identity as a basis for a feminist politics. For Beauvoir, the problematic is one of power rather than identity or difference. Women will forge their differential identity through their actions and choices in the world, once the barriers to their making such free choices have been removed.

Moi describes Beauvoir as offering in *The Second Sex* an extraordinary vision of freedom, a vision of an alternative to the status quo of the kind which every political movement requires. In her view this is one of the greatest strengths of the work. However, the nature of the utopia which Beauvoir elaborates is clearly itself shaped by its own historical moment and by Beauvoir's own situation: Moi analyses Beauvoir's speaking position as an exceptional intellectual woman, as a left-wing intellectual deeply committed to the socialist ideal, and as a woman in the throes of a sexual passion with a brilliant intellectual career. She can also be classed as an 'independent woman', in other words as falling into that category of woman described in *The Second Sex* as caught between the traditionally oppressed woman, to whose situation the greatest part of the essay is devoted, and the free woman of the future. As such, writes Moi, Beauvoir is herself caught in painful conflict between old and new, between patriarchal femininity and female freedom.

In the section on independent women which opens the following extract, Moi discusses Beauvoir's treatment of lesbianism and the critiques which have been made of it. Moi reminds us that just as Beauvoir does not accept the notion of a female essence, she does not accept the idea of a lesbian essence either, and she underlines the political position Beauvoir was adopting in discussing lesbianism as a valid choice. Nevertheless, Moi concedes that Beauvoir's discussion is riddled with theoretical and rhetorical confusions, and she analyses some of the reasons for Beauvoir's 'troubled response' to the subject.

In the section entitled 'Narratives of Liberation', Moi comes to the heart of her political analysis. Only three years after the publication of *The Second Sex*, Frantz Fanon published in Paris his essay on black alienation in a racist society, entitled *Black Skin, White Masks* (1952). Drawing on many of the same theorists as Beauvoir, and in particular on Sartre's essay 'Black Orpheus' published in 1948, Fanon manifestly has to contend with many of the problematics that Beauvoir had also faced. The confrontation of the two texts which Moi carries out is highly illuminating and allows her to pinpoint what she describes as 'the deepest political flaw in *The Second Sex*': Beauvoir's failure to grasp the political potential of a discourse of femininity. Where Sartre urges the necessity of a stage in the black struggle of 'antiracist racism' in which blacks temporarily recuperate their own blackness as a stepping stone to a future of depoliticised racial identity, where Fanon claims not only the political necessity but the emotional necessity of 'négritude', Beauvoir refuses to consider the uses of a stage of 'feminitude'. Moi explores with great sympathy how this refusal stems both from Beauvoir's intellectual positions and her personal experience, and underlines the historical obstacles to imagining an autonomous women's movement. Beauvoir cannot, she concludes, be criticised for not thinking the virtually unthinkable. Instead, she returns us to the powerful narrative of liberation which Beauvoir offers and to the vision of change which has inspired women all over the world.

Notes

1 T. Moi, *Feminist Theory and Simone de Beauvoir*, Oxford, Blackwell, 1990.
2 The extract printed here is taken from T. Moi, *Simone de Beauvoir. The Making of an Intellectual Woman*, Oxford, Blackwell, 1994, pp.197–213.

Independent women

For Simone de Beauvoir, economic independence is the *sine qua non* of women's liberation. As long as women are prevented from earning their own living, they will always be dependent on others. Women actually seeking paid work, however, are confronted with class exploitation and sexist oppression at every turn. Oppressed at home, they find themselves exploited, underpaid and alienated at work. Under capitalism, Beauvoir writes, there is nothing liberating in factory work: no wonder many working-class women would rather be housewives if only they could afford it, particularly since they usually have to do the housework anyway.[1] Under such conditions, women are caught in an internal double bind: without paid work they are delivered up to male exploitation; with paid work they find themselves working a double shift, with very little money to show for it at the end of the week. While some women heroically struggle to change their condition by becoming politically active in trade unions or various socialist parties, most – quite understandably – do not have the energy to spare.

A painful paradox thus emerges: only work can emancipate women, yet nothing enslaves them more completely. For genuine freedom to be possible, the social conditions of women's lives must be radically transformed. What is required, Beauvoir writes, is what the Bolshevik revolution promised but never delivered:

> Women reared and trained exactly like men were to work under the same conditions and for the same wages. Erotic liberty was to be recognized by custom, but the sexual act was not to be considered a 'service' to be paid for; woman was to be *obliged* to provide herself with other ways of earning a living; marriage was to be based on a free agreement that the contracting parties could break at will; maternity was to be voluntary, which meant that contraception and abortion were to be authorized and that, on the other hand, all mothers and their children were to have exactly the same rights, in or out of marriage; pregnancy leaves were to be paid for by the State [*la collectivité*], which would assume charge of

the children, signifying not that they would be *taken away* from their parents, but that they would not be *abandoned* to them.

(*SS*, pp.733–4; *DS* II, pp.653–4)[2]

Until such utopian conditions prevail – for this is the most complete description of Beauvoir's social utopia to be found anywhere in *The Second Sex* – women will remain economically and professionally disadvantaged.[3] While economic independence remains the fundamental starting point for liberation, Beauvoir is far from arguing that money alone guarantees happiness and freedom. This becomes particularly evident in her discussion of the status of 'independent women', that is to say, the 'fairly large number of privileged women who find social and economic autonomy in their professions' (*SS*, pp.691; *DS* II, p.600). Beauvoir herself, of course, is an outstanding example of just such a woman.

Independent women are not free. 'As yet they are only halfway there,' Beauvoir writes: 'The woman who is economically emancipated from man is not for all that in a moral, social, and psychological situation identical with that of man . . . The fact of being a woman today poses peculiar problems for an independent human being' (*SS*, p.691; *DS* II, p.600; TA). Theirs is a particularly contradictory situation, one in which they are, as it were, trying to live the future before the objective conditions are ripe. It is not surprising, then, that such women tend to be even more torn by conflicts and contradictions than their more traditional sisters.

'The independent woman of today is torn between her professional interests and the problems of her sexual life [*les soucis de sa vocation sexuelle*],' Beauvoir claims (*SS*, p.705; *DS* II, p.618). Whole, autonomous human beings are sexual beings: 'Man is a human being with sexuality; woman is a complete individual, equal to the male, only if she too is a human being with sexuality,' she writes. 'To renounce her femininity, is to renounce a part of her humanity' (*SS*, pp.691–2; *DS* II, p.601). Sacrificing their sexual needs and desires to the pressures of social conventions, women mutilate themselves, since freedom includes the right to sexual expression. For independent women in France in 1949, however, such freedom was hard to find. Contraception and abortion were illegal. To give birth out of wedlock usually amounted to professional suicide, while marriage, on the other hand, might well mean the end of any real independence for the woman. Even assuming that the woman somehow solved the problem of contraception, she could not simply pick up a man in the street without fear of venereal disease and violence. In smaller, more provincial towns, such behaviour would in any case be out of the question. Given the prevalence of patriarchal mythology, a truly successful woman might alienate potential sexual partners looking for more conventional incarnations of patriarchal femininity. An independent woman engaged in a stable relationship, on the other hand, might more or less unconsciously wish to avoid too much professional success, in order not to appear dominating in relation to her partner: 'split between the desire to assert herself and the desire for self-effacement,' Beauvoir writes, 'she is torn and divided' (*SS*, p.703; *DS* II, p.616; TA).

Arising from the woman's wish not to repress her own sexual needs, such conflicts are profoundly painful. But they also signal the presence of a will to struggle, and may produce great lucidity: an independent woman is likely to be more aware of her difficulties than a woman who buries her projects and her desires, but she is nevertheless infinitely better off.[4] Precisely because of her lived experience of the ambiguity of oppression, the independent woman becomes more authentic – but not more free – than most men. On this point, then, Beauvoir's political analysis rejoins her philosophical understanding of women's condition: as long as they are consciously experienced and accepted, women's contradictions and conflicts make them more acutely human than men.

For Beauvoir, lesbians make up one important category of independent women. Lesbianism, she writes, 'is one way, among others, in which woman solves the problems posed by her condition in general, by her erotic situation in particular' (SS, p.444; DS II, p.218).[5] According to The Second Sex, then, lesbianism may be understood as an existential choice like any other. Heterosexuality, one may add, is also a choice.[6] If anything, Beauvoir suspects lesbianism of being more, not less 'natural' than heterosexuality: 'And if nature is to be invoked, one can say that all women are naturally homosexual', she writes (SS, p.427; DS II, p.195). Lesbians may live their sexuality authentically or inauthentically: per se they are neither inferior nor superior to other women: 'Like all human behaviour, homosexuality will lead to make-believe, disequilibrium, frustration, lies, or, on the contrary, it will become the source of rewarding experiences, depending on how it is lived – whether in bad faith, laziness, and falsity, or in lucidity, generosity, and freedom' (SS, p.444; DS II, p.218; TA). While Beauvoir does not absolutely exclude the idea, often advanced by patriarchal discourse, that hormonal or anatomical factors may in some cases contribute to lesbian object choice, she resolutely rejects the idea that anatomy alone can determine sexual orientation: 'But anatomy and the hormones only define a situation and do not set the object towards which the situation is to be transcended' (SS, p.425; DS II, p.193; TA).

A number of lesbian feminists have been disappointed by the fact that Beauvoir fails to provide a theory of lesbian identity. Claudia Card, for instance, complains that Beauvoir 'assesses lesbian relationships simply as human relationships, not as specifically lesbian', and Ann Ferguson is unhappy with the fact that Beauvoir fails to 'make the historical distinction between lesbian practices and a lesbian identity'.[7] The question of whether it is in fact desirable to have a strong theory of lesbian identity will not be discussed here. Given Beauvoir's general application of the maxim that 'existence precedes essence' to every form of sexuality and identity, however, her understanding of lesbianism as an existentialist act expressed in a specific object choice is consistent with her general theoretical framework. Identity, for Beauvoir, does not precede but *follows from* our acts in the world. In so far as different women have different reasons for choosing to 'make themselves lesbian', to use a Beauvoirean expression, they will not all develop the same understanding of what it means to be a lesbian. Just as there is no general 'female essence' shared by all women, *The Second Sex* implies, there can be no common 'lesbian nature' either.

Beauvoir's discussion of lesbian life displays all the rhetorical and philosophical contradictions I analysed earlier. There is the same insistence on the passivity of female sexuality (on this point Beauvoir makes no difference between heterosexual and homosexual women), and the same tendency to take the masculine to be the universal, in spite of her own explicit warnings against that particular fallacy. In fact, her relatively brief chapter on lesbianism is exceptionally confused, structurally as well as thematically. Moving from trousers for women (now usual on beaches, Beauvoir notes) to the outlandish story of an aristocratic bisexual crossdresser in Austria, taken from the notoriously unreliable Wilhelm Stekel's 'study' of frigidity in women, Beauvoir also throws in glancing references to Radclyffe Hall, Sarah Ponsonby, wild jealous rages, and 'butch' and 'femme' behaviour and, finally, ascribes lesbian object choice to anything from a need for relaxation or a predilection for softness of skin (natural to all women, according to Beauvoir), to a desire to avoid being reduced to an object for men or a desire to compete with men on their own terrain.

The theoretical and rhetorical confusion of this chapter is indicative of deeper difficulties: it is as if the very subject of lesbianism makes Beauvoir incapable of organizing her thought. The revelation of Beauvoir's own homosexual practices in the posthumously published *Letters to Sartre* (1990) opens new perspectives on Beauvoir's troubled response to the subject. In this context, however, it is crucial to remember that she never considered herself a lesbian: the definition of lesbianism provided in *The Second Sex* also applies to her own case. According to Beauvoir, lesbians are not simply women who enjoy sexual relations with women; the decisive point is that is *all* they enjoy: '[The lesbian] is distinguished not by her taste for women but by the exclusive character of this taste,' she insists (*SS*, p.427; *DS* II, p.196). Or in other words: lesbians are women who *never* consider men potential objects of pleasure. On this definition, everybody else, including herself, is heterosexual.

There may be more than a touch of bad faith in this: Beauvoir's definition was after all formulated well after her major lesbian or, rather, bisexual period in the late 1930s and early 1940s. Perhaps it suited her to define lesbians as different from herself. Perhaps she simply could not face labelling herself as anything other than heterosexual, regardless of what her own sexual practices might be. Perhaps – and in the *Letters to Sartre* there is much evidence for this – she considered her own lesbian practices as purely 'supplementary' to heterosexual sex. Whatever her reasons may have been, the fact is that the author of *The Second Sex* answered every inquiry about her own sexual relationships to women in the negative for the rest of her life. In 1982, for instance, Alice Schwartzer asked her whether she had ever had a sexual relationship with a woman, and Beauvoir replied: 'No. I have had some very important friendships with women, of course, some very close relationships, sometimes close in a physical sense. But they never aroused erotic passion on my part.'[8]

There is a touch of Jesuitical casuistry about Beauvoir's answer here. But it is also true that it probably never occurred to her that a woman who also related to men might be thought of as a lesbian. This is confirmed by the curious episode in the *Letters to Sartre* where she denies that Natalie Sorokine is a lesbian, in spite of the fact that she herself carried on an unusually tempestuous affair with the very same Sorokine in 1939 and 1940. Under the morally repressive Vichy regime, in 1943 her affair with Sorokine even cost Beauvoir her job.[9] This is what Beauvoir writes to Sartre in her letter of 28 August 1950:

> When Sor. had left, Algren told me that his friends had been struck by her lesbian side. It has to be said, she does caress and kiss me in front of people in a way that must appear odd. But Christine had thought her a lesbian simply from hearing her voice on the telephone, and Algren says she made the same impression on him as soon as she got out of the taxi. She isn't one, though – she had one ludicrous, failed experience with a professional lesbian, that's all – she's above all sexually infantile.
>
> (*LS*, p.475; *LS* II, p.392).

After 1944, if the information currently in the public domain is anything to go by, there is not much evidence of lesbian practices in Beauvoir's own life. Sylvie Le Bon de Beauvoir – Beauvoir's adoptive daughter and the editor of the *Letters to Sartre* – does nothing to dissuade the reader from the idea that her life-long relationship with Beauvoir was also a sexual one: '[It was] love between Castor [Beauvoir] and myself,' she insists. 'What made it complicated is that neither one of us was prepared, especially me, to love someone who was a woman. But that's what it was, love, that's all.' Asked to specify whether they were in fact having a sexual relationship, Le Bon de Beauvoir would just say that, in public, Beauvoir always insisted 'that we were good friends because I didn't want her to say anything more, for many reasons, many bad reasons'.[10]

What, then, does Beauvoir have to say about lesbian sexuality? Is it truly an escape from the objectification imposed on women in a patriarchal world? In many ways, the answer would seem to be yes. It is in her discussion of lesbianism that Beauvoir produces one of the most positive descriptions of sexual relations to be found anywhere in *The Second Sex*: 'Between women love is contemplative; caresses are intended less to gain possession of the other than gradually to re-create the self through her; separateness is abolished, there is no struggle, no victory, no defeat; in exact reciprocity each is at once subject and object, sovereign and slave, duality becomes mutuality' (*SS*, p.436; *DS* II, p.208). On this account, lesbians would seem actually to achieve the existentialist ideal of reciprocity. The contrast to Françoise's heroic struggle to seduce Gerbert in a reciprocal mode is significant [in *She Came to Stay*]. Françoise found herself caught in a web of social hierarchies; here, on the other hand, the master–slave dialectics is undone, the struggle between the sexes plays no role: this is a true relationship of equals. This does not prevent Beauvoir from finding even more exciting values in *ideal* heterosexual sex:

> When woman finds in the male both desire and respect; if he lusts after her flesh while recognizing her freedom, she feels herself to be the essential in the very moment she makes herself object; she remains free in the submission to which she consents. . . . Under a concrete and carnal form there is mutual recognition of the other and the ego. . . . Alterity has no longer a hostile implication; it is this sense of the union of truly separate bodies that makes the sexual act so moving; it is the more overwhelming as the two beings, who together passionately deny and assert their boundaries, are similar [*semblables*] and yet different.
>
> (*SS*, p.422; *DS* II, p.189; TA).

Beauvoir's philosophical idealization of the male body leads her to find 'defeat' for women even in the most perfect instance of heterosexual intercourse. In this passage, it is as if the very difference between the two bodies adds intensity to the sexual encounter.

True reciprocity, Beauvoir implies, presupposes difference: too much similarity reduces sexual interaction to a narcissistic mirroring of the other: it is not a coincidence that she speaks of the 'miracle of the mirror' (*SS*, p.436; *DS* II, p.207) precisely in the context of lesbian sexuality. Overall, then, Beauvoir apparently believes that homosexual relations are preferable to the vast majority of heterosexual relations available to women under patriarchy. At the same time, however, she also comes dangerously close to equating lesbianism with narcissism. Ultimately, it would seem, Beauvoir stakes her sexual hopes on truly reciprocal sex with men: it is hard not to perceive the traces of Nelson Algren in Beauvoir's glowing praise of ideal heterosexual sex.

For Beauvoir, the advantage of her theoretical position is that it explains her own sexual practices in the 1930s and 1940s.[11] The disadvantage is that it is more than a little illogical. For if homosexuality truly represents one existential choice among others, and if such relations may potentially be lived in complete authenticity, as Beauvoir clearly believes, then there can be no reason to define lesbian relations as overwhelmingly narcissistic. For narcissism for Beauvoir is one specific mode of female alienation, one that always leads to bad faith: it is no coincidence that she devotes a whole chapter to narcissism as a false solution to women's dilemmas under patriarchy. Nor should it be forgotten that for existentialists, *every* subject is an Other: if the master–slave dialectics may be acted out in the encounter between two men, a point taken for granted by Sartre as well as by Hegel, then there can be no reason to assume that the tension of alterity would be absent between two women either. As Beauvoir suspects, under patriarchy, true reciprocity may in fact be easier to achieve between women than between women and men. There is no justification for assuming that women are somehow so marked by their sameness that instead of respecting – or fighting –

each other's difference they simply proceed to a harmonious, symbiotic merger with the Other.

In spite of its confusion, Beauvoir's chapter on lesbianism does make a number of valuable political points. In France in 1949, it took courage even to raise the subject. There can be no doubt that Beauvoir in fact sees lesbianism as a perfectly valid existential choice; she is clearly radically opposed to any kind of discrimination against women who choose to lead lesbian lives. A strong point of her chapter is her generous mapping of the many different ways of being a lesbian; the confusion of her writing is partly caused by the profusion of idiosyncratic examples jostling for space on her pages. Just as Beauvoir explicitly refuses to generalize about women's identity, she also, in principle, refuses to generalize about lesbian identity. Acutely sensitive to the difficulties encountered by lesbians and other independent women trying to protect their autonomy under patriarchy, Beauvoir describes their dilemmas – which are also her own – with sympathy and insight. The obstacles placed in the way of real freedom remain daunting, yet Beauvoir refuses to abandon the struggle. For her, everything remains possible: women's potential is unlimited; the future remains wide open.

Narratives of liberation

How, then, does Beauvoir envisage the future? What would count as liberation for the author of *The Second Sex*? In order to answer such questions, it is useful to consider *The Second Sex* in the context of Sartre's 'Black Orpheus' (1948) and Frantz Fanon's *Black Skin, White Masks* (1952). There can be no doubt that Beauvoir read Sartre's famous essay on *négritude*, published only a year before *The Second Sex*. To claim that *Black Skin, White Masks* can help to illuminate *The Second Sex* may be more surprising, yet the parallels between the two texts are striking. Just like *The Second Sex*, Fanon's epochal study of racism and colonialism explicitly invokes Lacan's theory of alienation in the mirror stage. Where Beauvoir draws on Lacan and Sartre to construct a highly complex theory of female alienation under patriarchy, Fanon mobilizes the same thinkers to theorize black alienation in a racist society. Centrally concerned with the question of the subjectivity of the oppressed, both theorists turn to a whole range of psychoanalytic writers in order to develop their own perspectives. Moreover, as we shall see, the authors' personal experience of oppression and marginality makes the question of *style* particularly important – and particularly problematic – for them.

Fanon himself makes absolutely no reference to *The Second Sex*. Nor does he seem even remotely interested in the question of women's liberation. Writing his essay as a medical student in Lyons, Fanon was influenced by existentialism, and – judging by his footnotes – clearly an assiduous reader of *Les Temps modernes*. In 1948 and 1949 the existentialist journal published many excerpts from *The Second Sex*, yet Fanon fails to mention any of them. Nor does he refer to the full-length book, although he could hardly have been unaware of its publication and the outraged response it provoked in France in 1949 and 1950.[12] Unfortunately,

Fanon's explicit invocation of Sartre and his total neglect of Beauvoir exemplify the usual response of male intellectuals to existentialism. In spite of the obvious historical connections between Fanon and Beauvoir, it would seem that present-day colonial and post-colonial critics have done nothing to change this unhappy state of affairs.

In *The Second Sex* Beauvoir often draws parallels between women's liberation and black liberation struggles. Her reaction to *Black Skin, White Masks* is not recorded. As far as I know, she never remarked on the Martiniquan theorist's neglect of her own work. In *Force of Circumstance* she gives a glowing account of her own meeting with Fanon shortly before his death in 1961.[13] In the late 1950s and early 1960s Beauvoir travelled extensively, and was constantly meeting some of the world's most influential politicians and intellectuals: Fidel Castro, Nkita Khrushchev, Albert Camus, Alberto Moravia, Jorge Amado, Nicolas Guillén and many others file through her pages. The only person truly to stand out in this glittering array, however, is Fanon, who by the late 1950s had become an important figure in the Algerian revolution. When Beauvoir met him, he was marked by illness, yet she found him 'intensely alive'. Praising Fanon's 'wealth of knowledge, his powers of description and the rapidity and daring of his thought', Beauvoir testifies to his intellectual stature (*FC*, p.611; *FC* II, p.427). 'He was an exceptional man,' she writes. 'When one was with him, life seemed to be a tragic adventure, often horrible, but of infinite worth' (ibid.).

Since Fanon's essay directly engages with Sartre's positions, it is necessary first to consider 'Black Orpheus'.[14] In order to free itself, Sartre argues, the working class must develop a consciousness of itself as a class, and then go on to oppose itself to its capitalist oppressors. The process of reaching the necessary proletarian class consciousness, however, is purely objective: it is simply a matter of recognizing the historical situation of the proletariat, and in no sense involves the subjectivity of the individual worker. Forced by racism to face their colour every day, blacks, on the other hand, realize that the first step towards liberation is to affirm and vindicate their very blackness: 'The final unity which will bring all the oppressed together in the same struggle, must be preceded in the colonies by what I shall call the moment of separation or negativity: this antiracist racism is the only road that will lead to the abolition of racial differences' (*Situations III*, p.237). For Sartre, the ultimate aim of the antiracist struggle is a 'society without privileges in which skin pigmentation will be considered purely accidental' (*Situations III*, p.236). Such 'antiracist racism' must necessarily produce a language of racial essentialism radically at war with its own ultimate goals. If racism alienates blacks from themselves, liberation requires them to recuperate their own blackness, to take it over for themselves, one might say. This is true even though the blackness recuperated is in no sense a 'pure' or 'essential' blackness, but the contradictory product of racism and colonialism. For Sartre, the 'antiracist racism' of *négritude* is an absolutely necessary ingredient in a process which will ultimately transform the abstract notion of universal humanity into a concrete reality. Or to put it differently: under truly non-racist conditions race will no

81

longer carry *political* implications. Sartre's model of black liberation, one might say, represents a utopian vision of the ultimate *depoliticization* of identity: his point, however, is that the way to this goal necessarily goes through the *radical politicization* of racial identity, however contradictory and conflictual the latter may be.

If we now turn to *Black Skin, White Masks,* the first and most striking aspect of it is its style. No doubt partly as a consequence of his marginal position in the French intellectual and cultural fields, Fanon's essay is deeply personal in tone. Shifting between poetic prose, irony, anecdote and relatively technical psychiatric and philosophical analysis, the multiplicity of voices in his text is such that the whole essay tends towards the centrifugal, only to be reined back by the intense staging – *mise en scène* – of the narrative and experiencing 'I'. The very plurality of Fanon's discourse enacts his complex relationship to his own experience and political situation. It also enables him to stage his arguments on a multiplicity of different levels: in *Black Skin, White Masks* the contradictions of black alienation and identity in a racist society are examined through narrative, literary criticism, polemics, personal experience and poetic musings. As a result, the reader grasps not only the contradictions of black subjectivity under colonialism, but also the pain, confusion and disillusionment which are part of the experience of blackness under such conditions. In this way, the very subjectivity at stake in Fanon's debate with Sartre is rhetorically enacted and placed at the centre of the text.

Through his highly idiosyncratic – and, to me, quite admirable – *écriture*, Fanon manages at once to signal his distance from and endorsement of Sartre's positions. Reflecting and refracting his theoretical investments, his rhetorical practice represents a radical break with the prevalent form of the philosophico-political essay in France at the time. If the Sartre of the late 1940s is the incarnation of French 'philosophy', Fanon's stylistic raids on that poetry of *négritude* which he clearly feels more than a little ambivalent about spell a subtle opposition to the very voice of the French master thinker. Deeply aware of the social and political implications of Sartre's distinguished speaking position, Fanon sees Sartre at once as a highly valuable political ally for the *négritude* movement, and as a crushingly condescending theorist. Objecting to Sartre's high-handed reduction of his own experience to a mere moment in the dialectics of liberation, Fanon shows that the existentialist thinker completely fails to grasp the emotional and experiential implications of black discourse:

> *Orphée noir* is a date in the intellectualization of the *experience* of being black. . . . Jean-Paul Sartre, in this work, has destroyed black zeal. In opposition to historical becoming, there had always been the unforeseeable. I needed to lose myself completely in negritude. One day, perhaps, in the depths of that unhappy romanticism . . . [. . .] The dialectic that brings necessity into the foundation of my freedom drives me out of myself. It shatters my unreflected position.[15]

Fanon's point, then, is not that *négritude* ('that unhappy romanticism') is a flaw-less theoretical position, but that it corresponds to an emotional and political need. In the very act of declaring his support for *négritude,* Sartre fails to understand that subjectivity and the body are inseparable. The result is that the *embodied* nature of black experience entirely escapes him: 'Not yet white, no longer wholly black, I was damned,' Fanon writes. 'Jean-Paul Sartre had forgotten that the Negro suffers in his body quite differently from the white man' (p.138).

The need for *négritude,* then, is not simply an abstract moment in the dialectics, but rather an inescapable aspect of the weave of black subjectivity, anchored as deeply in Fanon's body as is his need to partake of that general humanity where colour is only one variable among others: 'My black skin is not the wrapping of specific values,' Fanon writes at the end of his essay. 'I do not have the duty to be this or that' (pp.227, 229). Echoing fundamental existentialist themes, Fanon goes on to declare that 'No attempt must be made to encase [*fixer*] man, for it is his destiny to be set free [*lâché*]' (p.230), and to insist on his desire to liberate himself from the burdens of the past: 'I do not have the right to allow myself to be mired in what the past has determined. . . . The Negro is not. Any more than the white man' (pp.230–1). Fanon, then, does not object to the ultimate depoliticization of identity; his point is rather that Sartre's final utopia would seem to hold no space for black identity at all. While Fanon's critique of Sartre stops short of an explicit rejection of dialectics, his very *écriture* tends towards the non-dialectical. It is as if he is grasping for a way to theorize subjectivity in which the dialectical moments outlined by Sartre would all be constantly in movement, so that every element would ceaselessly cross the paths of others in new and unpredictable combinations. My point is that although Fanon's theory does not offer such a postmodern elaboration of the problem, his discourse comes close to enacting it.

What position does Beauvoir occupy in this picture? The oppression of women, Beauvoir argues, is in some ways similar to the oppression of other social groups, such as that of Jews or blacks. Members of such groups are also treated as objects by members of the ruling caste or race. Yet women's situation remains fundamentally different, above all because women are scattered across all social groups: 'The bond that unites her to her oppressors is not comparable to any other,' Beauvoir insists in the introduction to *The Second Sex* (*SS*, p.19; *DS* I, p.19).[16] As a result, women tend to feel solidarity with men in their own social group rather than with women in general. Under patriarchy there are no female ghettoes, no female compounds in which to organize a collective uprising: 'Women,' Beauvoir writes in 1949, 'do not say "We" . . . they do not authentically posit themselves as Subject' (*SS*, p.19; *DS* I, p.19). Opposing themselves to whites, blacks may posit blackness as a dialectical moment of revolutionary negation, in a way that women simply cannot do in relation to men who are their sons, brothers and fathers when they are not their husbands or lovers. 'Women lack concrete means for organizing themselves into a unit which would posit itself in the act of opposition,' Beauvoir writes (*SS*, p.19; *DS* I, p.19; TA).[17]

Precisely because the great majority of women have never lived in their own communities, segregated from men, women's alienation is much more ambivalent than that of other oppressed groups. The complex and contradictory outcome of patriarchal socialization, female subjectivity is an ambiguous mixture of transcendence and freedom. No other oppressed group experiences the same kind of contradiction between freedom and alienation.[18] *The Second Sex* in fact establishes an exact parallel between women's subjective and objective (social) positions. In both cases, their situation is characterized by the absence of a clear-cut opposition between the two first moments of the dialectic. It follows that women's liberation cannot be squeezed into the classically Hegelian narrative of freedom provided by Sartre.

What, then, is Beauvoir's alternative to Sartre's Hegelian narrative? On this point, *The Second Sex* becomes somewhat vague. On my reading of Beauvoir, the ambiguity of female subjectivity under patriarchy appears to be at once a political strength and a weakness. It is a strength in so far as it potentially enables women to achieve freedom with less violent struggle than other groups: in this scenario, change becomes a matter of seizing upon the multiple contradictions of patriarchal ideology and using them to undermine the system from within. It is a weakness in so far as it prevents women from constructing a revolutionary movement in which they clearly and squarely oppose themselves to men.[19] On this logic, women's very ambiguity makes the revolutionary option – which is precisely the development Sartre imagines for blacks as well as for the working class – impossible. Instead, women will have to keep up a continuous struggle against the contradictory manifestations of patriarchal ideology, as well as against outright violence and callous exploitation. On such a reading of *The Second Sex*, women's struggle for liberation emerges as a slow and contradictory process, the one truly non-violent revolution in history.

What, then, is the aim of this process? Remarkably clear and coherent, Beauvoir's utopia presupposes that the material conditions described above have been achieved. Firmly linking freedom to brotherhood, the last sentence of *The Second Sex* has often seemed problematic to feminists: 'Man must establish the reign of liberty in the world of the given. To gain the supreme victory, it is necessary, for one thing, that by and through their natural differentiation men and women unequivocally affirm their brotherhood' (*SS*, p.741; *DS* II, p.663; TA). In spite of appearances, this sentence cannot be reduced to a simple betrayal of the values of sisterhood.[20] Rhetorically as well as thematically, the last word of *The Second Sex* represents Beauvoir's final utopian gesture. 'All oppression creates a state of war,' she writes (*SS*, p.726; *DS* II, p.645). Only when oppression ceases will genuine solidarity be possible between men and women: Beauvoir's final *fraternité* must be imagined as situated in a space where patriarchy no longer rules, for only then can the word be given the truly universal meaning it ought to have had all along. In such a political space the word *sisterhood* will finally be taken to be just as universal as *brotherhood*.[21] There is here, of course, a deliberate allusion to the French Revolution: her utopia, Beauvoir is saying, would consist in a world in which the ideals of freedom, equality and brotherhood would finally be translated into reality. Equality here does not mean sexual *sameness*: hers is not a theory of a sexless society, in any sense of the word. For Beauvoir, political equality presupposes social and economic equality. Together, these three elements make up the *sine qua non* of ethical equality between the sexes. Ethical equality implies the mutual recognition of the other as a free, acting subject, and in *The Second Sex* this is usually called *reciprocity*, not *brotherhood*.[22] It may be necessary to add that what Beauvoir has in mind is *concrete* equality, not the purely *abstract* equality invoked by traditional bourgeois humanism. Concrete equality encompasses difference: maternity leave, for instance, signals the social recognition of women's specific role in procreation, but it also demonstrates the social will to ensure that such difference is not turned into a professional and economic liability. Or in other words: for concrete equality to be established, difference must be recognized.[23]

Much like Marx, Beauvoir dreams of a society in which the ostensibly universal values of the Enlightenment tradition will finally become available to all. Today, she writes, 'man ... represents the positive and the neutral – that is to say the male and the human being, whereas woman is only the negative, the female' (*SS*, p.428; *DS* II, p.197). As long as women are denied access to the universal, sexual difference is used against them. In Beauvoir's utopia, women would no longer be constantly reminded of their difference, no longer made to feel deviant from the patriarchal norm:

> When at last it will be possible for every human being to set his pride beyond sexual differentiation, in the difficult glory of free existence, then only will woman be able to let her history, her problems, her doubts, her hopes merge with those of humanity; then only will she, in her life and her works, be able to reveal the whole of reality and not merely her own person. As long as she still has to struggle to become a human being, she cannot become a creator.
>
> (*SS*, pp.722–3; *DS* II, p.640; TA)

Torn between their existence as women and their existence as human beings, women under patriarchy are obliged either to deny their specificity, or obsessively to focus on it. For Beauvoir, either option is unacceptable. To desire access to the universal, however, is not to deny difference. What Beauvoir wishes to escape is patriarchal femininity, not the fact of being a woman: 'What woman essentially lacks today for doing great things is forgetfulness of herself, but to forget oneself it is first of all necessary to be firmly assured that now and for the future one has found oneself (*SS*, p.711; *DS* II, p.626). There is in *The Second Sex* a recognition that women will never be free unless they establish a sense of themselves as female, as well as human. Beauvoir's insistence on women's right to full sexual expression points in the same direction.

Agreeing on the fact that oppression entails exclusion from the universal, Sartre, Beauvoir and Fanon differ markedly when it comes to the value they accord to the subjectivity of the oppressed. Inspired by Léopold Sédar Senghor's *Anthologie de la nouvelle poésie nègre et malgache*, Sartre insists that 'black subjectivity' must be explored for political purposes (*Situations III*, p.238), but casts this as a purely negative moment of 'antiracist racism'. Embracing *négritude*, Fanon argues, Sartre imprisons it in negativity. Stressing the profoundly interconnected roots of body and subjectivity, Fanon, on the other hand, warns that blackness will not simply wash away in the inexorable movement of the dialectics ('Not yet white, no longer wholly black, I was damned': p.138). For Fanon, then, liberation consists in gaining access to the universal *as a black human being*.

What political role, then, is to be assigned to female subjectivity in the transition from patriarchy to freedom? In their different ways, Sartre and Fanon both agree that the way to the ultimate, utopian depoliticization of identity goes through its radical politicization. Compared to their strong defence of the political uses of the subjectivity of the oppressed, Beauvoir's position remains curiously hesitant. In *The Second Sex*, there is no mention of a purely negative need for an 'anti-sexist sexism'. Nowhere does she explicitly posit the necessity of reaffirming the value of female contradictions under patriarchy, or of singing the praises of *féminitude* as a necessary step on the way to liberation. This does not prevent her, however, from developing one of the most ambitious theories of female – not 'universal' – subjectivity ever produced. Nor does it stop her from recognizing that women, in order to be free, must be able to assert themselves as women. Ultimately, however, she recoils from drawing the political consequences of such insights. It is as if Beauvoir finds herself uneasily suspended between her own pioneering recognition of the political importance of female subjectivity under patriarchy and an equally marked reluctance to cast that subjectivity as a *necessary* element in women's political struggle for freedom. In order to avoid having to confront the gap in her own thought, Beauvoir seeks refuge in Marxism: placing all her hopes in a socialist revolution, in 1949 she simply assumes that the demise of capitalism would spell the end of patriarchy as well.

In the end, then, the deepest political flaw of *The Second Sex* consists in Beauvoir's failure to grasp the progressive potential of 'femininity' as a political discourse. More than forty years after the publication of her epochal essay, it is easy to see that she vastly underestimated the potential political impact of an independent women's movement, just as she failed to provide an adequate analysis of female sexuality. Fanon may not have produced a fully developed alternative to Sartre's Hegelian dialectics, yet his rhetoric, at least, gestures towards an alternative story. By remaining unable to face the issue explicitly, whether on the level of style or on the level of theory, Beauvoir finds herself in a tighter theoretical impasse than Fanon. It is tempting to conclude that in the historical moment of France in 1950 it was not yet possible fully to reach beyond the confines of classical Marxist or traditionally bourgeois narratives of emancipation: Beauvoir's and Fanon's achievement consists in having demonstrated the impossibility of using such paradigms to theorize sexism and racism alike.

Beauvoir's failure explicitly to oppose Sartre's Hegelian narrative of liberation may not be surprising. From a purely personal perspective, the fact that she does not explicitly endorse it either is actually far more startling. Beauvoir's silence on the issue, however, is heavily overdetermined. At one level, her hesitations on the question of the political value of female subjectivity reflect her own position as an independent woman, a transitional figure arrested on the threshold of a new world. Having experienced the degradations of patriarchal femininity, Beauvoir is understandably reluctant to proclaim its world historical necessity. Her failure to posit femininity as a potentially positive force for change also springs from her excessively negative analysis of female sexuality. As such it is linked to her persistent tendency to overestimate the freedom of men, and to underestimate the power of traditional women. An even more important factor, however, is the historical situation of women in France in the 1940s. While the struggle against colonialism was gaining momentum throughout the decade, there was no sign of the future explosion of the women's movement. In 1949 it was far easier to envisage the necessity of an autonomous movement for blacks than for women. It would be uncharitable indeed to take Beauvoir to task for having failed fully to think through an issue not even broached by anybody else.

When she joined the women's movement in November of 1971, Beauvoir herself was quick to recognize some of her earlier mistakes:

> At the end of *The Second Sex* I said that I was not a feminist because I believed that the problems of women would resolve themselves automatically in the context of socialist development. By feminist, I meant fighting on specifically feminine issues independently of the class struggle. I still hold the same view today. In my definition, feminists are women – or even men too – who are fighting to change women's condition, in association with the class struggle, but independently of it as well, without making the changes they strive for totally dependent on changing society as a whole. I would say that, in that sense, I am a feminist today, because I realised that we must fight for the situation of women, here and now, before our dreams of socialism come true. Apart from that, I realised that even in socialist countries, equality between men and women has not been achieved. Therefore it is absolutely essential for women to take their destiny in their own hands. That is why I have now joined the Women's Liberation Movement.
>
> (Schwarzer, p.32)

In the 1970s, then, Beauvoir came to realize the necessity of independent feminist mobilization of women as women, both with and against the general socialist movement of which she considered herself a part. For her, however, such separatism remained wholly strategic: her general vision of liberation never changed.

In an interview from 1976, Beauvoir stresses the positive nature of certain 'feminine' qualities, such as lack of self-importance, the absence of vanity and arrogance, a sense of humour, disrespect for hierarchies and so on:

These 'feminine' qualities are a product of our oppression, but they ought to be retained after our liberation. And men would have to learn to acquire them. But we shouldn't go to the other extreme and say that a woman has a particular closeness with the earth, that she feels the rhythm of the moon, the ebb and flow of the tides . . . Or that she has more soul, or is less destructive by nature etc. No! If there is a grain of truth in that, it is not because of our nature, but is rather the result of our conditions of existence. . . . One should not believe that the female body gives one a new vision of the world.

(Schwarzer, pp.78–9)

Sceptical of the tendency to idealize reified images of 'women's culture' or 'women's tradition', the author of *The Second Sex* understands such phenomena as the contradictory products of patriarchy.[24] For Beauvoir, female sexuality does not have the wide-ranging cultural implications often asserted by later generations of feminists. Many of the qualities (openness, generosity, spontaneity, fluidity) considered by the proponents of *écriture féminine*, for instance, as grounded in feminine sexuality, Beauvoir does not consider particularly sexual at all. Even in the 1970s, then, her position remained wholly antagonistic to those feminists who chose to focus on women's difference, often without regard to other social movements, and certainly with distinct distaste for the 'old-fashioned' ideal of equality she herself incarnated.[25]

While Beauvoir is right to question the historical and theoretical value of feminist identity politics, I believe that she seriously underestimates the *strategic* value of a politics of difference. That is not to say, however, that I disagree with her ultimate vision of liberation. In the political and theoretical space of the 1990s, a real conflict remains between those who accept the strategic use of intellectual and political separatism in order to achieve a new, truly egalitarian society, and those who are convinced that women's interests are best served by the establishment of an enduring regime of sexual difference in every social and cultural field. What is at stake in current feminist debates, in other words, is different visions of liberation.

By casting the question in such terms, I am already doing homage to Beauvoir. In my view, the strongest legacy of *The Second Sex* is the fact that all its analyses and polemics are placed within a powerful narrative of liberation. By taking as her point of departure a story of historical and social transformation or, in other words, by giving feminism an end, by imagining a society in which there would no longer be any need to *be* a feminist, Beauvoir provided women all over the world with a vision of change. This is what gives her essay such power and such a capacity to inspire its readers to action, and it is also the reason why *The Second Sex* remains the founding text for materialist feminism in the twentieth century.[26]

Historically, narratives of freedom have been remarkably effective in producing social change: we abandon them at our peril. To raise the question of liberation in a postmodern intellectual field, however, is immediately to expose oneself to accusations of teleology and other metaphysical crimes: no wonder many feminists are rapidly losing faith in the future of feminism. But to deprive feminism of its utopias is to depoliticize it at a stroke: without a political vision to sustain it, feminist theory will hit a dead end.[27] The result will be a loss of purpose, a perfect sense of futility, and the transformation of feminism into a self-perpetuating academic institution like any other. Deprived of narratives of liberation, feminist theory becomes anaemic, theoreticist and irrelevant to most women. The great virtue of narratives is that they come to an end: *The Second Sex* helps me to remember that the aim of feminism is to abolish itself.

References and notes

Page references cited in brackets in the text refer to the following editions (the first reference is to the published English translation, the second to the French original):

SS   *The Second Sex*, translated by H. Parshley, Harmondsworth, Penguin, 1984. *DS* I/*DS* II   *Le Deuxième Sexe* vol.I/vol.II, Coll. Folio, Paris, Gallimard, 1949.
LS   *Letters to Sartre*, translated by Q. Hoare, New York, Arcade, 1991. *LS* I/*LS* II *Lettres à Sartre*, vol.I/vol.II, Gallimard, Paris, 1990.
FC   *Force of Circumstance*, translated by Richard Howard, Harmondsworth, Penguin, 1987. *FC* I/*FC* II   *La Force des choses*, vol.I/vol.II, Coll. Folio, Paris, Gallimard, 1963.
Situations III, Paris, Gallimard, 1949.

TA means translation adapted.

1 Claire Etcherelli's novel *Elise ou la vraie vie* (1967) gives a moving account of the situation of women and North African immigrant workers at the Citroën factories during the war in Algeria. As a result of her admiration for Etcherelli's novel, Beauvoir invited her to join the editorial board of *Les Temps modernes*.
2 It is interesting to note that this passage is written entirely in the past conditional tense, just like Françoise's final 'direct' proposition to Gerbert. It is as if Beauvoir's very style signals the fact that, for her, at least in the 1940s, direct and unambiguous expression of female desire, whether social or sexual, remained impossible.
3 In 1949, Beauvoir considered herself a socialist. In the English translation of *The Second Sex*, the extent to which she relies on Marxist and socialist thought is not always obvious to the reader. As Margaret Simons has shown, almost every reference to socialist feminism has been deleted from the English text (see M. Simons, 'The Silencing of Simone de Beauvoir: Guess What's Missing from *The Second Sex*', *Women's Studies International Forum*, 1983, vol.6, pp.559–64.
4 Beauvoir's account of the sexuality of independent women suffers from all the problems discussed in the previous chapter. Allusions to women's necessary passivity in sexual intercourse, for instance, are to be found throughout her discussion of women's sexual dilemmas. In spite of my misgivings about her analysis of sexuality in general, Beauvoir's discussion of women's *concrete* sexual dilemmas in France in 1949 still strikes me as sound.
5 Beauvoir also writes that: 'Woman's homosexuality is one attempt among others

to reconcile her autonomy with the passivity of her flesh' (*SS*, pp.426–7; *DS* II, p.195). While this statement unfortunately reiterates Beauvoir's belief in the fundamental passivity of female sexuality, it also casts lesbianism as one potential way forward for women reluctant to sacrifice their autonomy in exchange for sex.

6 I disagree with Claudia Card, who argues that 'Beauvoir seemed not to see that if "homosexuality" is a choice, heterosexuality is likewise a choice' ('Lesbian Attitudes and *The Second Sex*', *Women's Studies International Forum*, vol.8, 1985, p.209). Card forgets that within Beauvoir's existentialist framework, *everything*, including sexual orientation, is subject to choice. Choice *is* the use we make of our freedom, we might say. While Sartre's study of Jean Genet, for example, emphasizes his choice of homosexuality, his study of Flaubert stresses the latter's choice of heterosexual bachelorhood. Given her own existentialist premisses, it is quite unlikely that Beauvoir would take heterosexuality somehow to be given and not chosen.

7 Card, 'Lesbian Attitudes', p.213; A. Ferguson, 'Lesbian Identity: Beauvoir and History', *Women's Studies International Forum*, vol.8, 1985, pp.203–8 (p.207).

8 A. Schwarzer, *Simone de Beauvoir Today. Conversations 1972–82*, London, Chatto and Windus, 1984, pp.112–13. Discerning lesbian readers of *L'Invitée* nevertheless suspected that the truth was more complex. Focusing on the need for role models among lesbians, Jean Carlomusso's video *L Is For The Way You Look* has a short sequence where one woman describes her reaction to the relationship between Françoise and Xavière: 'I didn't know what it was,' she comments, 'but it was so damned attractive.' As revealed in the *Letters to Sartre*, Beauvoir and Olga Kosakiewicz, the model for Xavière, did in fact have a sexual relationship at the time of the 'trio' with Sartre (1935–37).

9 A number of the relevant bureaucratic dossiers are quoted in the otherwise highly sensationalist, historically inaccurate and thoroughly malicious book by G. Joseph, *Une si douce Occupation . . .: Simone de Beauvoir et Jean-Paul Sartre 1940–1944*, Paris, Albin Michel, 1991 (pp.197–222).

10 D. Bair, *Simone de Beauvoir. A Biography*, New York, Summit Books, 1990, pp.509, 510. Margaret Simons's 1992 essay 'Lesbian Connections: Simone de Beauvoir and Feminism', *Signs*, vol.18, 1992, pp.136–61 contains a useful summary of available information on Beauvoir's lesbian relationships.

11 I can think of no other chapter in *The Second Sex* where the political and the philosophical are so clearly involved with the personal – and I can think of no other chapter where Beauvoir's censorship of the personal aspects of her discourse is more massive.

12 In *Frantz Fanon: A Critical Study*, New York, Pantheon, 1973, Irene L. Gendzier stresses the importance of *Les Temps modernes* for Fanon in the period from 1947 to 1952: '[*Les Temps modernes*] carried articles on the subjects that Fanon was to concern himself with as time went on: communism and terror, the politics of the oppressed, black–white relations, the third world and the European left' (pp.20–1).

13 Her resolutely positive account of Fanon is clearly overdetermined. Although there can be no doubt of Beauvoir's personal admiration for him, the fact that she was writing immediately after his death obviously influenced her tone. Nor should it be forgotten that Beauvoir and Sartre's pro-Algerian stance forced them into a beleaguered minority position in France: it would have been out of the question for Beauvoir to undermine a political ally such as Fanon in print. (Published in

1963, *Force of Circumstance* was finished in the summer of 1962, only a few months after the Evian agreements [which paved the way for full independence for Algeria being achieved the same year].)

14 At about the same time (1947–48) as he was writing 'Black Orpheus', Sartre also drafted another text on black liberation, particularly in the context of slavery in the United States. Published in 1983 under the title 'La Violence révolutionnaire', this paper now constitutes the second appendix to Sartre's *Cahiers pour une morale*.

15 Quotations from Fanon refer to *Black Skin, White Masks*, translated by C. Lamm Markmann, New York, Grove Weidenfeld, 1967; originally published as *Peau noire, masques blancs*, Paris, Seuil, 1952. The quotation here is from pp.134–5.

16 To argue, as Elisabeth Spelman does in her *Inessential Woman: Problems of Exclusion in Feminist Thought*, Boston, Beacon, 1988, that Beauvoir's comparison of women with blacks and Jews is sexist because it implies that Beauvoir excludes the existence of black and Jewish women from her categories is to make the mistake of taking a statement about *oppression* (that is to say, about power relations) for a statement about *identity*. What Beauvoir is saying is that the relationship of men to women may in some ways (not all) be seen as homologous to that of whites to blacks, anti-Semites to Jews, the bourgeoisie to the working class. In such a statement there is absolutely no implication that these other groups do not contain women, nor that all women are white and non-Jewish: nothing prevents us from arguing that the position of a black Jewish woman, for instance, would form a particularly complex intersection of contradictory power relations. In her chapter on Beauvoir, Spelman also confuses the idea of otherness and the idea of objectification. Spelman's book in general is an excellent example of the consequences of treating the word *identity* as if it represented a simple logical unit, and of mistaking the opposition of *inclusion* and *exclusion* for a theory of power relations. Such strategies tend to backfire: while criticizing Beauvoir's 'exclusivism', Spelman herself excludes women who are not citizens of the United States from her categories. Thus the figures intended to illustrate different categories of people all have the suffix 'American' appended to them ('Afro-American', 'Euro-American', 'Hispanic-American', 'Asian-American' and so on; see Spelman, pp.144–6).

17 In this sentence Parshley's translation entirely fails to capture the Hegelian flavour conveyed by Beauvoir. 'Elles n'ont pas les moyens concrets de se rassembler en une unité qui se poserait en s'opposant,' Beauvoir writes (*DS* I, p.19). 'Women lack concrete means for organizing themselves into a unit which can stand face to face with the correlative unit,' Parshley translates: *SS*, p.19).

18 Beauvoir is not interested in producing a competitive hierarchy of oppression. Her point is not that women are necessarily more *or more painfully* oppressed than every other group, but simply that the oppression of women is a highly specific *kind* of oppression.

19 In this sense, Monique Wittig's utopian novel, *Les Guérillères*, is an excellent – and highly dialectical – commentary on *The Second Sex*: by imagining outright warfare between a society of women and a society of men, ending with the celebration of a new solidarity – *fraternity* – between men and women, Wittig shrewdly posits a truly utopian solution to Beauvoir's dilemma. After all, Wittig seems to say, this would be the *easy* way out of the patriarchal quagmire.

20 English-language readers should note that, in French, the word *sororité* never took on the political and feminist connotations achieved by 'sisterhood' in English in the

late 1960s and early 1970s. To argue that Beauvoir *ought* to have written *sororité* in 1949 is absurd: since Beauvoir truly dreams of a society marked by solidarity – not struggle – between men and women, she could hardly end her book on a term which in 1949 would have been perceived as exclusively pertaining to females.

21 Only under such utopian conditions, I would add, would the word 'he' be a true universal. Under current social conditions, 'he' remains a false universal. As long as current patriarchal conditions prevail, my own usage is to use 'she' as a gender-neutral pronoun in order to signal my (utopian) desire to construct a society in which the feminine finally would be as universal as the masculine.

22 Reciprocity in fact represents for Beauvoir the incarnation of the highest human value: 'Authentic love,' she writes, 'ought to be founded on the mutual [*réciproque*] recognition of two freedoms; the lovers would then experience themselves both as self and as other: neither would give up transcendence, neither would be mutilated; together they would reveal values and aims in the world' (*SS*, p.677; *DS* II, p.579; TA).

23 Beauvoir's own position is influenced by the socialist tradition, but one hardly needs to be a Marxist to accept the argument for maternity leave. Most Europeans find the widespread American equation of equality with abstract equality quite shocking. When I first discovered that American women do not have an automatic, legal right to maternity leave – let alone to maternity leave on full pay – my reaction was one of profound disbelief. Only the most abstract idea of equality can allow such blatant discrimination against women.

24 To argue that women's development under patriarchy should be valorized as the norm and standard for free femininity, one may add, is to generalize from the particular case by turning the experience of one group of women into the norm for others.

25 For a perspicacious analysis of the French women's movement in the 1970s and 1980s, including dominant accounts of Simone de Beauvoir, as seen from the perspective of a young Frenchwoman in the 1990s, see Sandrine Garcia's 'Le féminisme, une revolution symbolique?' (Thesis. Ecole des Hautes Etudes en sciences sociales, 1993). Garcia particularly emphasizes the intellectual excitement provoked by the 'sexual difference' faction, even among women who did not share the political analysis of that group.

26 My analysis of the current situation in feminism is close to Edward Said's impatience with the 'depoliticization of knowledge' occurring in the postmodernist rejection of every great narrative ('Representing the Colonized: Anthropology's Interlocutors', *Critical Inquiry*, 15, 1989, p.222).

27 Although I argue for the production of feminist utopias, I do not feel obliged to *endorse* them all. I have no quarrel with Margaret Whitford, for instance, who stresses the utopian aspects of Luce Irigaray's thought (see Whitford, *Luce Irigaray*, London, Routledge, 1991, pp.9–25). I too see Irigaray as a truly utopian thinker, offering a powerful political vision to contemporary feminism. Unfortunately, however, I shudder to think what it might be like to live in the fully 'sexuate' culture which makes up the stuff of Irigaray's dreams. Whether I am right or wrong to feel this way remains to be seen. My point is simply that unless we are willing openly and forcefully to *debate* questions of utopia and liberation, feminist theory will lose sight of the political.

THE MASTER–SLAVE DIALECTIC IN *THE SECOND SEX*

Eva Lundgren-Gothlin

Eva Lundgren-Gothlin's *Sex and Existence* (1996) offers a lucid and detailed analysis of the philosophical sources of *The Second Sex*.[1] Demonstrating the way in which Beauvoir sought to combine Hegelianism, Marxism and phenomenological existentialism, Lundgren-Gothlin subverts the notion of Beauvoir as primarily a disciple of Sartre and sets her work within the wider intellectual climate of France in the 1930s and 1940s. She is thus able to explain how Beauvoir was able to break out of the individual perspective and ahistoricity of Sartre's *Being and Nothingness*. However, she also emphasises that the writing of *The Second Sex* took place in a male-dominated intellectual environment and discusses problems inherent in the fact that in using the philosophical tools of her time Beauvoir inevitably imported androcentric elements which continue to pose problems for a reading of *The Second Sex* today.

The chapter presented here focuses on Beauvoir's use of Hegel's master–slave dialectic and demonstrates that, rather than being mediated by Sartre's reading of Hegel, Beauvoir's argument is influenced by the Hegelian scholar Alexandre Kojève, a Russian émigré who played a major role in the renaissance of French interest in Hegel which developed during the 1930s and 1940s until, by 1945, Hegel had gained a central place in French intellectual life. Lundgren-Gothlin points out that neither Beauvoir nor Sartre had the opportunity to study Hegel at university and that it was during the war years that Beauvoir studied *Phenomenology of Spirit* at the Bibliothèque Nationale, where she also read Kojève's *Introduction to the Reading of Hegel*. Kojève utilised concepts from Marxism and existentialism in his interpretation of Hegel, and, focusing on Hegel's early work, presented his philosophy as radical and liberating.

Kojève saw the process of struggle for recognition by another self-consciousness which Hegel's master–slave dialectic enacts as the key to the origins of humanity and of history. Lundgren-Gothlin shows that Beauvoir also insists on the fundamental importance of the struggle for recognition, using it as an explanation of why oppression is ontologically satisfying. Yet at the same time, and again following Kojève and against Sartre, she posits a solution to the master–slave dialectic, which is that of reciprocal recognition. Thus she allows for the abolition of oppression as well as for an explanation of how it arises. Other commentators on *The Second Sex* have often assumed that in her use of Hegel Beauvoir simply locates man as the master and woman as the slave. However, Lundgren-Gothlin establishes that, despite some passages in which Beauvoir points to similarities between the master–slave and the male–female relationship, Beauvoir in fact presents woman as having historically been outside the process of recognition, a fact which explains the unique nature of her oppression and accounts for the way in which man has been able to cast her as the absolute other.

The origins of women's failure to enter the process of recognition – for failure it is in Beauvoir's terms if the entry into the process is an essential feature of humanity – have to be sought historically in women's reproductive role. Combining Kojève with a Darwinian view of nature, Beauvoir identifies the risking of life which men undertook in primitive times as giving them an advantage in moving away from the animal towards the human, whilst women's role in giving and preserving life kept them closer to nature. Finally, in her 'feminist reflections', Lundgren-Gothlin considers the problems inherent in Beauvoir's acceptance of the Hegelian struggle for recognition as a model for the advent of humanity, but underlines that in so doing Beauvoir was employing the progressive philosophy of her time to break out of a Sartrean mould which was unsuited to her purposes.

Note

1 The extract which follows is taken from E. Lundgren-Gothlin, *Sex and Existence. Simone de Beauvoir's 'The Second Sex'*, translated by L. Schenck, London, Athlone, 1996, pp.67–82.

In this chapter, I argue that the influence of Hegel evident in *The Second Sex* is mediated via the French tradition of Hegelianism, and particularly by the interpretation of Kojève.[1] In claiming that *The Second Sex* contains more than a secondary influence of Hegel passed along via Sartre I oppose the opinion expressed in the majority of the literature on Simone de Beauvoir.[2] While others assert that the fundamental theme of conflict in *The Second Sex* is ahistorical and eternal, I maintain that in the work of Beauvoir, as opposed to Sartre's *Being and Nothingness*, it is counterbalanced by belief in the possibility of transcending the conflict through reciprocal recognition – in accordance with Kojève's philosophy. I thus claim that Beauvoir's interpretation of Hegel differs from Sartre's.

In *The Second Sex*, the process of recognition is referred to as one explanation of the origin of oppression and inequality and is seen as characteristic of the origin of humanity. In this, Simone de Beauvoir is clearly in agreement with Kojève. In reflecting on such phenomena as conflicts, division into classes, and otherness, Beauvoir states:

> These phenomena would be incomprehensible if in fact human reality were simply a *Mitsein* based on solidarity and friendliness. Things become clear, on the contrary, if, following Hegel, we find in conscious-ness itself a fundamental hostility towards every other consciousness; the subject poses himself only in setting himself up against another – he sets himself up as the essential, and constitutes the other as the inessential, the object.
> But the other consciousness sets up a reciprocal claim.
>
> (*SS*, p.17, TA; *DS* I, p.16f.)[3]

The individual or the group thus discovers that its efforts to assert itself as sove-reign, as master, are met by similar claims from its counterparts. This means, Beauvoir maintains, that it must 'recognize the reciprocity' of the relationship to the Other. In only one relationship has no demand for reciprocity been raised: that between men and women (see below).

Simone de Beauvoir traces the origin of oppression to these demands for sovereignty, which, she claims, characterize primordial human consciousness, and in doing so, she also enters into polemics with Engels and the Marxist view of human nature. Arguing against Engels's explanation of the oppression of women, she maintains:

> If the original relation between a man and his fellows was exclusively a relation of friendship, we could not account for any type of enslavement; this phenomenon is a result of the imperialism of the human conscious-ness, seeking to accomplish objectively its sovereignty. If the human consciousness had not included the original category of the Other and an original aspiration to dominate the Other, the invention of the bronze tool could not have caused the oppression of woman.
>
> (*SS*, p.83, TA; *DS* I, p.101)

Beauvoir asserts that if we are to explain oppression, we must supplement the Marxist view with the Hegelian view. Although she regards productive activity as playing an important role, she, like Kojève, sees the struggle for recognition as more fundamental, particularly in explaining the origin of oppression.

Kojève and Hyppolite had exemplified how Marx and Hegel could be syn-thesized, an idea that also permeated Merleau-Ponty's essays of the same period.

Simone de Beauvoir was thus not the first thinker to attempt such a synthesis in the Paris of the 1940s. In an essay in *Les Temps modernes*, Hyppolite, like Beauvoir, criticized the inadequacy of the Marxist explanation of the origins of oppression. He maintained that Marx does not explain 'the foundation of his dialectics' and that it is therefore necessary to go back to Hegel to understand how oppression originates and what are the conditions for the existence of self-consciousness or for human existence itself.[4]

Masters, slaves and women

A thorough textual analysis of a central section of *The Second Sex* reveals exactly what use Beauvoir makes of Hegel/Kojève. In my opinion, at the beginning of the myth chapter in *The Second Sex*, the basic elements of the Hegelian master–slave dialectic in Kojève's interpretation are recapitulated, without this being stated. Simone de Beauvoir explains in this section why it is ontologically satisfying for men to have women be the Other.

Beauvoir begins this section by stating that the subject cannot 'assert himself' until he meets an Other, who 'limits and denies him'. She sets out the basic elements of the process of recognition, going on to say that 'man's life is never abundance and quietude; it is dearth and activity, it is struggle' (*SS*, p.159; *DS* I, p.231). Man needs an Other because he cannot 'appropriate' nature, as he wants to do. Nature 'cannot fulfill him' (*SS*, p.159; *DS* I, p.231).

Here Beauvoir is repeating the original insight of the process of recognition. As self-consciousness, as desire, a human being cannot be enduringly satisfied by acquiring, by swallowing up, that which surrounds it: food, the bodies of others, things. The independence of objects means that desire is constantly renewed.

This interpretation is strengthened when Beauvoir goes on to explain why humans cannot be satisfied in relation to nature; either nature appears as 'a purely impersonal opposition', an 'obstacle' and something which 'remains a stranger', or else 'submits passively to and permits assimilation'. Nature can be possessed only by being 'consumed', being destroyed. Like Hegel, Beauvoir is led to state that 'There can be no presence of an Other unless the other is also present in and for himself: which is to say that true alterity – otherness – is that of a consciousness separate from mine and substantially identical with mine' (*SS*, p.159; *DS* I, p.231).

Certainty cannot be reached without the presence of another self-conscious being. This, then, means that the meeting of two self-consciousnesses is imperative. According to Simone de Beauvoir, 'It is the existence of other men that tears each man out of his immanence and enables him to fulfill the truth of his being, to complete himself as transcendence' (*SS*, p.159, TA; *DS* I, p.231) and we should recall in this context that transcendence is defined as characteristic of the human being.[5] The Hegelian nature of this way of thinking becomes increasingly evident:

But this other freedom, that confirms my freedom, also conflicts with it: there is the tragedy of the unfortunate human consciousness; each separate consciousness aspires to set itself up alone as sovereign subject. Each tries to fulfill himself by reducing the other to slavery. But the slave, through his work and his fear, also experiences himself as essential; and, by a dialectical reversal, it is the master who appears to be the inessential.

(*SS*, p.159f., TA; *DS* I, p.231f.)

To recapitulate the process of recognition described above: each one attempted to confirm themselves as self-consciousness by proving to be such, to be not bound to nature, to life, and this led, via a life-and-death struggle, to a division between masters and slaves, between an essential and independent consciousness and an inessential and dependent one. However, given the fear of death, and through work carried out to serve the master, the slave came gradually to experience himself as essential, came actually to attain a certainty as self-consciousness; conversely the master, confirmed by an inessential consciousness, and unformed by labour, found himself at an impasse. This reveals the dialectical aspect of the relationship.

Like Hegel and Kojève, but unlike Sartre in *Being and Nothingness*, Beauvoir saw a solution to this conflict:

It is possible to overcome this conflict if each individual freely recognizes the other, each regarding himself and the other simultaneously as object and as subject in a reciprocal manner.

(*SS*, p.160, TA; *DS* I, p.232)

However, this solution, the *reciprocal recognition*, requires certain presuppositions. It cannot be realized without 'friendship and generosity', which are 'man's highest achievement' and 'his true nature'. Simone de Beauvoir emphasizes that this solution demands constant effort; the human must incessantly 'master himself' *(se surmonte)*.

This passage, then, contains two different statements of the truth of the human being. One is that the true being is transcendence, project, and that one can appear as such only in the encounter with other human beings, an encounter which leads to conflict and to the master–slave division of humanity. The other is that the true nature of the human being is realized through reciprocal recognition, recognition of one another as subjects in friendship and generosity. This is something the human being must constantly strive to obtain.

Beauvoir's picture of the human condition is in accord with Kojève's as he considers that the struggle for recognition is fundamental to and recurrent in history, but also that it can be transcended through reciprocal recognition. (Only in the origin of humanity are humans regarded as really entering into life-and-death struggles; the conflict continues later under different, less extreme conditions.) In *The Second Sex*, the two images of the truth of the human being serve as an explanation both of how oppression arises and how it may be abolished.

The passage analysed above is not about oppression of women. The nature of that oppression is determined a few lines later, when Beauvoir reflects on the nature of man's relationship to woman and says that via this relationship man hopes to avoid his human conditions, i.e. the constant tension and conflict in the human relationship, the need of others and the concomitant risk of being subordinated.

> This dream incarnated is precisely woman; she is the wished-for inter-mediary between nature, which is foreign to man, and the fellow being who is too closely identical. She opposes him with neither the hostile silence of nature nor the hard requirement of a reciprocal recognition; through a unique privilege she is a conscious being and yet it seems possible to possess her in the flesh. Thanks to her, there is a means for escaping that implacable dialectic of master and slave which has its source in the reciprocity that exists between free beings.
>
> (*SS*, p.160, TA; *DS* I, p.232f.)

It is evident in this passage that the 'man' referred to in the master–slave dialectic is a male. Female human beings do not seek recognition; it is males who are confirmed as human, as self-consciousness in relation to other males, males who become either masters or slaves. Beauvoir is saying here that man, in the relation-ship to woman, nurtures the hope of achieving confirmation without engaging in this kind of dialectics; logically, therefore, woman has not engaged in a struggle for recognition, and thus neither has become essential nor has had her self-consciousness confirmed. In other words, she remains at a more animal level. Woman has not raised a reciprocal demand for recognition.

Thus Beauvoir describes two different forms of otherness or alterity (*altérité*): one applying to men, the other to women. In this she does not disagree with Hegel. Neither Hegel nor Kojève discusses how the relationship between men and women is related to the master–slave dialectic, nor does either explicitly state that the latter applies only to men. But other passages in *The Phenomenology of Spirit* lead the reader to conclude that women are not conceived of as partici-pants in the struggle for recognition. Women belong to the private sphere, and the question of their self-consciousness is of no interest to Hegel.

We might even say that when Beauvoir reflects on the relationship between man and woman, she reveals the inherent androcentricity of the Hegelian view of the human being. To Hegel, man is unquestionably the head of the family and it is he who relates to society. This distinction between the sexes is made explicit when Kojève says: 'The family is a *human* family by the fact that its (male) mem-bers struggle for recognition and have slaves; they are accordingly Masters.'[6]

Thus we may conclude that, at least during antiquity, the relationship between men and women within the family was not strictly 'human', as there was no fight for recognition. Kojève refers to a kind of natural, mutual 'recognition' and an 'animal sexuality'. He says that the relationship of a couple becomes 'human' when they share children, labour and property.[7]

I am therefore claiming, in contrast to other scholars,[8] that while Beauvoir uses the Hegelian master–slave dialectic to explain the origins of oppression, she does not locate man as master and woman as slave in this dialectic. Instead, woman is seen as not participating in the process of recognition, a fact that explains the unique nature of her oppression. Although the man is the master, the essential consciousness in relation to woman, the woman is not a slave in relation to him. This makes their relationship more absolute, and *non-dialectical*, and it explains why woman is the *absolute Other*.

This interpretation finds direct support in *The Second Sex*, when Beauvoir claims:

> To regard woman simply as a slave is a mistake; there were women among the slaves, to be sure, but there have always been free women – that is, women of religious and social dignity. They accepted man's sovereignty and he did not feel menaced by a revolt that could make of him in turn the object. Woman thus seems to be the inessential who never goes back to being the essential, to be the absolute Other, without reciprocity.
>
> (*SS*, p.160f.; *DS* I, p.233)

The relationship between man and woman is, thus, unique. There is no other with which it may be compared. Neither as individuals nor as groups do men and women challenge one another. Rather, Simone de Beauvoir asserts, they are a *Mitsein* within the collective.[9]

Another expression of this stance can be found in Simone de Beauvoir's objections to Engels's comparison between class and the oppression of women. She argues that

> it is impossible to confuse the two. For one thing, there is no biological basis for the separation of classes; in his work, the slave acquires self-consciousness against his master; and the proletariat has always experienced its condition in revolt, thereby returning to the essential, constituting a threat to its exploiters.
>
> (*SS*, p.83; *DS* I, p.101, TA)

The importance of work is emphasized both in the development of self-consciousness and in the creation of new conditions which may lead to a renewal of the struggle for recognition on the side of the slaves or the proletariat. This is in accordance with the Hegelian and the Marxist view and, like Kojève, Beauvoir sees slaves and the proletariat as comparable categories.

In view of this, it is not surprising that, in Beauvoir's opinion, women must enter into the master–slave dialectic – that is, participate in work and demand recognition – in order to liberate themselves.

The master–slave dialectic, or a Hegelian view of human nature, thus explains the occurrence of oppression.

As mentioned above, it has often been assumed that Beauvoir applied the master–slave dialectic to the relationship between men and women, and, on the basis of this assumption, she has been accused of inconsistency, since she does not maintain that, like the slave, women develop actual independent consciousness.[10] I want now to examine in greater detail a passage often referred to and generally assumed to prove that Beauvoir places women and slaves in equivalent positions. It reads:

> Certain passages of the dialectic by which Hegel defines the relation of master to slave apply much better to the relation of man to woman. The privilege of the master, he says, comes from his affirmation of Spirit as against Life through the fact that he risks his own life; but in fact the conquered slave has known the same risk. Whereas woman is basically an existent who gives Life and does not risk *her* life; between her and the male there has been no combat. Hegel's definition would seem to apply especially well to her. He says: 'The other consciousness is the dependent consciousness for whom the essential reality is the animal type of life'.
>
> (*SS*, p.90; *DS* I, p.112, TA)

Clearly Beauvoir rejects the idea that men and women have engaged in a mutual struggle for recognition, since she characterizes woman as the one 'who gives Life and does not risk *her* life'. For this very reason, she asserts, 'certain passages' of the master–slave dialectic are better suited to describing the relationship between men and women. She is referring here to the first phase of the dialectic, where the master has proved himself as pure self-consciousness by not having set life up as supreme, and where the slave is apparently the party for whom the significant reality is sheer survival, life. Beauvoir concludes that this phase of the master–slave dialectic is an excellent illustration of the relationship between the sexes. In the next phase of this dialectic, however, it turns out that the slave, who has experienced the fear of death, who has actually been engaged in the struggle although not prepared to go all the way, has taken a step away from the animal, a step he fulfils through his labour in the service of his master. But what applies to the slave does not apply to woman.

Beauvoir thus stresses one aspect of the dialectic in the passage quoted above as an illustration of the fundamental difference between the sexes. She relates this difference to the reproductive functions of the two sexes, claiming that this explains why woman does not become engaged in a struggle for recognition, and why she became the subordinate sex. What is this difference? It is that women as a sex are destined to *give*, not take or risk, life.

In one other passage Beauvoir makes similar use of the master–slave dialectic to illustrate the differences between sex and class relations. Here, too, she sees a particular phase of the dialectic actually reflecting the relationship between the sexes better than the one between master and slave: the confirmation of his sovereignty sought by the master from the slave. Beauvoir states:

> being *other* than man and sharing the disturbing character of the *other*, woman in a way held man in dependence upon her, while being at the same time dependent upon him; the reciprocity of the master–slave relation was what she *actually* enjoyed, and through that fact she escaped slavery. But the slave . . . he was nothing but a man in servitude, not different but inferior: the dialectical expression of his relation to his master was to take centuries to come into existence.
>
> (*SS*, p.103; *DS* I, p.129)

The Hegelian insight of the reciprocal dependence in the master–slave relationship is used here to illustrate the uniqueness of the relationship between man and woman. In principle, or conceptually, this dependence is originally reciprocal, but it has not yet been realized for the master in relation to the slave. From the first, the slave is dependent on the master, in whose hands his life rests, but the master, who has all the power, has not experienced his dependence on the slave and does not realize that without the slave's labour, without the slave's recognition of him, he would be nothing. Centuries must elapse before the slave can challenge the master and make him aware of his dependence. Woman, on the other hand, has never been an enslaved equal, but has always been an Other; in the relation between her and man, mutual dependence has been actual from the very outset, although without leading to her freedom.

Why, then, according to Beauvoir (and Hegel) did woman remain outside the process of recognition? Why did she become subordinate, the absolute Other?

While Hegel and Kojève claimed that men were originally fundamentally equal, and that nothing (such as physical strength) disposes one to concede to the other in the struggle for recognition, when Beauvoir uses this struggle to explain the origins of the oppression of women she simultaneously foregrounds a fundamental *difference* between the sexes. The importance that Beauvoir attaches to women's biological role as mothers has already been mentioned, but she also traces this difference all the way back to the animal kingdom. This explanation is rooted both in a Hegelian conception of the difference between the sexes and in a Darwinistic view of nature. Females are physically weaker and their role in the reproductive process predisposes them not to participate in the struggle for recognition.

The significance of biology

In the chapter on biology in *The Second Sex* recurs an idea of a conflict between the *life of the individual* and the demands on the individual from the *species* (*l'espèce*), a conflict which is said to exist for both sexes but to be manifested differently by each. Simone de Beauvoir maintains that in the lower species of animals, both male and female are 'enslaved to the species', i.e. they are hardly more than reproductive organs (*SS*, p.46; *DS* I, p.51). The higher in the animal kingdom we look, however, the more marked becomes the conflict between species and individual, and the greater the differences between the sexes, because the organism no longer simply reproduces itself and life has become more individualized. The more transient role of the male in propagation makes it possible for him to assert his independence to a greater extent and to integrate his reproductive role into his individual life. Because of her reproductive function, on the other hand, 'the individuality of the female is opposed by the interest of the species' (*SS*, p.53; *DS* I, p.61). In relation to reproduction, the female represents continuity and care, the male separation and creativity.

According to Beauvoir, the importance of these fundamental differences between the sexes is augmented because separation and individuality tend to lead to conflict. While the male animal is more aggressive, strives to assert his individuality in combat with other males and seeks out the female, she rarely has any 'combative instinct' (*SS*, p.51; *DS* I, p.58), nor does she seek to thrust forward her individuality in relation to males or other females. This is why, in most animal communities, the males reign.

Human beings exhibit the greatest differences between the sexes. Beauvoir claims that woman suffers most from her 'enslavement' to the species and that in woman the conflict between the interests of individual and species is most notable, as exemplified in difficult pregnancies or in the fact that puberty is a critical time for the female. For man there is no such conflict between sexual life and personal existence (*DS* I, pp.61–9). In addition, woman is weaker, slower, less emotionally stable, etc., than man, and 'she cannot challenge him in combat' (*SS*, p.61, TA; *DS* I, p.72f.).

Beauvoir does not claim that these differences between the sexes lead *per se* to the subordination of women, but that they are significant in the original historical situation.

To Beauvoir, human beings are distinguished from animals by their constant state of 'becoming' (*devenir*); they can transcend what is immediately given: 'humanity is not an ordinary natural species: it does not seek to maintain itself *qua* species; its project is not stagnation, instead, its aim is to go beyond itself' (*DS* I, p.109f.).

In line with Kojève, Simone de Beauvoir maintains that what an animal values most highly is its own life and the preservation of this life, while humans assert themselves as human by risking life. Her chapter on biology shows the male asserting his individuality and subjectivity in the battle for females and territory, while the female is preoccupied with reproducing life and her individuality is subordinate to that of the species; it is obvious which sex is to take the step from being animal to being human.

Thus, in the early days of humanity, man transcended mere life in his demands for recognition. Simone de Beauvoir states this explicitly in several passages; for example:

> The warrior put his life in jeopardy to elevate the prestige of the horde, the clan to which he belonged. And in this he proved dramatically that life is not the supreme value for man, but on the contrary that it should be made to serve ends more important than itself. The worst curse that was laid upon woman was that she should be excluded from these war-like forays. For it is not in giving life but in risking life that man is raised above the animal; that is why superiority has been accorded in humanity not to the sex that brings forth but to that which kills.
>
> (*SS*, p.89; *DS* I, p.111)[11]

Since Beauvoir, like Kojève, sees risking one's life as basic to the appearance of humanity, to belong to the sex whose biological orientation is towards giving birth, towards representing the re-creation and preservation of life, rather than the sex that puts life at risk in the struggle for recognition, is a 'curse'. Moreover, man realizes himself as human through productive activity, activity which subjugates nature and shapes an anthropogenic world:

> The female, to a greater extent than the male, is the prey of the species; and the human race has always sought to escape its specific destiny. The support of life became for man an activity and a project through the invention of the tool; but in maternity woman remained closely bound to her body, like an animal. It is because humanity calls itself in question in the matter of living – that is to say, values the reasons for living above mere life – that, confronting woman, man assumes mastery.
>
> (*SS*, p.90f.; *DS* I, p.113)

In primitive societies man took the lead, and never again relinquished this leadership. Because woman during primitive times was never engaged in the struggle for recognition, and did not experience the fear of death, she was, and had to be, more animal than man. Woman was and remained closer to nature, and could thus also serve as a mediator between nature and man. Like Hegel, Beauvoir contrasts Life and Spirit, and refers to a male and a female principle in prehistoric times, according to which man was characterized by a higher degree of consciousness – of spirit in the Hegelian sense. In historical development, man was one step ahead in moving away from nature and towards spirit.

Male principle	*Female principle*
Spirit (*Esprit*)	Life
transcendence	immanence
technique	magic
reason (*raison*)	superstition

creation   maintenance
order   confusion
project, activity   contingency[12]

Had the female principle not been subordinated to the male principle, society would not have developed. Simone de Beauvoir is explicit about this; she maintains that 'The devaluation of woman represents a necessary stage in the history of humanity' (SS, p.100; DS I, p.125). New means of production, particularly the bronze axe, meant that the male principle was able definitively to vanquish the female one. Man was now able to realize himself through labour and to liberate himself in relation to nature. In line with Hegelian tradition, Beauvoir emphasizes the importance of work to rational, conceptual thinking, and to human and social development. From this time woman's role in society was clearly subordinate and her rights and freedom of movement were restricted.

Concluding comments

Because Beauvoir attaches such importance to the struggle for recognition, her explanation of the origins of oppression tends to be Hegelian and idealistic rather than Marxist and materialistic.[13] This is the only aspect of The Second Sex which Beauvoir herself later criticized with some severity, although she went on to maintain that a more materialistic explanation would not have altered the subsequent argument.[14] If the conflict between consciousnesses is seen as a Hegelian theme rather than a Sartrean one, Beauvoir's insistence on the possibility of reciprocal recognition is not, as claimed, philosophically excluded. This implies a philosophy of history, an element normally neglected when Sartre's ahistorical philosophy is read into The Second Sex.

In summary, we may say that in The Second Sex the master–slave dialectic occurs on both the individual and the social levels, being combined on the latter with a philosophy of history inspired by Marx. Simone de Beauvoir asserts that the conflict can and should be transcended on both levels. On the social level, this results from the bringing about of socialism. Beauvoir maintains, in line with Kojève, that an original conflict does not exclude the possibility of subsequent mutual recognition. This interpretation is strengthened by the fact that the master–slave dialectic, described as an implacable conflict between consciousnesses, mainly occurs in the parts of The Second Sex dealing with the origins of humanity and oppression.

However, unlike Kojève, Beauvoir never presumes the 'end of history' or the absolute abolition of all human conflict. On the other hand, unlike Sartre in Being and Nothingness, she claims that human relations are not necessarily conflict-laden. Reciprocal recognition requires a moral effort, as well as a society in which individuals may realize themselves as free, and relate as such. But, even in a socialist society, conflict will occur.

A question remains: according to the Hegelian conception of the human being, is it possible for woman to become truly 'human', before she has demanded recognition and has participated in those activities which are defined as work or labour? Beauvoir appears to believe that this becomes possible for woman only with the industrial revolution. Just like man, woman must liberate herself from nature, something which she achieves not only through work but also through a rational control of her own fertility.

Thus, according to Beauvoir, the traditional relationship between man and woman is not dialectical in itself, and it is only in the public sphere of production that new terms and conditions for changing the relationship between the sexes are created.

Feminist reflections

Beauvoir's description of basic differences between the sexes in humans and animals reproduces ideas from androcentric biological science. Although she criticizes sexism in biology, this sexism plays its part in the 'facts' she accepts. She rejects prejudiced conclusions drawn from these facts, but fails to realize, as contemporary feminist critics have done, that even when scientists have described, interpreted, selected and performed studies on animals, they have done so from a male perspective.[15] Beauvoir accepts, for example, the traditional view of motherhood which associates it with incompetence and weakness. The Darwinistic picture of the basic struggle for existence in nature may, in turn, be questioned from a feminist point of view; so may the glorification of aggression, in line with both social Darwinism and the Kojèvian view of human nature.

Another problematical area lies in Beauvoir's tendency to employ parallels between man and animals when describing differences between the sexes.[16] Although in doing so she establishes a greater fidelity to the Hegelian view than the dualism represented by Kojève and Sartre, regarding the relationship between human and nature and animal, at the same time she runs the risk of falling into the trap of a biological determinism which she generally rejects.

As we have seen in this chapter, in combination with the Hegelian view of the original human conditions for existence, the differences between the sexes determine the position of woman as subjected, as the absolute Other. The biological differences, with the male representing individuality, subjectivity and greater vocal strength, predestine the male to engage in a struggle for recognition, and the female to remain outside that fight.

Although a recurring theme in *The Second Sex* is the relative physical weakness of woman and her 'enslavement to the species', Beauvoir emphasizes that these 'facts' are significant only in relation to a historical situation. At the end of the chapter on biology, she declares herself to be against biological reductionism and stresses a qualitative difference between humans and animals which, she maintains, implies that the differences between the sexes must always be seen in a social context.

The Second Sex conceives a continuity between human and animal similar to that described by Marx and Hegel. This continuity is broken by a decisive quali-tative step: the struggle for recognition and productive activity, respectively. Both Hegel and Marx saw motherhood, and the activities related to it, as closer to the animal than were the activities of men, and since unfortunately Beauvoir does not criticize this androcentric view, she is apt to reproduce it. There is a tendency to regard woman as more animal, closer to nature *per se*, than man, and thus as inevitably subordinate in the historical process.

In accepting the Hegelian struggle for recognition as a model for the advent of humanity, without criticizing it from a feminist perspective, Beauvoir has also taken on board its androcentricity.[17] This has a paradoxical consequence: her reasoning sometimes verges on being misogynist. How else can her statement that the sex that kills is superior to the sex that gives birth be described?

In order to explain the origins of the oppression of woman, Beauvoir turned to what appeared to be the progressive philosophy of her times: a Hegelianism with an existentialist and Marxist bent. Using this philosophy, she was able to break out of the individual perspective and the ahistoricity that characterized Sartre's *Being and Nothingness*. Had she remained within that frame, an explanation of the oppression of women as a collective, social phenomenon would have been virtually impossible.

In post-war Paris, where the occupation and the Resistance were still fresh in everyone's mind, the Kojèvian insistence on the importance of risking one's life for values other than life itself probably sounded less strange than it does today. In her novel *The Blood of Others*, written during the war and dealing with the Resistance, Beauvoir had personally grappled with the difficult problem of whether or not one should sacrifice one's own life and the lives of others to combat oppression. Post-war France admired the heroic deeds of the war years and Kojève's message was in tune with the times.

Notes

1 This is noted in the literature on Simone de Beauvoir to my knowledge only by Carol Craig in her 'Simone de Beauvoir's "The Second Sex" in the light of the Hegelian Master–Slave Dialectic and Sartrean Existentialism' (University of Edin-burgh dissertation, 1979) and by Betty W. Ross in *Simone de Beauvoir's Idea of Transcendence and its Applicability to Women Who Work as Nurses* (University Microfilms International, Ann Arbor, 1982), whose theoretical stance follows that of Craig.

2 The opinion that what is to be found in *The Second Sex* is Hegel mediated via Sartre is maintained, for example, by Geneviève Lloyd, 'Masters, Slaves and Others', *Radical Philosophy*, no. 34, 1983, p.5; Kate Soper, *Humanism and Antihuman-ism*, London, Hutchinson, 1986, p.63; Aino Saarinen: 'The Dialectics of Master and Slave from a Feminist Standpoint', in *Wom Werden des Wissens: Philosophie–Wissenschaft–Dialektik*. Kongress der internationalen Gesellschaft für dialektische Philosophie, Societas Hegeliana, Helsinki, 4.–8. (Oulu, 1987), p.265; Solvig

Saetre, *Kvinnen–det annet Kjønn? En studie: Simone de Beauvoir filosofi*, Gylden-dal, Oslo, 1969, p.47.

3 S. de Beauvoir, *The Second Sex*, translated by H. Parshley, London, Jonathan Cape, 1968, p.17. Subsequent references are given in the text as *SS* (TA indicates that the translation has been modified), and followed by reference to the French text, *Le Deuxième Sexe*, 2 vols, Paris, Gallimard, 1949, abbreviated as *DS*.

4 See 'Situation de l'homme dans la phénoménologie hégélienne', *Les Temps modernes*, no. 19, April 1947, p.1286f.

5 This central concept defines the specifically human capacity to go beyond given conditions, the freedom to conceive, to act, to create.

6 A. Kojève, *Introduction à la lecture de Hegel: leçons sur la 'Phénoménologie de l'Esprit', professées de 1933 à 1939 à l'Ecole des Hautes-Etudes, réunies et publiées par Raymond Queneau*, Paris, Gallimard, 1985 [1947], p.98.

7 Ibid. p.100f.

8 M. O'Brien, *The Politics of Reproduction*, London, Routledge & Kegan Paul, 1981, p.70; P. Jagentowicz Mills: 'Hegel and "The Woman Question"', in *The Sexism of Social and Political Theory. Women and Reproduction from Plato to Nietzsche*, ed. L. M. G. Clark and L. Lange, Toronto, University of Toronto Press, 1979, p.79f; Saarinen, p.264 f.; see also A. Jaggar and W. McBride: '"Repro-duction" as Male Ideology', *Women's Studies International Forum*, vol. 8, no. 3, 1985, p.190f; and J-A. Pilardi Fuchs: 'On the Warpath and Beyond: Hegel, Freud and Feminist Theory', *Women's Studies International Forum*, vol. 6, no. 6, 1983, p.569. According to Lloyd, 1983, Beauvoir saw women as engaged in this struggle, but as having agreed to be defeated rather than as serious opponents: see p.7. While Lloyd claims that Beauvoir was still trying to make women fit into the master–slave dialectic (p.4f.), I assert that she was not. O'Brien, 1981, sees Beauvoir's view of what characterizes woman as being closer to Hegel's, i.e. that woman is in a sphere of her own. See p.70ff. Yet she makes no effort to match this with her statement that Beauvoir applies the master–slave dialectic to the relation-ship between men and women. J. Okely in *Simone de Beauvoir. A Re-Reading*, London, Virago Press, 1986 notes, with a reference to Craig, that woman is contrasted with the Hegelian slave. On this point Craig's and my interpretations are in agreement; see Okely, p.73. Saetre notes that woman should be seen more as a vassal than a slave, but she does not analyse the master–slave dialectic. See p.47. None of these analyses is detailed.

9 Simone de Beauvoir describes the couple as 'a primordial *Mitsein*', *SS*, p.19; *DS* I, p.19, and argues that 'The couple is a fundamental unity with its two halves riveted together': ibid. On another page it is also stated that 'the couple is an original *Mitsein*', *SS*, p.62; *DS* I, p.74.

10 Saarinen, p.264f., maintains that Beauvoir did not take the time to learn her Hegel thoroughly. Mills makes the same accusation of inconsistency, p.79f., as do Jaggar and McBride, p.190f.

11 It should also be noted that Beauvoir uses the term 'prestige' here, which originates from Kojève. See also: 'Her misfortune is to have been biologically destined for the repetition of Life, when even in her own view Life does not carry within itself its reasons for being, reasons that are more important than the life itself' (*SS*, p.90; *DS* I, p.112). See also the summary: *SS*, p.90f.; *DSI*, p.113.

12 For these principles, see *Le Deuxième Sexe*, pp.122–8.

13 Feminists have criticized Beauvoir for giving an idealistic explanation; see, for example, M. Lowenthal Felstiner: 'Seeing the Second Sex through the Second Wave', *Feminist Studies*, vol. 6, no. 2, 1980, p.265.

14 'As for the content, I should take a more materialist position today in the first volume. I should base the notion of women as *other* and the Manichaean argument it entails not on an idealistic and *a priori* struggle of consciences, but on the facts of supply and demand . . . This modification would not necessitate any changes in the subsequent developments of my argument'. *Force of Circumstance*, Harmondsworth, Penguin, 1981, p.202.

15 See Seigfried's detailed discussion of the chapter on biology and its prejudices, C. Haddock Seigfried: 'Second Sex: Second Thoughts', *Hypatia*, vol. 8, no. 3, 1985. Like myself, Seigfried sees an opening in Beauvoir's concept of situation. See also criticism of Beauvoir's acceptance of biological facts in E. Hoffman Baruch: 'The Female Body and the Male Mind', *Dissent*, 1987, p.351f. and, not least, Suzanne Lilar's consistent criticism of Beauvoir's devaluation of female biology in *Le Malentendu du Deuxième Sexe*, Presses Universitaires de France, Paris, 1969.

16 See also M. Evans's criticism of biological reductionism in *The Second Sex*, in *Simone de Beauvoir: A Feminist Mandarin*, London, Tavistock, 1985, pp.62–6. As Evans ignores the concept of situation, she portrays Beauvoir as being more reductionist than she actually is.

17 For a critique of Hegel from a feminist perspective, see also Lloyd, 1983, and G. Lloyd: *The Man of Reason: 'Male' and 'Female' in Western Philosophy*, London, Methuen, 1984; O'Brien, 1981; and Mills.

READINGS OF THE
AUTOBIOGRAPHY

THE FATHER IN *MEMOIRS OF A DUTIFUL DAUGHTER*

Francis Jeanson

Francis Jeanson first met Simone de Beauvoir when she was almost 40 years old, and just beginning to emerge as a well-known writer and left-wing intellectual. They worked alongside each other as co-members of the editorial team of *Les Temps modernes* from 1951 to 1956, and in 1960 Jeanson called on her to support him in his clandestine activities on behalf of the FLN (the Algerian nationalist front and guerrilla movement) in Algeria. She immediately accepted. Jeanson had written a number of highly regarded analyses of Sartre's work; in 1965 he conducted two lengthy interviews with Simone de Beauvoir, which have been much cited, and went on to write one of the earliest books devoted to her work, *Simone de Beauvoir ou l'entreprise de vivre* (1966).[1]

Jeanson's position *vis-à-vis* Simone de Beauvoir is thus that of friend, collaborator and political ally. He had been one of the first to defend *The Second Sex* when it was published in France; he had a background in philosophy and was interested by the philosophical dimension of Beauvoir's work, as well as by her fiction. Yet, as he writes in his introduction, his decision to focus on the 'extraordinarily rich' three volumes of the memoirs published by 1966 derives from his conviction that they stand as 'the centre of gravity of her work'.[2] His approach is above all that of the sympathetic analyst, strongly influenced by Freudian thinking, and he produces an intelligent and highly sensitive reading which makes few distinctions between author and text, treating Beauvoir's account much as an analyst might treat his patient's discourse. His interest in the early formation of personality leads him to focus primarily on the first volume of memoirs, covering Beauvoir's childhood and adolescence. In this extract his discussion centres on Beauvoir's relations with her father, and on the significance of the father's reaction to his daughter's first menstruation – a frequent and often highly charged topos in women's autobiographical writing.

Jeanson's approach can be interestingly compared with the approach adopted by Alex Hughes, in the next piece in this section. Following recent shifts in feminist appropriations of Freudian thinking, Hughes places the mother, rather than the father, at the centre of her analysis, and examines the way relations with the mother affect later emotional bonds.

Notes

1 The extract which follows is taken from F. Jeanson, *Simone de Beauvoir ou l'entreprise de vivre*, Paris, Seuil, 1966, pp.97–108. Translated by Elizabeth Fallaize.
2 Ibid., p.10.

'My father was thirty, my mother twenty-one, and I was their first child.'[1] The very first mention that Simone de Beauvoir makes of her relationship to others, to her parents, is one which underlines its privileged character, a privilege arising from the fact that *no-one else participates in it on equal terms with her*. Almost as soon as she becomes aware of her own existence, her presence in the world is immediately valorised by an absence, as it were: that of her sister, the baby who is two and a half years behind her. If she was jealous of the baby, the sentiment was of short duration: 'I felt myself to be much *more interesting* than an infant bundled up in a cradle. *I had* a little sister: that doll-like creature didn't *have me*' (p.5). We will be coming later to the details of the role which, on this basis, the young Poupette was called upon to play; we can simply note, for the moment, that the relationship between the two sisters from which her role was to derive was, from the outset, one of an unequal dependency.

But first of all we need to look at the people who were the first to exist for her as autonomous beings. We can begin by ruling out her nursemaid Louise, a pure symbol of '*unalterable security*' (p.5). And equally 'a numerous family' (grandparents, uncles, aunts, cousins) which, taken as a whole, offered her above all a guarantee of her own '*importance*' (and who later she referred to as the 'familias' as they became more and more burdensome to her). Can her father equally be put to one side? The first few lines that she devotes to him might well lead one to think so. We are presented first with the image that had already appeared in *America Day by Day* of the very young child spending hours curled up in the 'knee-hole under the desk' (p.5): here the father is simply identified with a particular atmosphere, that of the 'holy sanctum' (p.10, TA) in which he works, which the child can escape to, where she can envelop herself 'in its dusty glooms' and feel '*safely ensconced*'. But the reader may remember that in recalling this memory Beauvoir had refused to attribute to it any so-called desire to 'recover the maternal breast' (a notion equally rejected to describe the situation which provokes the memory, in which she is snuggled up in the cosy solitude of a train cab). In the version given in the memoirs, I note, first of all, that her childhood refuge takes on a much more positive value: 'Safely ensconced, I watched, I touched, *I took stock of the world*' (p.10). On the other hand I must confess to being rather disturbed to see the father appear for the first time in the shape of a vague entity whose only attribute is one which implies a maternal function . . . Had the child already managed to invert the roles of her parents? She goes on straight away to make clear, if I can put it this way, that her father had no 'very well-defined role in my life' (p.60). And she confides that her mother, 'distant' and 'capricious' (in comparison with Louise who seemed to the child to exist only in order to look after her and her sister) inspired 'the *tenderest feelings of love* in me; I would sit upon her knee, enclosed by the perfumed softness of her arms, and cover with kissses her fresh, youthful skin . . . I needed her smile' (p. 6, TA).

A father who represented for her both security and gaiety, a mother with whom she was in love: it would be unwise to draw any conclusion at all from this at this juncture. Instead, let us note in passing a crucial detail about the *closeness between the couple*, of which their daughter was well aware: 'When he came home in the evening he used to bring my mother a bunch of Parma violets, and they would laugh and kiss' (p.6).

Later she began to feel a certain admiration for her father:

> Since I had started going to school, my father had become interested in my progress and my successes, and he was beginning to mean much more in my life. . . . No one in my circle of acquaintances was nearly as funny, as interesting and as brilliant as he . . . I took him to be a kind of magician.
>
> (p.25)

But this was because he was playing a comic role and made her '*cry with laughter*' dressed up in a Pierrot costume, or as a waiter, or a soldier, or an actress, or 'in the role of a simple-minded cook named Rosalie' (p.25). However, the war came along, and her father was called up for active service with the Zouaves : 'he had let his moustache grow, and under his tarboosh his face had a gravity which made a great impression on me' (p.27). It seems that it was indeed around this time that a new dimension developed in their relationship: 'While I was still very small, he had won me over by his gaiety and gift of the gab; as I grew older, *I came to admire him for more serious reasons*. I was amazed at his culture, his intelligence, and his infallible good sense. . . . he paid more and more attention to me. In particular he took great pains with my handwriting and spelling . . . he told me with great satisfaction that I was a natural speller. . . . he read the classics aloud to me . . . I asked him many questions which he answered willingly' (p.36).

This new development in their relationship does not seem to have brought about any emotional perturbation: 'He never intimidated me, in the sense that I never felt the slightest unease in his presence; but I did not attempt to bridge the distance that lay between us; there were many subjects that I could not imagine myself discussing with him; *to him I was neither body nor soul, but simply a mind. Our relationship was situated in a pure and limpid atmosphere where unpleasantness could not exist.* He did not condescend to me, but raised me up to his level, *and then I was proud to feel myself a grown-up person'* (pp.36–7). It was in fact from here on that she began to feel something resembling passion for him; he had acknowledged her, she was wildly grateful and immediately set about admiring him even more. On an outing with him one Sunday afternoon (to a play at the Comédie Française) she felt a tremendous sense of complicity: 'for a few hours *I had the intoxicating impression that he belonged to me alone'* (p.71).

And as it became more and more apparent that he had not made a success of his life, she raised this into a source of hidden glory, a counterproof of his value – this 'silent wound' conferred upon him a 'new prestige'. 'About this period, *my feelings for my father became more intense* . . . I was moved by the spectacle of a man of such superior attainments adapting himself so simply to the shabbiness of his new position in the world . . . *I adored him with a romantic fervour'* (pp.71–2, TA). A little further on we read: *'My own passion for him had continued to grow'* (p.106). And the way in which this admiration worked is detailed for us as follows:

> The more difficult it became for him, the more I was dazzled by my father's superior character; it did not depend on money or success, and so I used to tell myself that he had deliberately ignored these; that did not prevent me from being sorry for him: I thought he was not appreciated at his true value, that he was misunderstood and the victim of obscure cataclysms. I was all the more grateful to him now for his outbursts of gaiety, which were still quite frequent.
>
> (p.106)

It does not come as a great surprise to discover that this peak of Simone's feelings for her father coincided with her puberty. And it was precisely in this period that the *first crack* in their relationship appeared, the first of many, but one which can be seen as particularly significant in so far as it set a pattern.

An event must have taken place at some time in Simone de Beauvoir's childhood which was responsible for transforming her initial sense of happiness into her almost primary optimism – an aspect of her personality so fundamental as to be second nature. I should now make clear that I consider this event to be *mythical*; I have no intention, therefore, of trying to give it a precise date.

The most that can be said about it is that it was an experience of *separation*, of 'a final break' (p.104) and that it included a number of experiences of different kinds which took place on separate occasions. It is possible, for example, to imagine that the origin of this experience may be anterior to the critical stage in relations between Simone and her father which we have now reached. It is undeniable that even during the period when her feelings for him were just beginning to intensify, they also had the downside of a distressing sense of imposition, of boredom and suffocation: an event as insignificant as a summer evening's walk with her father in the Luxembourg Gardens struck her as just as surprising as if she had found 'a hawthorn in flower in the middle of winter' (p.72). The young Simone must have felt singularly emotionally deprived to have seized so avidly on this spark of warmth. 'My daily routine was as unalterable as the rhythm of the seasons: *the slightest deviation transported me almost into the realms of fantasy*' (p.72). And a similar feeling is recorded in the period in which her passion for her father reached its height: 'When he stayed at home he read us Victor Hugo and Rostand; he talked about the writers he liked, about the theatre, great events of the past, and a host of other improving subjects *which transported me far away from the everyday drabness of life*' (p.106). But these two remarks recall a third which predates them: '*I couldn't tolerate being bored: my boredom soon turned to real distress of mind*' (pp.67–8).

It will be remembered that as a child Simone had already evolved a strategy to cope with inactivity (breeder of boredom) which consisted in a full utilisation of self and objects, and a strict administration of her time and money: in this way her duty coincided with what she wanted. It should be understood that if doing her duty suited her it was strictly in so far as it served her wants; and we have just noted that it distressed her to experience imposition. She required, certainly, a world ordered by necessity, but that meant a world centred on herself and furnishing an absolute justification for her existence: she wanted to be sure that she was occupying her proper place, and doing what had to be done. She *expected*, we are told, and later we are shown her *expecting herself*. The fact is that her situation as a child (and then as an adolescent) struck her as a misfortune: a misalignment, a discrepancy, an inner contradiction endured with difficulty. As consciousness, she felt herself to be and wished to be sovereign; as a little girl, her sovereignty was not acknowledged by adults.[2] But when it is impossible to step outside a situation the only solution is despair or recourse to magic, to some powerful way out guaranteed by divine right and already almost there: '*I was expected*'. In other words she thought of herself as being (she was determined to be), somewhere or other, a fully constituted person: all that she needed was to be eventually reunited with herself; and since she *insisted* that she would be, a *promise* had been made that she would. She soon received confirmation of the promise (and by the same token it became more concrete) in so far as her father appeared to her to be capable of keeping it. No doubt the task suited him: in any case, he willingly and fully entered into the game.[3]

However, if it is easy to understand how the young Simone's *impatience to be herself* soon hooked into her father's willingness to offer her an abstract acknowledgement, we still have to explain how, through him, the difficulties which he was intended to protect her against instead became more cruelly wounding.

That first crack in their relationship is situated by her as occurring at the time of her first menstruation. The physiological event in itself – which initially made her 'horror-stricken' because her mother had not prepared her – seemed to her on the whole to be positive, once she was quite sure that there was no implication of fault: she even felt 'a sort of pride' (p.101). She did not really mind when she heard her mother talking about it to her female friends. But she did not expect that her father would be informed, and she took it very badly when he made a joking reference to her condition: '*I was consumed with shame . . . I thought of myself in relationship to my father as a purely spiritual being; I was horrified at the thought that he suddenly considered me to be a mere organism. I felt as if I could never hold up my head again*' (p.101).

The second identifiable crack is closely connected to the first : 'As long as he approved of me, I could be sure of myself. . . . *But when I entered the "spotty" stage, he was disappointed in me*' (p.107, TA).[4] And the third is probably also linked, since the conflict which it brought to light (and which could in theory have taken place at any period) actually only appeared at the very beginning of puberty: 'I dreamed of having a more intimate relationship with my father' (p.107) but '*I soon lost this illusion*' (p.108). This time the conflict was directly between the child and her mother, with the child unable to accept that her mother's relationship with the father was a special one – one which constantly *relativised* the child's own relationship with the father: 'even on the rare occasions when we found ourselves alone together we talked as if she was there with us' (p.107).

If we wish to chart the progressive deterioration in her relationship with her father to its end, and to see how it modified her relationships with others and her view of the world, we need first to return to the mother and to try to define what her mother represented for her in her early years. After having written about them in a way which always distinguishes between them, almost to the point of opposing each to the other, she begins to be much more inclined to refer to *her parents* – to lump them together, so to speak. But even before reaching this stage, she found herself obliged to redistribute the roles which she had originally assigned to them. The reassuring father, whose masculinity was singularly unimportant to her, came as we have seen to be the object of her feelings of passion; simultaneously, the mother whom she initially adored, whose presence brought her such pleasure, became strangely distant from her, to the point of representing for her that unjust imposition which she saw as keeping her separated from herself. And these two apparently inverse developments eventually led to a common crowning conclusion in which the father and mother are merged into one: a conviction that the relationship is a failure, or at the least has serious shortcomings. We have noted the sudden decline of the relationship with the father which had been developing positively; we now need to turn to the mother.

The most immediately striking element in the feelings that the mother inspired in the child seems to me to be the *anxiety* which underlies them. Bursting with pride when she was congratulated on having grown a few centimetres, the child nevertheless 'sometimes felt frightened . . . I would look at Mama's armchair and think: *I won't be able to sit on her knee any more if I go on growing up*' (p.7). And then there is also the fact that this 'laughing, lively young woman', who believed a wife should obey her husband in everything, nevertheless had quite a sharp manner: 'She also had about her something wilful and imperious . . . with Louise, my sister, and myself she showed herself to be dictatorial and overbearing, sometimes passionately so' (p.37). Timid and conformist in public, 'if one of her intimate friends or relations happened to cross her or offend her, she often reacted with anger and outbursts of violent frankness' (p.37). One can imagine why her daughters felt obliged to be '*prudent*': 'whenever her eyes had that stormy look or even when she just compressed her lips, I believe that I *feared* the disturbance I was causing in her heart more than my own discomfiture' (p.40).

But that feeling of 'discomfiture' was nevertheless feared by the young Simone, dependent as she was on a mother for whom she in some ways felt *responsible*: 'At every instant of the day she was present, even in the most secret recesses of my soul, and I made no distinction between her all-seeing wisdom and the eye of God himself' (p.38). The difference was, however, that whereas she had never feared that God would abandon her, simply detaching herself from him once she had understood that he could not be the guarantor of the kind of absolute which she required, she was terrorised by the idea of her mother rejecting her: 'any reproach made by my mother, even her slightest frown was a threat to my security: without her approval, I no longer felt that I had any right to live' (p.39).

By the time that puberty came along, a few years later, this crucial relationship had turned into something very different: 'My mother's eternal solicitude began to weigh on me. She had her own "ideas" which she did not attempt to justify, and her decisions often seemed to me quite arbitrary' (p.105). The result was that Simone, despite her customary docility, sometimes contested an authority in which she no longer believed; when she was obliged to give in 'it was with *rage in my heart*, vowing never to forgive her for what I considered to be an *abuse of her power* over me' (p.105). Even more radically, '*I held it against her for keeping me so dependent upon her and continuing to impose her will upon me*' (p.106). Her rage, on top of her anxiety, had the effect of intensifying and further exposing the deep-rooted feeling which was already worrying her: the feeling of being imprisoned by derisory boundaries and strictly limited in her freedom. She had managed to cope with this feeling, more or less, throughout the earlier period in which her father had given her a recognition which she took to be absolute; but, when this resort failed her, crisis became inevitable.

It failed her, as we have seen, when she became conscious that in her father's eyes she had a *bodily* existence, one that she was just discovering. The 'sovereign' judge on the intellectual plane ('I couldn't imagine a more intelligent man than my father', p.106), he saved her from contingency – from the fate of being held to be inessential, relative – by feigning to establish a relationship of intellectual equality with her. The moment that he betrayed her expectations, her *confidence*, by relegating her to the physical dimension of her existence, he found himself cut down to size in his turn and removed from his safekeeping function, quickly transferred to another – a fictional hero (as a provisional stopgap), a male teacher older than the young heroine and 'endowed with the highest qualities', who understands her, comforts her, advises her and marries her: 'This superior individual . . . was the incarnation of that *supreme Judge by whom I hoped one day to be acknowledged*' (p.105).

All was now lost with her father. She spent a certain amount of time making quite sure that it was the case – the time necessary, in a favourite expression of hers, to *work through the failure*. This is why, as I argued earlier, no exact date can be put on the 'primary event', the decisive break with the happiness of her childhood.

In the first stage of her new awareness, in fact, we see her trying to substitute for the close relationship she wanted with her father a 'silent complicity' – against her mother, of course. But the only result achieved was that she found herself obliged to measure the difference between the real *solidarity* of her parents and the derisory *complicity* which she had hoped to fall back on. In a sense, nothing more serious would ever happen. Her father had struck a double blow in taking her mother's side against her – wrongly – when she had precisely counted on him in judging her mother ('Mother is ridiculous!'). She felt betrayed twice over: once for being passed over for someone else, and again for losing the 'absolute infallibility' in his eyes which had acted as a guarantee of redemption. In another sense, however, things continued to go from bad to worse in as far as she did not immediately feel able to take the break on board. 'My parents still had the power to make me feel guilty; I accepted their verdicts while at the same time I looked upon myself with other eyes than theirs. My essential self still belonged to them as much as to me' (p.108). Between the ages of 13 and 17, Simone *had to discover several times* that her father was not infallible, 'that it was possible to be of another opinion than my father', in which case 'one could not even be sure of what the truth was' (p.133); or that her parents supported each other, that they opposed her by mutual consent, that they shook their heads in unison in agreeing, 'what a pity Simone wasn't a boy!' (p.177); or, yet again, that her father was disappointed by her appearance, that he thought her ugly, not a credit to him, and, finally, that he disagreed with her about everything.

We have seen how deeply disappointed she had been at 13. As a student of literature at the Sorbonne and of maths at the Catholic Institute, we can still see her registering her disappointment, recording it as if it were a new element in her life:

> My captivity seemed all the more unbearable because I no longer felt happy at home. Her eyes raised imploringly heavenwards, my mother would pray for my salvation; she was always moaning about the errors of my ways: we had completely lost touch with one another. At least I knew the reasons for her distress. *But my father's reticence astonished and wounded me much more. He should have been taking some interest in my work, in the progress I was making: he might, I thought, have talked to me in a friendly way about the authors I was studying: but he was merely indifferent, and even vaguely hostile, in his attitude towards me.* My cousin Jeanne was far from intelligent, but she was very pretty and always smiling; my father never tired of telling everyone that his brother had a delightful daughter; then he would give a sigh. *I was very put out. I*

couldn't understand what had come between us and was to cast a heavy
shadow over my youth.

(p.175)

'He had wanted me to study and reproached me for always having a book open: I kept wondering what I had done wrong; I felt unhappy and ill at ease, and nursed resentment in my heart' (p.179). It was at this point that she discovered, through her cousin Jacques, the joys and beauties of literature. Her mother immediately reproached her for reading novels; her father criticised her choice of authors: 'I was vexed by these attacks. The conflict that had been smouldering between us was beginning to leap into flame. *My childhood and adolescence had passed fairly smoothly . . . but now it seemed that there had been a decisive break in the course of my life*' (p.187).

Notes

1 S. de Beauvoir, *Memoirs of a Dutiful Daughter*, trans. James Kirkup, Harmondsworth, Penguin, 1987, p.5. All subsequent references to this are given in brackets in the text. Italics are all in the original.

2 'As soon as I was able to think for myself, I found myself possessed of infinite power, and yet circumscribed by absurd limitations' (p.68).

3 This is moreover one of the two classic attitudes fathers take up to daughters: it seems to me that it tends both to deny the child in favour of the woman (of whom the child is merely a disappointing reduction) and to deny, in the name of morality, the woman who is after all prefigured in the child. The synthesis of this double negation is the attribution to the child of an adult consciousness, totally asexual: 'My father treated me like a fully developed person' (p.39) and 'to him I was neither body nor soul, but simply a mind' (p.36).

4 Her father liked women: 'he appreciated elegance and beauty in women' (p.107). And this is precisely why he chose from the beginning to ward off his daughter's femininity by denying it. As long as she remained a child, he could not seriously resent her for reminding him that she was a woman and looking so little like one, but when the gap between his daughter and womanhood began to narrow, the threat became more present and was accompanied by resentment. She was about to become a woman (and could not be one for him); she nevertheless frustrated him by not yet being, by refusing to be, a woman. 'Not only did he fail to conceal his disillusionment, but he began showing more interest than before in my sister, who was still a pretty girl' (p.107). One of the most remarkable aspects of his attitude is that he contributed to his own disappointment, forcing her into the 'difficult' age sooner than she would have done if left to herself. His joke about his daughter's menstruation was probably intended to put her at her ease (in a situation which embarrassed him himself in a somewhat irrational way), but it is also evident that he took pleasure in humiliating her by suddenly reducing her to her body, and in an unpleasant way, as if to punish her for approaching so close to the femininity which it would be impossible for him to recognise. It is clear, in any case, that his attitude made worse the disturbances which frequently occur in girls at the time of puberty.

MURDERING THE MOTHER IN
MEMOIRS OF A DUTIFUL DAUGHTER

Alex Hughes

Alex Hughes has published a number of studies of different aspects of Beauvoir's work, including a stimulating psychoanalytic study of *The Blood of Others*, Beauvoir's second novel.[1] In the article which follows, published in 1994, she focuses on *Memoirs of a Dutiful Daughter* in order to ask whether it can be considered to be a matricidal text; whether, in other words, the text carries out the kind of exorcism of the mother which theorists such as Luce Irigaray consider to be crucial to the achievement of the daughter's subjectivity.[2] Considering much of the same material as Francis Jeanson, thirty years later and from an explicitly feminist theoretical position unavailable to Jeanson, Hughes notes as he does the memoirs' construction of an early close bond between Simone and her mother and reads it as a characteristic example of the specular relation between mother and daughter posited by Irigaray and Nancy Chodorow (albeit from different perspectives). Yet, within this specular bond, Hughes also detects an extreme anxiety on the part of the daughter, a fear of engulfment which Simone protects herself against by seeking out doubles – in her sister, Poupette, in God, in her schoolfriend Elisabeth Mabille and, finally, in Sartre. Hughes focuses on the figure of Elisabeth Mabille – Zaza – to show that Zaza operates as an ambiguous double, serving both as an emancipatory protection against the mother and as a repetition of her mother's dominance. Zaza's death can thus be read not only as tragedy but also as the necessary removal of a quasi-maternal obstacle to the daughter's autonomy.

The father, central to Jeanson's reading, is almost non-existent in Hughes's account, and this emphasis reflects the way in which feminists have moved on from the Freudian insistence on relations to the father to an emphasis on the mother, and on other female relationships. Finally the way in which Hughes builds on the work of Alice Jardine, and points forward to the way in which the figure of Sartre can be read in the final autobiographical text, *Adieux: Farewell to Sartre*, creates interesting links with the article by Elaine Marks which closes this section.

Notes

1 See A. Hughes, *Le Sang des autres*, Glasgow, University of Glasgow French and German Publications, 1995.
2 A. Hughes, 'Murdering the Mother: Simone de Beauvoir's *Mémoires d'une jeune fille rangée*', *French Studies*, 1994, vol.48, no.2, pp.174–83. Adapted by Elizabeth Fallaize.

In her provocative essay 'Death Sentences: Writing Couples and Ideology', Alice Jardine suggests that Beauvoir's *A Very Easy Death* and her *Adieux: A Farewell to Sartre* emblematize 'the poetics of an ideology that insists upon killing the mother'.[1] Jardine's argument is that in these texts, the maternal body is dissected, exorcized and purified through language, so that Beauvoir may continue to write and may simultaneously preserve the integrity of a disembodied textual realm in which she is definitively shielded from the snares of the maternal/material. It is easy to see how Jardine's thesis is applicable to *A Very Easy Death*, since this text charts the (shocking) physical disintegration of Beauvoir's mother Françoise; however, Jardine's perception of *Adieux: A Farewell to Sartre*, as a 'matricidal' work is unexpected, to say the least. Jardine justifies her reading of Beauvoir's last autobiographical volume as an assault upon the maternal body by positing its key player, the moribund Sartre, as a 'maternal' entity – as a 'phallic', rather than biological, mother. The concept of the phallic mother, to which I shall return in the course of my discussion, is Freudian in origin,[2] but is more developed in the work of Julia Kristeva who, as Jardine indicates, theorizes maternal phallicity as 'an organizing fantasy for the denial of sexual difference'.[3] Broadly speaking, the phallic mother, in Freudian terms, constitutes, as Jane Gallop explains, 'the pre-Oedipal mother, apparently omniscient and omnipotent, until the "discovery of her castration", the discovery that she is not a "whole" but a "hole"'.[4]

Jardine's foregrounding of Sartre's phallic/maternal status (the basis for which will be indicated below) permits her to interpret *Adieux: A Farewell to Sartre*, as much as *A Very Easy Death*, as a vehicle for Beauvoir's matricidal impulses, and to take both texts as evidence that Beauvoir represents a classic example of a woman author operating within a 'masculine' writing economy which necessitates a rejection of the Mother and an identification with the Father. Jardine concludes her discussion with a series of questions. These are destined to encourage her readers to reflect upon whether, in a culture predicated upon the Oedipal Family Romance and the act of symbolic matricide that subtends it, it is possible (for Beauvoir? for any woman? for anyone at all?) to write 'without dismembering the female body; without killing other women in the name of epistemological purity; without killing our mothers, the mother in us?'[5] This article represents an effort to respond to Jardine's inquiry. In it I focus on the treatment meted out to the mother, and to her substitutes/doubles, in Beauvoir's first autobiographical work, and endeavour to establish whether the *Memoirs* constitute, in the last analysis, a 'matricidal' opus. A focal point of my discussion will be the significance of the stories to which Beauvoir was exposed in childhood and adolescence and which she retells as she weaves the narrative of her youth; stories which attest to her deepest and most secret preoccupations.

In the opening section of Beauvoir's *récit*, it becomes quickly apparent that the relationship between the young Simone and her mother was characterized, in its early stages, by intersubjective interpenetration, continuity and entanglement. That the two women shared a 'mirror-bond' of peculiar intensity should come, perhaps, as no surprise, particularly to readers familiar with the work of Luce Irigaray and Nancy Chodorow, both of whom claim – albeit for different reasons – that the dynamics of the mother/daughter relation are predicated upon specularity, symbiotic identity and boundary merging, and fusionality.[6] It seems at first that Beauvoir merely offers us a detached account of the symbiotic tie that bound her to her maternal parent during her childhood; an account in which her infantile dependency upon her mother – and the response her mother's 'hold over [her]' (*Memoirs*, p.39) aroused in her – are lucidly analysed:[7]

> Any reproach made me by my mother, and even her slightest frown was a threat to my security: without her approval, I no longer felt I had any right to live. . . . Certainly, the reason for my timidity was a desire to avoid her derision. But at the same time, whenever her eyes had that stormy look or even when she just compressed her lips, I believe that I feared the disturbance I was causing in her heart more than my own discomfiture. . . . My responsibility towards her made my dependence even greater. And that is how we lived, the two of us, in a kind of symbiosis. Without striving to imitate her, I was conditioned by her.
>
> (pp. 39–40)

Yes, the adult Beauvoir appears to be saying, I did share a powerful, identificatory relationship ('une sorte de symbiose') with my mother, which complicated my sense of my own autonomous, individual selfhood, but my resultant feeling of insecurity was neither unusual nor especially significant. However, other elements of the first part of the *Memoirs* tell a rather different story. In Part I, Beauvoir articulates an anxiety focused upon the maternal/filial bond, whose intensity is discernible and yet is never properly acknowledged. This anxiety is first hinted at, obliquely, at the very start of Beauvoir's autobiography, when she evokes her infantile eating difficulties and her mother's efforts to feed her in a way which, arguably, is indicative of a sense on her part of unwelcome intrusion/ engulfment:[8]

> The principal function of Louise and mama was to feed me; their task was not always an easy one. . . . The insipidity of milk puddings, por-

ridge, and mashes of bread and butter made me burst into tears; the oiliness of fat meat and the clammy mysteries of shellfish revolted me.

(p.6)

The fear implied by this extract is comparable to that which, in *The Second Sex*, Beauvoir analyses in terms of the *male* subject's disgust at his own 'contingence charnelle', which he projects onto/into the mother who comes to embody the threat of *engloutissement* and *viscosité*.[9] However, the mother-related anguish that permeates Part I of the *Memoirs* – a daughter's story, not a son's – is a function rather of issues of invasion and absorption which are commonly associated with the mother/daughter dynamic. It is considerably more apparent in Beauvoir's accounts of fictional or cinematic narratives encountered by her childhood self which, once re-narrated, form *micro-récits* within the main body of the text. From these *micro-récits*, which Beauvoir remembers and which, with elaborate casualness, she reproduces in her narrative – the tale of the child Charlotte who eats an egg which is both 'stomach' and 'cradle' and whose ingestion reduces her to a foetal state (p.8); the story of Bob, 'the jungle explorer', who is 'swallowed alive' in a 'subterranean passage' by a python (p.52); and that of the heroine of a silent film (watched by the young Simone with her mother and grandmother), who is swallowed up by the marshes (pp.53–4) – there emerges a disquieting vision of the mother as a subjugatory, invasive entity, whose engulfing potential must be conjured at all costs. What, then, is actually at stake in these narratives-within-the-narrative, with whose protagonists Beauvoir clearly identified in childhood, and which, as an adult, she feels compelled to disinter and insert into Part I of her *Memoirs*?

The opening section of Beauvoir's autobiography contains a message which is ultimately not dissimilar to that offered by Luce Irigaray's poetic, distressing exploration of mother/daughter bonding, *Et l'une ne bouge pas sans l'autre* (1979). Through her personal recollections of the tales that 'appealed' to the child she was, the mature Beauvoir fearfully and instinctually evokes a mother/ mirror/marsh perceived as capable (still?) of absorbing her. Irigaray, on the other hand, creates a complex, focused account of the impossibility in our culture of mediated relationships between women, and of the absence of processes whereby daughters may achieve an identity distinct from that of the mother. Leaving these differences aside, both women are essentially addressing the anguish of the daughter who senses herself to be filled/fed by her mother so excessively that she is deprived of autonomy and threatened with extinction. What is at issue, in other words, in the early stages of the *Memoirs* as much as in Irigaray's short text, is the inscription of resentful dread – a daughter's dread of a maternal figure who menaces her with obliteration.

At the same time that Beauvoir's autobiographical *récit* chronicles – however implicitly – extreme daughterly anxiety, it also points to strategies adopted by its narrator/heroine in an effort to undermine maternal authority and to emancipate herself from the maternal orbit, via a process of differentiation and liberation. In Parts I and II of the *Memoirs* Simone seeks out doubles or companions whose reassuring presence combats the terror of being swallowed up (*engloutissement*) and annihilation the mother incarnates. Her account of her dealings with these individuals confirms the point made by Freud in 'The Uncanny' that the 'invention of doubling [is] a preservation against extinction' and that the double constitutes 'an insurance against the destruction of the ego' (*Standard Edition*, XVII, p.235). In the first section of the text, the 'liegeman [. . .], alter ego, [. . .], double' (p.42) in question is Poupette, Beauvoir's sister; in Part II, Poupette is replaced by God. Sister and divine Father (Beauvoir's biological father has curiously little to do with the trajectory I am outlining) are initially represented as capable of shoring up Simone's sense of identity and uniqueness, and of relieving her unconscious fear of being (re)absorbed into the maternal:

> What I appreciated most in our relationship was that I had a real hold over her [my sister] . . . . She alone endowed me with authority; adults sometimes gave in to me: she obeyed me. . . . Thanks to my sister I was asserting my right to personal freedom; she was my accomplice, my subject, my creature.
>
> (pp. 44–5)

> His [God's] sovereign power did not cancel out my own authority. He knew all things after his own fashion, that is to say, in an absolute sense: but it seemed to me that he needed my eyes too in order that the trees might have their colours. . . . Far from wishing to dethrone me, he assured me that I could go on reigning.
>
> (p.126)

Unfortunately for the young Simone, neither her sister – the first acknowledged object of an intense desire for a double which resurfaces later in the *Memoirs* – nor God proves to be a satisfactory partner in her quest for freedom and individuation. The latter is too reliant upon her ('He needed my eyes') to hold out a genuine possibility of liberation. Poupette, as Catherine Portuges argues in her discussion of attachment and separation in Beauvoir's autobiography, does at first appear to 'enable her elder sister, simply by virtue of her existence, to pursue the single-minded search for self-realization that is one of the subjects of the *Memoirs*'.[10] Ultimately, however, she is too close to the mother and too involved in the symbiotic paradigm to offer a means of escape from it. This is why, as Portuges points out, Simone's encounter with Zaza Mabille, her first and only school friend, seems so decisive. In Zaza, it appears, she finds at last the emancipatory companion she has been seeking; a companion whose non-familial status and admirable independence will ensure that 'symbiotic and enmeshed relationships with m/others [are] first challenged and then rapidly replaced'.[11] A brief examination of the terms in which Zaza, and Simone's reaction to her, are described in Parts I and II of the *Memoirs* helps us quickly to see why the other girl is, initially at least, so attractive to Simone:

> In Zaza I could glimpse a presence, flashing as a spring of water, solid as a block of marble, and as firmly drawn as a portrait by Dürer.
>
> (p.112)

> At the musical and dramatic performance which was given every year round about Christmas, we played in a sketch. I, in a pink dress, my hair in ringlets, impersonated Mme de Sévigné as a little girl; Elisabeth took the part of a high-spirited boy cousin; her young man's costume suited her, and she enchanted the audience with her vivacity and ease.
>
> (p.92)

> For ten to fifteen days I dragged myself somehow, on legs that seemed as weak as water, from hour to hour, from day to day. One afternoon I was taking my things off in the cloakroom at school when Zaza came up to me . . . So total had been my ignorance of the workings of the heart that I hadn't thought of telling myself: 'I miss her'. I needed her presence to realize how much I needed her. . . . I allowed myself to be uplifted by that wave of joy which went on mounting inside me, as violent and fresh as a waterfalling cataract, as naked, beautiful, and bare as a granite cliff.
>
> (p.95)

The attributes which Simone associates, explicitly or implicitly, with her friend – whose captivating personality transforms an early reunion, evoked in the last of the extracts cited, into 'a fete, a celebration, a moment of almost mystical revelation'[12] – emerge forcefully from the passages I have selected. Zaza embodies (pseudo-) maleness, hardness and firmly contoured distinctness – characteristics that are the antithesis of those imputed to the mother in the *micro-récits* of Part I of the *Memoirs*. It is precisely because Zaza seems to Simone to have the (masculine) qualities of 'a granite cliff' that she promises to constitute the perfect, liberatory love-object Portuges considers her to be. If the female, engulfing mother/ marsh that is Françoise de Beauvoir must be spurned by Simone, because she threatens *engloutissement*, Zaza can be loved wholeheartedly, because she in no way embodies the risk of absorption or invasion. If Simone rediscovers Zaza with a quasi-erotic joy after a two-week separation, it is because she perceives her as offering the possibility of 'a satisfactory integration of [the] desire for closeness and differentiation, for attachment and separation',[13] and, more importantly, the means by which Simone may begin to escape her mother and all she represents. As long as Zaza exists, the mother can (apparently, at least) be cast aside.

In the light of the above, it becomes clear why Zaza's role in Simone's development has been interpreted as more or less emancipatory.[14] However, the Zaza/Simone relation is a good deal more complex than critics have generally allowed. Beauvoir's narrator certainly invites us to read her adolescent bond with her friend positively, i.e. as the vehicle for a necessary break with mother and milieu; indeed, she directs us towards just such a reading, by emphasizing at the end of Part I of her *récit* her great good fortune in meeting Zaza.[15] However, there are a number of indications in the *Memoirs* that what Simone discovers in her dealings with Zaza is an interpersonal dynamic which is identical to that linking her to her mother, and which is consequently far from liberatory. If Simone eludes invasion and absorption in the presence of her 'distant' (p.144), granite-hard school friend, she none the less finds herself involved in a bond in which she is once again mirror-image, subordinate and vassal:

> And once again the glaringly obvious struck me: 'I can't live without her'. It was rather frightening: she came and went unconcernedly in my life, and all my happiness, my very existence, lay in her hands. . . . I had gone as far as to admit the extent of the dependence which my attach-ment to her placed upon me: I did not dare envisage all its consequences.
>
> (pp.95–6)

> I loved Zaza so much that she seemed to be more real than myself: I was her negative; instead of laying claim to my own characteristics, I had to have them thrust upon me which I supported with ill grace.
>
> (p.112)

Since Zaza effectively affords Simone renewed dependency, and reinforces rather than eliminates problems already encountered *vis-à-vis* the mother – compare, for example, the first of the above extracts with the narrator's earlier comment, in Part I of the *Memoirs*, that 'without her [mother's] approval, I no longer felt that I had any right to live' (p.39) – what is her actual function in the *récit*? What, regardless of her apparent status as adored, exemplary classmate, does she really represent? Clearly, she cannot be viewed simply as an extension of the absorbing mother/marsh whose threatening aspect emerges so intensely from Beauvoir's *micro-récits*. None the less, within the psyche of the narrator/heroine of the *Memoirs*, Zaza evidently stands in a relation of some kind to the figure of the mother. Arguably, therefore, what Zaza signifies for Simone is not a *replacement* for the mother but rather a different *sort* of mother; one who, to use Jane Gallop's terminology, is not a 'hole', likely to engulf and obliterate, but a 'whole'. Is Zaza, with her hardness and 'maleness', the pre-Oedipal mother, the mother who precedes the discovery of castration, who is possessed of the phallus; the mother who, to quote Gallop, 'is more phallic [than the Primitive Father] precisely by being less obvious'?[16] If this is the case – and it is extremely tempting to 'read' her in this way – why does she attract Beauvoir's narrator/heroine? Conceivably, Simone is drawn to and seeks out in Zaza this archaic mother-figure precisely because, for all her fear of maternal *engloutissement*, absolute *loss* of the mother is also terrifying. Turning to Zaza, the phallic mother, is the one means by which Simone hopes (erroneously) to elude the mother-related anguish evoked in Part I whilst avoiding the 'exile' to which she knows definitive mother/ daughter separation condemns her.[17]

All of the above suggests that what the reader is offered in Parts I and II of the *Memoirs* is the same binary, oppositional configuration of phallic/non-phallic mothers that Jardine discerns in *A Very Easy Death* and *Adieux: A Farewell to Sartre*. There is, however – apparently – a distinction between the latter text and the *Memoirs*. In *Adieux: A Farewell to Sartre*, according to Jardine, the phallic mother, in this instance the incontinent, ailing Sartre, is immolated, cut up by the violence of Beauvoir's razor-edged discourse. In the *Memoirs*, on the other hand, his equivalent, Zaza – the beloved confidante, the vivacious tomboy who suc-cumbs to the manipulations of family and class and finally takes on the role of 'dutiful daughter' her friend refuses – seems to emerge as the object of Simone's enduring love and gratitude. Or does she? As we saw earlier, interaction with Zaza actually involves Simone in a subjugation she has already experienced – and resented – in her dealings with her biological mother, and consequently menaces her with (re)exposure to feelings of *néantisation*. What is her reaction to the renewal of the threat of obliteration? In order to gauge this, we need to look further at the account we are given of the Simone/Zaza relation, and at what happens to Zaza in the course of the *Memoirs*.

Simone's dependency upon Zaza is articulated for the first time at the end of Part I, in the declamatory passage where Beauvoir recalls the epiphanic moment during which she became aware of her love for her friend. In the same section of the text, Zaza's (imagined) death is evoked, also for the first time:

I imagined Mlle Gontran coming in, her long black skirts sweeping the floor, and saying: 'Children, let us pray; your little companion, Elisabeth Mabille, was called away to the arms of God last night'. Well, if that were to happen, I told myself, I should die on the spot.

(p.95)

The possibility of Zaza's disappearance resurfaces in Part II of the *Memoirs*, shortly after Beauvoir's narrator petulantly describes herself as the 'negative' of her cherished companion (p.112). In the passage in question, Beauvoir evokes another narrative that captivated her youthful imagination, *Schoolboy in Athens*, by André Laurie. In the course of the re-narration of this *micro-récit*, Zaza is linked to Euphorion, an extraordinarily gifted youth who none the less dies pre-maturely, leaving his more pedestrian friend, Théagène, to tell his story, and to become in so doing 'both mind and memory, the essential Subject' (p.114) – a position which Simone clearly claims as her own by the end of the *Memoirs*. The *Memoirs* close with the account of Zaza's actual demise, and with the following, passionate tribute from Beauvoir:

She has often appeared to me at night, her face all yellow under a pink sun-bonnet, and seeming to gaze reproachfully at me. We had fought together against the revolting fate that had lain ahead of us, and for a long time I believed that I had paid for my own freedom with her death. (p.360)

The final words of the *Memoirs* have engendered speculation about the moral debt Beauvoir felt she owed to the companion whose 'fall' paralleled her own conquest of freedom,[18] and have led to comment regarding the 'reparative function'[19] of her text – which, on one level, can indeed be read as a tribute to the girl who offered Beauvoir a model of exemplary independence and unconventionality and then died in her stead. Critics who have analysed Beauvoir's account of Zaza's death have interpreted it moreover as the source of her life-long revolt against the bourgeoisie (to whose restrictive moral codes she attributed blame for her friend's tragic end),[20] and have located in this revolt the stimulus for her highly successful literary endeavours.[21] Emphasis has been placed therefore both on the intensity of Beauvoir's grief and (guilty, loving) gratitude and on the positive consequences of these sentiments. It is possible, however, to read Beauvoir's narration of Zaza's fate (m)otherwise, in a way which places the conclusion of her *Memoirs* in the context of the seemingly premonitory visions that assail Simone in Parts I and II in connection with her friend's death. Arguably, for all her idealization of Zaza, Beauvoir's narrator/heroine is manifesting through these visions and their textual reproduction an implicit but powerful need to remove a resented obstacle to her own autonomy. This need, which is already discernible at the end of Part I (when Zaza's death is first evoked) and palpably informs the Euphorion/Théagène *micro-récit*, is murderous and, given that Zaza functions as the phallic mother, is above all matricidal. Once we recognize its nature and force, we can no longer interpret Zaza's demise simply as the unexpected, ironic realization of what was, in Part I, an 'improbable hypothesis'.[22] Inevitably, her 'fall' takes on the appearance of an actualization – however fantastic – of an unconscious, mother-related death wish born out of Simone's (daughterly) rage and sense of subjugation. The *Memoirs*, in other words, offer a confirmation of the point made by Irigaray's narrator in *Et l'une ne bouge pas sans l'autre* that for a daughter (Simone) to achieve subjectivity and identity, the mother (Zaza) has somehow to cede her place and disappear.[23] Obviously, it would be overstating the case to argue that Zaza's death is willed, on a conscious level, or that the closing sentences of Beauvoir's first autobiographical volume are in any way overtly triumphalist. However, the 'maternal' interpretation I am offering makes it impossible to read the end of the *Memoirs* as exclusively loving or reparative, or even simply as the acknowledgement of a moral debt. In addition, my reading situates Beauvoir's *Memoirs* as the first element within an autobiographical sequence whose end point is the matricidal 'Tomb-Books' Jardine discusses, *Adieux: A Farewell to Sartre* and *A Very Easy Death*.[24]

Apparently, then, for Beauvoir, discursive matricide and the textual decomposition of the maternal body – in death, Zaza's hands are 'as fragile as an ancient mummy's' (p.360) – have the value of an imperative. At the end of the *Memoirs*,

Zaza, the archaic phallic mother who displaces/liquidates the biological mother/ marsh, is not only dead but has been displaced, as love-object, in her turn – by Sartre, the male lover/father dreamed of by Simone in adolescence ('Sartre corresponded exactly to the dream-companion I had longed for since I was fifteen: he was the double in whom I found all my burning aspiration raised to the pitch of incandescence' (p.345). The Oedipal family romance has evidently prevailed. Or has it? Are things so simple? Sartre, after all, corresponds to an ideal incarnated in the first place by a woman, Zaza herself ('My chosen one must, like Zaza, impose himself upon me, prove he was the right one; otherwise I should always be wondering: why he and not another?': pp.144–5). He is a 'double', consequently a partner in a mirror-relationship – and Simone's primordial specular tie was clearly that which bound her to her biological mother ('Without striving to imitate her, I was conditioned by her': p.40), even though it is Poupette, hapless sister-vassal rather than mother or mother-substitute, whom Beauvoir presents as her first double. So perhaps the 'matricidal' work of the *Memoirs* is not as complete as all that, and the mother is still present as primary object, in the person of Sartre? Sartre's phallic/maternal status is even made belatedly explicit by Beauvoir, in *A Very Easy Death,* when she refers to dreams she has after her biological mother dies, which explains, *inter alia,* why Jardine reads in the way that she does Beauvoir's positioning of Sartre in her last autobiographical *récit.* It seems therefore that neither the death of Zaza, in the *Memoirs,* nor that of Françoise, in *A Very Easy Death,* actually kills off the mother – the one with the phallus, at least – permanently and definitively. As Jardine demonstrates, it is not until *Adieux: A Farewell to Sartre,* with its visions of Sartre's putrefying body, that Beauvoir succeeds in liquidating the most phallic mother of all.

Notes

1 A. Jardine, 'Death Sentences: Writing Couples and Ideology', *Poetics Today,* vol. 6, 1985, pp.119–31 (p.121).

2 The notion of the maternal phallus – and of the recognition/non-recognition of its absence is central to Freud's work on fetishism (see *The Standard Edition of the Complete Psychological Works of Sigmund Freud,* translated and edited by James Strachey, 24 vols, London, Hogarth Press, 1953–74, XXI, pp.152–3). Laplanche and Pontalis present the figure of the phallic mother as an integral element of the Freudian account of infantile psychosexuality, as well as a common feature of dreams and phantasms, and argue that 'la mise en évidence progressive d'une "théorie sexuelle infantile" puis d'une phase libidinale proprement dite, dans lesquelles il n'y aurait pour l'un et pour l'autre sexe qu'un seul organe sexuel, le phallus, vient donner son fondement à l'image de la femme phallique'. J. Laplanche and J-B Pontalis, *Vocabulaire de la psychanalyse,* Paris, PUF, 1967, p.310. Henceforth references to the *Standard Edition* will be given in the text.

3 Jardine, 'Death Sentences', p.128.

4 J. Gallop, *The Daughter's Seduction: Feminism and Psychoanalysis,* Basingstoke and London, Macmillan, 1982, p.22.

5 Jardine, 'Death Sentences', p.130. Jardine's perception of the Oedipal Family Romance as intrinsically 'matricidal' relates to the fact that the breaking of the (incestuous, pre-Oedipal) mother/child dyad which both sexes must effect in order to gain access to the Symbolic order (i.e. the order of language, culture and society) involves a repudiation of the mother that may be read as somehow 'murderous'. Luce Irigaray's remarks concerning the nature of the sociocultural/ linguistic order into which the subject is inserted at the Oedipal moment bear Jardine's contention out: 'Freud says our culture is built on a parricide. More fundamentally, our culture is built on a matricide: the matricide of the mother/ lover'. Luce Irigaray, 'Interview', in *Women Writers Talking*, ed. J. Todd, New York, Holmes and Meier, 1983, pp.232–45 (p. 238).

6 Irigaray and Chodorow come to similar conclusions about the fusional nature of the mother/daughter bond, but their conceptual contexts are very different. In *The Reproduction of Mothering: Psychoanalysis and the Sociology of Gender*, Berkeley and Los Angeles, University of California Press, 1978, Nancy Chodorow explores at length, from the standpoint of Object Relations theory, the problems of self/ other differentiation women experience in their dealings with their mothers, and links identity/boundary blurring between mothers and daughters to the different treatment sociocultural norms lead mothers to offer their male and female offspring. Hers is, therefore, essentially an empirical, psychosociological analysis. Irigaray's approach, on the other hand, is related to her extensive, speculative and philosophical exploration of the place of the female subject in the current social, cultural and linguistic order, and its imaginary. As Margaret Whitford explains, Irigaray's argument is that in the Symbolic order as it stands, there is no recognized space for women outside the place of the mother. The mother/ daughter relationship remains unsymbolized, i.e. 'there is an absence of linguistic, social, cultural, iconic, theoretical, mythical, religious, or any other representations of that relationship', and non-symbolization 'hinders women from having an identity in the symbolic order that is distinct from the maternal function'. Consequently, 'women's ontological status in this culture is *déréliction*, the state of abandonment', and 'women have difficulty in separating from their mothers'. What is required, between mothers and daughters and women in general, is an 'interval of *exchange*', permitting differentiation and individual subjectivity. M. Whitford, 'Rereading Irigaray', in *Between Feminism and Psychoanalysis*, ed. T. Brennan, London and New York, Routledge, 1989, pp.106–26 (pp.108–12).

7 Page references are to the English translation, *Memoirs of a Dutiful Daughter*, translated J.Kirkup, Harmondsworth, Penguin, 1987.

8 A similar, eating-related unease is conveyed by the daughter/narrator of Irigaray's *Et l'une ne bouge pas sans l'autre*. In the section of this short text which focuses on maternal nurturing, Irigaray's manipulation of pronouns foregrounds clearly the theme of mother/daughter identity-merging: 'Tu as préparé à manger. Tu m'apportes à manger. Tu me/te donnes à manger. Mais tu me/te donnes trop, comme si tu voulais me remplir toute entière avec ce que tu m'apportes. Tu te mets dans ma bouche et j'étouffe. . . . Ne t'engloutis pas, ne m'engloutis pas, dans ce qui passe de toi en moi'. Luce Irigaray, *Et l'une ne bouge pas sans l'autre*, Paris, Editions de Minuit, 1979, pp.9–10.

9 For Beauvoir's exploration of the way in which the mother is perceived and represented in the patriarchal imaginary as the source of menacing engulfment,

absorption and contingent materiality, see the section entitled 'Myths' in *The Second Sex*, vol. I, translated by H. Parshley, Harmondsworth, Penguin, 1986.

10 Portuges, 'Attachment and Separation in *Memoirs of a Dutiful Daughter*', *Yale French Studies* 72, 1986, pp.107–18 (p.113).

11 Ibid., p.117.

12 E. Marks, *Simone de Beauvoir: Encounters with Death*, New Brunswick, Rutgers University Press, 1973, p. 50.

13 Portuges, p.114.

14 This is the view adopted by Marks and Portuges, and also by Deborah MacKeefe, in a further discussion of the Beauvoir/Zaza relationship entitled 'Mission and Motive in Simone de Beauvoir's *Mémoires*', *Contemporary Literature*, vol. 24, 1983, pp.204–21.

15 'I had had the good fortune to find a friend' (p.91). Elaine Marks notes the presence of almost identical phraseology in Beauvoir's accounts of her encounters with two other key figures in her life, Sartre and Sylvie Le Bon, and comments that it is used to evoke 'privileged relationships [that] have the effect of breaking routines associated with . . . stagnation'. Elaine Marks, 'Transgressing the (In)cont(in)ent Boundaries: The Body in Decline', *Yale French Studies* 72, 1986, p.186.

16 Gallop, *The Daughter's Seduction*, p.118.

17 'I kept on growing and I realized that my fate was sealed', *Memoirs*, p.8.

18 See Marks, *Encounters with Death*, pp.54–5, and L. Hewitt, *Autobiographical Tightropes*, Lincoln and London, Nebraska University Press, 1990, pp.34–9.

19 Portuges, p.114.

20 Marks, Hewitt and Portuges endorse this view.

21 'Had Zaza not died, it is possible to imagine that Simone de Beauvoir would not have carried with her, after her adolescent liberation, such strong feelings of revolt. Nor would she perhaps have felt so deeply the need to bear witness, through literature, to her own life and that of her generation. Zaza's death was the social evil that no triumph could erase.' Marks, *Encounters with Death*, p.51.

22 Ibid.

23 'Quand l'une vient en monde, l'autre retombe sous la terre. Quand l'une porte la vie, l'autre meurt.' Irigaray, *Et l'une ne bouge pas sans l'autre*, p.22.

24 Jardine, 'Death Sentences', p.128.

ENCOUNTERS WITH DEATH IN *A VERY EASY DEATH* and THE BODY IN DECLINE IN *ADIEUX: A FAREWELL TO SARTRE*

Elaine Marks

Elaine Marks has published extensively on French women's writing and on Beauvoir's work. In 1973 she published an influential book entitled *Simone de Beauvoir: Encounters with Death*, examining the obsession with mortality which Marks identifies across a range of Beauvoir's fiction, essays and memoirs.[1] Despite the evident seriousness with which Marks treats Beauvoir's work, the tone of her 1972 study is at times overtly hostile: in the extract which follows, focusing on Beauvoir's account of her mother's death in *A Very Easy Death*, Beauvoir is accused of narcissism, naivety, arrogance and a lack of imagination in relation to the suffering of others. Some of this antipathy can be explained by political differences between the critic and her subject; more broadly, however, it can be taken to represent the risk which Marks was taking as a female American academic in the early 1970s in devoting a book to Simone de Beauvoir. As Marks herself writes somewhat ruefully as late as 1987, 'the study of women writers is still not taken seriously by many scholars within academia, and the prestige that accrues to work done on women writers is considerably less than the prestige associated with research related to a major male writer'.[2] It is perhaps unsurprising then that Marks's nervousness about her subject explodes into her early study.

The second piece is taken from an article published more than a decade later, in 1986, in the prestigious context of a special volume of *Yale French Studies* devoted to Simone de Beauvoir.[3] The academic canon has become less rigidly male, considerable developments have taken place in feminist and literary theory, and Marks herself signals the way in which her position on Beauvoir's writing on mortality has shifted. Her central argument here is that, in Simone de Beauvoir's writing, there is a paucity of explicit discourses on sexuality; she proposes that it is through the discourses on ageing that sexuality covertly emerges. The uncontrollable body in decline is for Beauvoir a body manifesting both a disgusting and a fascinating sexuality, and it is presented through obsessive rhetorical strategies.

Marks's reading focuses on *Adieux: A Farewell to Sartre*, Beauvoir's last 'autobiographical' text published in 1981, five years before her death. The text recounts the last ten years of Sartre's life, as seen through Beauvoir's eyes, and is largely based on a diary which she kept throughout the period. One of the interests of Marks's reading is that it enables her to analyse the critical hostility which the text provoked and to account for it in terms of the transgressive nature of Beauvoir's subject matter. Writing about incontinence, Marks suggests, is a transgression of boundaries which limit the acceptable contents of texts. In focusing on content in this way, Marks is well aware that she is taking a different tack from psychoanalytic readings such as that of Alice Jardine which discuss the text in terms of a denial of the maternal function.[4] What Marks is able to do, however, through her approach, is to recover a Beauvoir who as a writer 'revels in the referential fallacy', in defiance of the 'ruling protocol for important writing in the 1970s and early 1980s'.

Finally Marks discovers at the centre of the discourses on ageing and sexuality what she calls a 'homo-sexual' secret – the narcissism at the heart of Beauvoir's bond with 'Sylvie Le Bon', and, by extension, the secret of feminine sexuality. All proper names are placed in quotation marks by Marks to underline the fact that we are dealing with textual figures.

Notes

1 The first extract is taken from E. Marks, *Simone de Beauvoir: Encounters with Death*, New Brunswick, Rutgers University Press, 1973, pp.100–12.

2 Quoted from E. Marks, ed., *Critical Essays on Simone de Beauvoir*, Boston, G.K. Hall, 1987, p.2.

3 Extract taken from an article first published by E. Marks, 'Transgressing the (In)cont(in)ent Boundaries: The Body in Decline', *Yale French Studies*, 1986, 72, pp.181–200.

4 A. Jardine, 'Death Sentences: Writing Couples and Ideology', *Poetics Today*, 1985, vol.6, pp.119–31.

The death of Simone de Beauvoir's mother is the most detailed of all the encounters with death. It is the only death to which an entire book is devoted although it might be said that the memoirs are, in fact, about the death of Simone de Beauvoir. This book, in which there is more mother and less I, is perhaps Simone de Beauvoir's best. Neither fiction nor memoir, *A Very Easy Death* is a *récit-reportage* shorter in length and more tightly constructed than

Simone de Beauvoir's other writings. The reader follows the thirty or more days of the intestinal cancer's final evolution, the thirty or more days of modern medicine's attempts to preserve lingering life, the thirty or more days of two sisters in their mid-50s watching their 78-year-old mother die, the last days of a woman who does not want to die.

The death of a mother is always a very special death. Psychoanalytic evidence and hypothesis have accustomed us to recognize the complex feelings of desire, guilt, and horror that a mother's death arouses in a child – of any age. Modern literature has both suggested and confirmed psychoanalytic theory with abundant examples. The death of the mother is a crucial event that determines attitudes and behaviour and that brings the 'child' to an anguished awareness of human precariousness and solitude. In the case of Simone de Beauvoir there is no fictional transposition, although there is, of course, the essential distance between an experience that does and does not exist in words. Once the story is written down it makes little difference whether it was invented by the author or lived through and told. In both cases the facts which we confront are verbal.

The reader who is familiar with the three volumes of Simone de Beauvoir's memoirs is familiar, too, with the figure of Françoise de Beauvoir. Simone de Beauvoir portrays her mother as a rather attractive but silly woman, a willing victim of the Catholic milieu to which she belonged and enthusiastically adhered. The reader shares Simone de Beauvoir's resentment of the innumerable prejudices that clogged Françoise de Beauvoir's mind and heart and that restricted her capacity to feel and to see. Simone de Beauvoir is quite explicit about her own preference for her nonconformist father. She was never very close to her mother, and one senses that her revolt against the despicable bourgeoisie is, in part, an outgrowth of her revolt against Françoise de Beauvoir. And yet when Georges de Beauvoir, deeply shocked by the defeat of France and by the Occupation, died quietly in July 1941, Simone de Beauvoir was but little affected; her father's indifference to *his* death may be largely responsible for her indifference to it. Her mother was not indifferent to her death and neither was Simone de Beauvoir. What she thought she felt about her mother does not coincide with what she feels during the long agony.

The pity, horror, and helplessness the reader of *A Very Easy Death* feels, corresponds both to the author's central emotion and to the underlying theme. No attempt is made at any moment in the main body of the *récit* to transcend the facts of dying or the sentiments, gestures, and words of the woman who is dying and the daughters who are watching her die. The irony of both the Dylan Thomas quotation which is used as an epigraph, 'Do not go gentle into that good night', and of the title is continued throughout the book in a courageous desire to break through some of the simplistic left-wing ideology that often replaces intelligent analysis in her other books. When the bourgeois Catholic images which she had so firmly and so conveniently affixed to her mother are displaced, a human being begins to die, and Simone de Beauvoir begins to suffer for someone other than herself. Sartre is absent from all but two scenes in the *récit*, and this significant absence helps to explain Simone de Beauvoir's ability to sustain, for so long a time, an excruciating lucidity. Is it that she has nothing and no one to turn to for solace or as a means of evasion? Is it perhaps that this time none of the usual havens are sufficient because reality is so blatant?

A Very Easy Death is the only one of Simone de Beauvoir's books in which the hectic rhythm which she projects on the world is abruptly interrupted and the interruption prolonged. There is an outlandish contrast between the joyful scenes of mass demonstrations in the preceding volume, *Force of Circumstance*, the frenetic tempo of Simone de Beauvoir's voyages alluded to in the opening pages of *A Very Easy Death*, and the scene of the hospital bed on which Françoise de Beauvoir lies. The image of a human being agonizing on a bed which Simone de Beauvoir has been avoiding since *L'Invitée* and which is her central obsession is forced upon her by the event.

Before the fall that disclosed her mother's cancer, Simone de Beauvoir was a faithful but inattentive daughter. Between trips to Rome, Prague, and elsewhere she would visit her mother for a few hours. Their relationship was affectionate but distant.

The quotations that follow reveal the manner in which this encounter acts upon Simone de Beauvoir's usual defences, how they crumble, and which ones, nevertheless, remain intact.

'I was not much affected. In spite of her frailty my mother was tough. And after all, she was of an age to die'.[1] Simone de Beauvoir's first reaction to the dangers of three months in bed for an elderly woman who has apparently broken her pelvic bone is straightforward and abstract. She felt that her mother was basically strong and in no mortal danger – she could not feel her mother as mortal. This reaction was inaccurate; Françoise de Beauvoir was far from 'tough'. She had an intestinal cancer whose signs – pallor, odour, loss of weight – were detected by friends and completely unsuspected by Simone de Beauvoir and the blundering doctors.

At the same time that she felt that her mother was not going to die, Simone de Beauvoir felt that 78 was after all a proper age for death. It is a well-known cliché that the death of a young person is tragic but that the death of an older person is in the natural order of the biological world and is therefore acceptable. Simone de Beauvoir never uses this cliché when she imagines her own death or Sartre's. Her use of it in connection with her mother reveals a lack of imagination for the suffering of others, a refusal to feel the world as another feels it.

Thirteen pages later, Simone de Beauvoir realizes the vacuity of her own words: 'When I said to myself, "She is of an age to die," the words were devoid of meaning, as so many words are. For the first time I saw her as a dead body under suspended sentence' (p.20). What is curious is that it should take so many years and an old body on a hospital bed before Simone de Beauvoir can recognize that her mother is mortal, before she can think the corpse behind the body.

'I pictured her distress. She believed in heaven, but in spite of her age, her feebleness, and her poor health, she clung ferociously to this world, and she had an animal dread of death' (p.14). Only a few pages separate the second quotation from the first, yet the difference between them is impressive. The story, which Françoise de Beauvoir tells over and over again, of how she fell in her bathroom and crawled for two hours before reaching the telephone, has an immediate and painful impact on Simone de Beauvoir and consequently on the reader. The image of the old woman on all fours seeking help is an image that symbolizes our apprehension of solitude and old age, of pathetic animal helplessness. It is difficult not to identify with this image. When Simone de Beauvoir writes 'I pictured her distress', she is describing what is for most people a fairly routine mechanism and what is, for her, a rare occurrence: the possibility of imagining what it is like to be someone else, to see and feel differently.

On the first page of the *récit* Simone de Beauvoir writes: 'I was putting papers away when the telephone rang. It was Bost calling me from Paris: "Your mother has had an accident," he said. I thought: she has been knocked down by a car; she was climbing laboriously from the roadway to the pavement, leaning on her stick, and a car knocked her down' (p.9). Simone de Beauvoir's immediate reaction suggests that she was prepared for some accident to befall her mother. She sees her mother as a lonely, pitiable victim. She thinks in concrete terms: the car, the sidewalk, the street, the cane. Her anxiety about her mother, whatever she may say to the contrary, antedates her mother's fall and the diagnosis of her illness. This anxiety, composed essentially of anticipation and guilt, is disclosed in the repetition of 'she has been knocked down by a car. . . . A car knocked her down.' Simone de Beauvoir had for some time thought about how it would come. Still 'I thought' is not nearly as strong as 'I pictured her distress.' The second verb goes beyond obsession to identification and compassion. What Simone de Beauvoir is able to identify with is the 'animal dread' of death. This is stronger than the barriers erected between them by her mother's religious beliefs and the differ-ence of generation. From the moment that Simone de Beauvoir realizes that her mother does not want to die and is afraid of dying, Françoise de Beauvoir is transformed from a prig and a bigot into a suffering human being.

> It was a lovely autumn day with a blue sky: I made my way through a lead-coloured world, and I realized that my mother's accident was affect-ing me far more than I had thought it would. I could not really see why. It had wrenched her out of the framework, the role, the set of images in which I had imprisoned her: I recognized her in this patient in bed, but I did not recognize either the pity or the kind of disturbance that she aroused in me. . . . I bristled when the privileged classes spoke through my mother's mouth; but I felt wholly on the side of the bedfast invalid struggling to thrust back paralysis and death.
>
> (pp.20–2)

This is the first and only time in the writings of Simone de Beauvoir that a feeling of solidarity exists for another human being who is neither a part of a mass (as in the mass demonstration) nor Jean-Paul Sartre. The information divulged here is crucial to our understanding of why 'my mother's accident was affecting me far more than I had thought it would'. A particular accident had been foreseen. What was not foreseen was the degree to which Simone de Beauvoir would react to it. The essential revelation in this passage is not the revelation of another Françoise de Beauvoir, but the disturbing revelation of another Simone. It is she who is 'wrenched out of the framework, the role, the set of images in which I had imprisoned her' and what appears, troubling and unforeseen, is 'the pity . . . the kind of disturbance'. 'Disturbance' and disorder are what Simone de Beauvoir has always ferociously tried to avoid. The very words 'privileged classes' and 'wholly on the side of' tell us something about Simone de Beauvoir's philosophical, ideological orientation. On the side of Satan is the evil elite, including Françoise de Beauvoir. On the side of God, the good oppressed and the good authentic lucid beings, including Simone de Beauvoir. This version of the human world is not altered by the 'pity' and the 'disturbance'. Instead, Françoise de Beauvoir's dying is shifted from Satan's camp to God's. The verb 'struggling' makes of Simone de Beauvoir's mother an agonizing, oppressed victim. She is saved. The problem now is how Simone de Beauvoir will cope with her own unexpected reactions that have awakened the old anguish concerning nothingness and death.

Between the passages already quoted and those that follow an important fact is disclosed in the book. Françoise de Beauvoir's illness was finally diagnosed: she had intestinal cancer and was dying. We learn, too, that Françoise de Beauvoir had for a long time been fearful that she herself would one day have cancer.

The diagnosis brings to the hospital and to the bedside of Françoise de Beauvoir her younger married daughter Hélène, or Poupette, to whom *A Very Easy Death* is dedicated. Simone de Beauvoir's initial solitude is thus broken by the presence of her sister, who, closer to their mother, now bears a major part of the waiting and watching. Poupette's first words when she arrives at the hospital establish a significant difference between the two sisters: '"But what's the good of tormenting her, if she is dying. Let her die in peace," said Poupette, in tears' (p.27). More spontaneous, more direct, less encumbered by ideological and intellectual constructions, Hélène, as seen by her elder sister, is also less prone to sudden hysteria.

I went home; I talked to Sartre; we played some Bartok. Suddenly, at eleven, an outburst of tears that almost degenerated into hysteria.

Amazement. When my father died I did not cry at all. I had said to my sister, 'It will be the same for Maman.' I had understood all my sorrows up until that night; even when they flowed over my head I recognized myself in them. This time my despair escaped from my control: someone other than myself was weeping in me. I talked to Sartre about my mother's mouth as I had seen it that morning and about everything I had interpreted in it: greediness refused, an almost servile humility, hope, distress, loneliness – the loneliness of her death and of her life – that did not want to admit its existence. And he told me that my own mouth was not obeying me any more: I had put Maman's mouth on my own face and in spite of myself, I copied its movements. Her whole person, her whole being, was concentrated there, and compassion wrung my heart. (p.31)

Like her sister, Simone de Beauvoir also cries. When she does, she is on the verge of hysteria. These crises have been a part of Simone de Beauvoir's behaviour pattern since her childhood, so the reader who is familiar with her memoirs is less amazed than Simone de Beauvoir. When all the props (Sartre and Bartok) are useless, and the situation is extremely painful, Simone de Beauvoir falls apart. That is her way of dealing with the most distressing encounters.

The reader's wonder is at her reiterated naiveté and arrogance: 'it will be the same for Maman.' This mania for planning and plotting emotional reactions in advance can only be a sign of fear, the fear that if there is no organized plan there will be no means of controlling her emotions and that she will be subject to the dreaded 'hysteria', drowned by sorrows, her heart wrung with compassion. Simone de Beauvoir's insistence that before this she has always understood her most severe crises does not convince anyone who has read her memoirs. These past crises seem intimately related to the one provoked by her dying mother, which is easier to understand because of the circumstances: mother, a hospital, cancer. Simone de Beauvoir's inability to understand her grief and her despair on this occasion can be attributed to the immense weight of ideological conditioning and prejudice.

It is almost as if Simone de Beauvoir were ashamed to admit consciously both the process of identification and the degree to which she identifies with her mother. She is betrayed by her own mouth. Sartre, here, is not a refuge but a perceptive critic. Indeed, this process of identification has been going on since the opening page of the *récit* that announced the accident. Simone de Beauvoir's resistance to it accounts for much of the work's tension. What Simone de Beauvoir has read into the expression of her mother's mouth and imitates unconsciously is her own unavowed solitude. In becoming her dying mother Simone de Beauvoir has momentarily known compassion. It is a rare and precious state, because we are at the same time ourselves and another. Without leaping we can move naturally from the solitude of every human being to some sense of solidarity. Simone de Beauvoir is too upset to move beyond defeat, solitude, and silence. When she recovers she will not make the move because, with recovery, the old conditioning and prejudices return, and the inevitable tendency to leap with words.

This compassion marks the critical moment of this encounter with death. It is the moment when the emptiness at the heart of all things, which for so long had been hers alone, is finally shared. It is the difference between saying and knowing that all men are mortal. In this awareness sustained is the possibility of a new sensibility.

After this episode, Simone de Beauvoir has several moments of heightened consciousness that again break through the protective façade. During a period of relative calm in her mother's agony, Simone de Beauvoir flies to Prague with Sartre. A telegram and a painful telephone call from her sister precipitate her return to Paris. ('I held Maman's hand all the time and she kept begging me not to let her go. She said, "I shall not see Simone again."')

> I asked the porter to reserve me a place in the aeroplane that was leaving the next morning at half past ten. Engagements had been fixed; Sartre advised me to wait a day or two. Impossible. I did not particularly want to see Maman again before her death; but I could not bear the idea that she should not see me again. Why attribute such importance to a moment since there would be no memory? There would not be any atonement either. For myself I understood, to the innermost fibre of my being, that the absolute could be enclosed within the last moments of a dying person.
>
> (pp.62–3)

Sartre's advice is useless. He is evidently outside the drama and his comments on it are irrelevant. The 'porter', the 'aeroplane', the 'engagements' form an appropriate contrast to Hélène de Beauvoir's laconic account of her mother's condition. They belong to the world of the committed intellectual busily travelling, conferring, lecturing, writing, saving souls, and solving problems which take precedence over the annoying intrusion of death. Simone de Beauvoir's reaction is immediate and simple. Her need to justify it takes us back to the image she has of who she is, or should be, and how she should behave, her suspicion of her own motive, her apparent distrust of spontaneity. The self-consciousness surrounds a decision that is based on doing something to please someone else, particularly her mother, and reveals how much she has to struggle to reach the most evident and simplest conclusions. She finds, in this case, a rather pompous formula: 'I understood . . . that the absolute could be enclosed within the last moments of a dying person.' She does fight through and she does manage to juggle with an apparent paradox that opposes logic and feeling. But is the word 'absolute' which she struggles against using and finally uses really the proper word? The central fact in this paragraph is 'I could not bear . . . to the innermost fibre of my being.' This is another way of saying that Simone de Beauvoir was drowned by sorrows, her heart wrung with compassion. The danger is that the haughty maxim about the 'last moments of a dying person' will usurp the place that rightfully belongs to the direct and moving words: 'She said: "I shall not see Simone again."'

Simone de Beauvoir returns to Paris and finds that her mother has moved closer to death.

My real life took place at her side, and it had only one aim – protecting her. . . . What tried us more than anything were Maman's death-agonies, her resurrections, and our own inconsistency. In this race between pain and death we most earnestly hoped that death would come first. Yet when Maman was asleep with her face lifeless, we would anxiously gaze at the white bedjacket to catch the faint movement of the black ribbon that held her watch: dread of the last spasm gripped us by the throat.

(pp.73–5)

Never, as companion to Sartre, or mistress or passionate friend, did Simone de Beauvoir allow herself to be caught in a situation in which someone else was so dependent on her. Never, in the brief accounts in the memoirs of those she loved do we sense the tenderness of 'protecting her' and the repetition of 'maman'. There is no sentimentality here, only an extreme human compassion which moves the reader more profoundly than her ponderous maxims. The situation described is located at the limit of human endurance: wishing for death to end suffering and dreading death above all else; seeing the appeal in the eyes of the dying who want neither to suffer nor to die and knowing the inevitability of their suffering and their death. However different dying may be in fact from our imaginings about it, watching someone die who is suffering is worse than our worst fantasies. 'Nothing on earth could possibly justify these moments of pointless torment' (p.81). This Simone de Beauvoir has been able to express.

'The only comfort I have,' she [Poupette] said, 'is that it will happen to me too. Otherwise it would be too unfair.' Yes. We were taking part in the dress rehearsal for our own burial. The misfortune is that although everyone must come to this, each experiences the adventure in solitude. We never left Maman during those last days which she confused with convalescence and yet we were profoundly separated from her.

(pp.99–100)

Hélène's words go further in their implications than her sister's comments on them would suggest. Hélène is saying what she has learned from the experience, a sense of communion with her mother through mortality, whereas Simone de Beauvoir is repeating an eternal verity: 'each experiences the adventure in solitude'. She finds evidence for this in the fact that her mother was not told that she was dying of cancer, whereas those who watched her die knew. Yet many things in Françoise de Beauvoir's behaviour suggest that she did know – not that she had terminal cancer but that she was indeed dying. There are, in this kind of situation, different ways of knowing. The importance of this encounter with death, as Hélène seems to have understood, is that a deep awareness of mortality tends to violate the law of solitude. Again Simone de Beauvoir is separated from her experiences by the language she uses. Language is perhaps the most efficacious instrument of evasion.

Sometimes, though very rarely, it happens that love, friendship, or com-
radely feeling overcomes the loneliness of death: in spite of appearances,
even when I was holding Maman's hand, I was not with her – I was lying
to her. Because she had always been deceived, gulled, I found this ultimate deception revolting. I was making myself an accomplice of that fate
which was so misusing her. Yet at the same time in every cell of my body
I joined in her refusal, in her rebellion: and it was also because of that
that her defeat overwhelmed me. Although I was not with Maman when
she died, and although I had been with three people when they were
actually dying, it was when I was at her bedside that I saw Death, the
Death of the dance of death, with its bantering grin, the Death of fireside
tales that knocks on the door, a scythe in its hand, the Death that comes
from elsewhere, strange, and inhuman: it had the very face of Maman
when she showed her gums in a wide smile of unknowingness.

(p.105)

Simone de Beauvoir begins by making exceptions to the general truth she had
enunciated earlier, but she gives us no precise example. What she's doing is setting
up ideal situations opposed to the one she has just lived through with her mother.
The point seems to be that because her mother was always guilty of 'bad faith'
there was no possibility of an authentic relationship with her. 'I was lying to her' is
a curious perversion of what did in fact take place and was witnessed by the reader.

Simone de Beauvoir describes her encounter with her mother's death in these
terms because, when she comes to the last part of her *récit*, the summing up, she
feels obliged, certain laws of composition oblige her, to draw relevant conclusions and she falls back once again on a language that does not relate to the facts
of her experience. It is a language within which the elite that Françoise de Beauvoir represents must be eternally damned. 'I was making myself an accomplice of
that fate which was so misusing her' seems to have no relation at all to the
preceding events: 'accomplice' and 'fate' refer to the animistic prescientific world
of primitive man. The 'fate which was so misusing her [lui faisait violence]' was
old age and intestinal cancer; Simone de Beauvoir was not and could not have
been their accomplice. She sets up images of her mother and herself that obscure
the problems. The conclusion does not emanate from the phenomena described
but from a hypothesis held prior to the experiment. This hypothesis is based on
the positive or negative charge of certain words. 'I joined in her refusal, in her
rebellion'; but is it possible to use words like 'refusal' and 'rebellion' to describe
the behaviour of an old woman afraid of dying and of death?

There is a similar though more subtle abuse of language in the last long sentence of the quotation. The parallels established between certain traditional
death themes and the expression on her mother's face are subjective and valid.
However, the last word, 'unknowingness', is ideologically rather than poetically
charged. It goes back to 'lying', 'deceived', 'deception'. It does not relate to the
death of Françoise de Beauvoir, but to a notion of how an elitist bigot should die.

What has occurred, then, in *A Very Easy Death* is not essentially different from what occurred in the other encounters with death; the encounter is followed by an evasion. Here, the encounter is more direct and more profound. Simone de Beauvoir is involved as she never was before, and yet there is the moment when the exploration of the unknown becomes unbearable and she goes back to what is, after all, her fundamental project as a writer: building an acceptable image of herself. This image gets in the way of serious analysis and in the end is quite useless.

Note

1 S. de Beauvoir, *A Very Easy Death*, London, André Deutsch, 1966, p.12. All subsequent references to this are given in brackets in the text.

In 1973, in a book-length essay entitled *Simone de Beauvoir: Encounters with Death*, I argued that Simone de Beauvoir was obsessed with mortality. I attempted to describe how this obsession took the form of exploring encounters with death at the same time as these encounters were aborted by the construction of an ideology that emphasized commitment to a cause. In the dialectical movement between mortality and commitment, mortality was, temporarily at least, subsumed and obliterated, only to emerge again at a later moment in the same or another text. My 1973 essay apparently accused Simone de Beauvoir, the woman and the writer, of refusing to deal with mortality until the bitter end, as it were, and of veering off into a reassuring rhetoric.

In 1985 I take up some of my earlier positions and argue, but differently, that even though Simone de Beauvoir's texts do not go as far as I would have liked them then to go, they do go further than most. The critical reception of *La Cérémonie des adieux* has obliged me to rethink my earlier interpretations and to conclude that *La Cérémonie des adieux*, like *Une mort très douce* (1964), *La Vieillesse*, and certain passages of *Tout compte fait*, is a text that transgresses the (in)cont(in)ent boundaries. *La Cérémonie des adieux* goes beyond the limits of what is considered legitimate for a woman or a man to write. For ageing and dying, when presented referentially, are taboo topics within phallocentric discourse: it is permissible to write about the sexual practices of a famous man; it is not permissible to write about his loss of control over his excretory functions. Through an analysis of the reviewers' discourse and of selected passages in Simone de Beauvoir's texts, I shall attempt to show what is involved in the systematic disparagement of this content and conclude with some generalizations on content, continents, incontinence. I shall also come back to the theoretical discussions that surround the death of the author, the death of the referent, and argue that for all their seductive subtlety they may also be a means of obliterating once again women, sexuality, old age, dying, and death.

While preparing the selection of book chapters, essays, and book reviews that will appear in a volume of *Critical Essays on Simone de Beauvoir* to be published by G. K. Hall, I have been reading and rereading what has been written about the author-narrator Simone de Beauvoir and about her corpus (the three are rarely differentiated). I am impressed by the repetition of the word 'too', in the sense of more than sufficient, excessively. Whether the critics are French, British, or North American, whether they are Catholic, right-wing literati, left-wing intelligentsia, or devotees of *l'écriture féminine*, they seem to agree that there is a problem of excess: Simone de Beauvoir's texts are, in general, too long; there are too many lists in the volumes of memoirs; there are too many unpleasant details about her mother's body ravaged by cancer; too many repugnant details about 'Sartre's' food spilling and incontinence (and the incontinence of their longtime friend 'Camille' [Simone Jolivet]); too many anecdotes about characters in *Les Mandarins* who were on the borderline between the fictional and the factual (for example, Albert and Francine Camus); too many negative attacks on marriage and maternity; too much narcissism. Here are the words of some reviews: 'Among other things, Simone de Beauvoir shares with Sartre, a tendency to write too much', in *Books Abroad*, 1965; 'a merciless record of the trivia of death – old age and bed wetting, pubic baldness, enemas . . .' in *Time*, 1966; 'such an exhaustive and practically all-embracing manner', in *The French Review*, 1970; 'she supplies a baker's dozen of facts, she provides exhaustive analyses', in *The Atlantic*, 1972; 'excessively lengthy parts', in *The Economist*, 1972; 'just short of five hundred obsessive and ultimately negative pages', in *The Spectator*, 1972; 'the merciless realism of the description of the final degradation of her friend Camille', in the *New Boston Review*, 1977. As for *La Cérémonie des adieux*, from the moment it appeared, the book created a furore. Simone de Beauvoir was accused of illegally seizing an inheritance, of voyeurism, almost of necrophagia in *Magazine littéraire*, 1982. 'Mme de Beauvoir spares us, and herself, nothing: the dribble on his shirt, the food spilt over his shoes, the wet patch on chairs, the soiled pyjamas at night,' in *Sunday Times*, 1984. Add to this the writer Nelson Algren, an ex-lover, now dead, who accused the woman, Simone de Beauvoir, of talking too much, even suggesting, in an article in *Harper's* (May 1965), that after a devastating atomic bomb explosion one voice would remain, indestructible, the voice of Simone de Beauvoir.

Other readers might agree with some or all of these charges of excess. These charges are usually couched in aesthetic terms and suggest that Simone de Beauvoir is not really an artist, or a novelist, or a philosopher, but over and over again an autobiographer, a label used pejoratively for women, or that she is, at her best, a memorialist. What interests me are the connections between the charges levelled at Simone de Beauvoir and those discourses that denigrate the importance of content and are uneasy (as we have all become) with unexamined commonsense notions of language. The question is then: to what degree is Simone de Beauvoir being accused of transgressing boundaries established by both phallocentric discourse and the concept of *l'écriture féminine*, boundaries that have made and maintained certain content areas taboo: incontinence, old age, dying?

In a brilliant essay by Alice Jardine entitled 'Death Sentences: Writing Couples and Ideology', a psychoanalytic reading uncovers violence against the mother in *Une mort très douce* and the representation of Sartre as the phallic mother in *La Cérémonie des adieux*.[1] These are challenging interpretations. The dream sequence in *Une mort très douce* in which Sartre and the mother blend is a particularly convincing example of the blurring of gender lines and of the power of the pre-Oedipal mother. But, at another level, these interpretations might also be read as an example of theory trivializing 'content', making it impossible for 'new' or another content to emerge by immediately reducing this other content to a familiar situation and paradigm. The problem then is how to write (about) ageing, suffering, death in the first person without their being subsumed by those psychoanalytic concepts which demand a return to structures determined by childhood and which argue that the Real is not writable. The concerted attack against the conventions of realism, against the naturalizing of culturally constructed modes of thinking and behaviour, and the insistence on the mediating role of language have undermined the importance of material life and its structuring influences on social life. The ageing body, the body in decline, the dead body have no place in contemporary fictional and autobiographical texts read by poststructuralist, psychoanalytic critics because the apparent 'story' is always secondary.

I would argue that to translate these texts on incontinence, old age, and dying into Simone de Beauvoir's 'denial of the mother' or rage against the maternal function is perhaps to eliminate, with a very powerful and convincing theory, dramas other than those of the Oedipal family. I would not, therefore, so much argue against Alice Jardine's interpretations, but I would retrieve what is thereby excluded, the new kind of content that Simone de Beauvoir has been proposing and that almost no one has any desire to read.

Annette Kolodny, in her essay on Kate Millett's autobiographical text *Flying*, entitled 'The Lady's Not for Spurning: Kate Millett and the Critics', contends that the critics had difficulty in dealing with Millett's text *Flying* because it pushed aside 'the accepted boundaries of narrative content'.[2] The introduction of a new content about women's lives was perceived as a transgression. We face a similar phenomenon in the critical response to many of Simone de Beauvoir's texts. A closer reading of these texts reveals that a tendency to transgress boundaries has always characterized her work. Indeed, the first narrative section of *La Cérémonie des adieux* with its particular examples of 'Jean-Paul Sartre's' ageing and incontinence recalls examples of the physical disintegration of women in other autobiographical or fictional texts, particularly 'Camille' and 'Violette Leduc' in *Tout compte fait*. In the second part of *La Cérémonie des adieux*, Simone de Beauvoir interviews Sartre on his relations to and with the big, embarrassing questions: the body, men and women, money, time, death, and God. These interviews remind us that in her fiction as well as in her essays

Simone de Beauvoir has consistently broken with decorum and has written directly about those topics one does not write or speak about today except in the discourse of empirical social science, of jokes, or through metaphor. It could, therefore, be maintained that the originality of Simone de Beauvoir's discourse is precisely this act of trespassing. She has not obeyed the taboos placed by the institutionalization of specialized discourses on the body, sexuality, ageing, and God; she has not remained within the acceptable boundaries marked by level of style or genre that tell the reader this is a poetic text, a scientific text, a philosophical text. The result is that Simone de Beauvoir has often been accused of 'bad taste'. Furthermore, the reaction against popular existentialism and against humanistic universalizing has added to the derogatory criticism of Simone de Beauvoir's discourse and to the accusation that she is, as a writer, incontinent with respect to topic, content, and style boundaries. Simone de Beauvoir, therefore, provides an excellent case study for one of the central problems that has emerged in Western Europe and the United States since the late 1960s and that continues to challenge theorists and critics: the relationship between language and ideology, on the one hand, and 'le vécu', questions of sex, gender, race, class, age, and the possibilities of change, on the other. Although the emphasis on the signifier as the sign of the unconscious has relegated the signified, and with it the notion that language translates experience, to an ancillary position, Simone de Beauvoir remains one of the few major figures on the contemporary French intellectual scene to support the signified and its representations.

A few examples will reinforce these points and suggest others. In *Le Deuxième Sexe* (1949) Simone de Beauvoir transgressed the boundaries of what was then considered permissible to write about male–female relations, about marriage and motherhood, and about female sexuality, particularly lesbianism.

In her chapter on 'La Lesbienne' Simone de Beauvoir transgresses the boundaries of accepted discourse at several points: she writes against that commonsense discourse whose reliance on nature and what is natural nullifies any serious analysis of ideology and makes political constructions impossible; she writes against the reigning determinist discourse of psychoanalysis with its case histories and its established categories of masculine and feminine; she opposes, by not mentioning it, any religious discourse in which procreation becomes the definition of woman's function. Her own negative attitudes towards reproduction, marriage, motherhood, and the nuclear family do not prevent her from imagining other living arrangements. At the same time, however, as these boundaries are transgressed, as official discourse appears to be shaken and sexual practices liberated from repressive patterns, other repressive habits are reinforced. If psychoanalytic theories are dismantled in Simone de Beauvoir's discourse, the examples of case histories from psychoanalytic literature, from Renée Vivien, Colette, Radclyffe Hall are used to illustrate the experience of lesbians in 1949 without any conscious attempt to understand the relation between the literary text and lived experience. Lesbianism, in this essay, continues to be viewed as an individual experience separate from any political and community considerations. And, as the most repressive of all possible gestures, throughout the essay reappears the figure of the ideal woman, the heterosexual, virile woman who lives and loves among men: Ninon de Lenclos, Madame de Staël. Must the reader add to this list another woman who prides herself on male connections: the narrator? Is this the way the narrator puts herself into the chapter? Men, throughout *Le Deuxième Sexe*, are presented as the privileged class, outstanding men as the human elite. This does not change the chapter on the 'lesbienne', but it is more blatant there than elsewhere in the book. My reading is, of course, a 1985 re-reading, and my criticisms must be understood in light of the new research on homosexuality and lesbianism that has appeared since 1968. If I try to construct my 1949 reading of 'La Lesbienne', I can find again the radical, transgressive aspects of the essay. Indeed, in the history of discourses on lesbianism, Simone de Beauvoir's 'La Lesbienne' retains status as precursor, as a text that has made it possible to formulate other discourses and to think against those that have been and continue to be in place. The fact that Simone de Beauvoir ventured into a new territory, even though she may have been holding the guiding hand of virile heterosexual women, has itself the status of a disruptive, discursive event.

In *Mémoires d'une jeune fille rangée* the narrator relates in the same paragraph the trials of puberty and the revelations made to her by her cousin Madeleine about how babies are produced; she ends with a comparison between herself and Gulliver:

> That year, when we moved to the rue de Rennes, I began to have bad dreams. Had I not properly digested the revelations made by Madeleine? Only a thin partition now divided my bed from the one in which my parents slept, and sometimes I would hear my father snoring: did this promiscuity upset me? I had nightmares. A man would jump on my bed and dig his knees into my stomach until I felt I was suffocating; in desperation, I would dream that I was waking up and once again I would be crushed beneath the awful weight of my aggressor. About the same time, getting up became such a painful ordeal that when I thought about it the night before, my throat would tighten and my palms would grow damp with sweat. When I used to hear my mother's voice in the mornings I longed to fall ill, I had such a horror of dragging myself out of the toils of sleep and darkness. During the day, I had dizzy spells; I became anaemic. Mama and the doctor would say: 'It's her development'. I grew to detest that word and the silent upheaval that was going on in my body. I envied 'big girls' their freedom; but I was disgusted at the thought of my chest swelling out; I had sometimes heard grown-up women urinating with the noise of a cataract; when I thought of the bladders swollen with water in their bellies, I felt the same terror as Gulliver did when the young giantesses displayed their breasts to him.[3]

In *Tout compte fait* the pages on the narrator's new intimacy with 'Sylvie Le Bon', 'She is as thoroughly interwoven in my life as I am in hers', are followed by the pages on the decline, the alcoholism, the filth, and death of 'Camille' (Simone Jolivet, ex-mistress of Dullin and of Sartre):

> One day when we were waiting for her in my flat we heard heavy uncertain footsteps in the street; they came nearer, then moved away. She took a quarter of an hour to find my door. She was staggering and she could not articulate properly. She went upstairs to the bathroom, and although she was usually so modest she left the door open: we heard her urinating loudly.[4]

Here the move from sexuality to urination and back to sexuality is explicitly made. Urination, abundant, excessive urination by women, becomes the metaphor for everything that is embarrassing in sexuality. The body grows on its own, so to speak, proliferates without permission, makes noises, in the same way as incontinence takes over the body in decline. And the metaphor always involves the feminine. It is, therefore, not surprising that when Sartre's behaviour is described in terms of 'his lack of aggressiveness and his resignation', it involves his metamorphosis into a woman as she is negatively defined both by culture and cultural stereotypes and by Simone de Beauvoir in *Le Deuxième sexe*. 'Sartre', incontinent, is passive, incapable of transcendence, no longer a creator but reduced like women to immanence and urinating in a sitting position.

'Françoise de Beauvoir' is also incontinent in *Une mort très douce*. She is the prey of a body in decline and ravaged by cancer. In this earlier text there are also reasons to evoke the family name Beau/voir of the narrator as the desire to see and not to see her mother's 'bald pubis' and 'the garden' outside.[5] Sartre is present in this text as a quiet witness of the narrator's unwitting imitation of her mother's mouth (p.28), and in the last chapter he appears in a dream with the narrator's mother: 'She blended with Sartre, and we were happy together. And then the dream would turn into a nightmare: why was I living with her once more? How had I come to be in her power again? So our former relationship lived on in its double aspect – a subjection that I loved and hated' (p.89).

Une mort très douce transgresses yet another set of boundaries. Simone de Beauvoir persists in her jibes against the institutions of marriage and motherhood that began in *Le Deuxième sexe* in 1949 and that continue through the interviews with Alice Schwarzer, *After The Second Sex*, in 1984. Simone de Beauvoir has not abandoned her earlier positions and her conviction that these institutions are traps for women. Her most significant example is the case of her mother, Françoise de Beauvoir, whose miniature biography as a 'corseted woman' she presents in the second part of *Une mort très douce*.

Both Mary Evans (*Simone de Beauvoir: A Feminist Mandarin*, London and New York: Tavistock, 1984) and Alice Jardine (1985) have read these challenges to the institutions of marriage and motherhood as symptoms in the writing and in the psyche of Simone de Beauvoir. Mary Evans reads them as a fear of female biology and of the irrational and the emotional. Alice Jardine, as we have seen earlier, reads them as violence against the phallic mother whom Simone de Beauvoir needs to destroy and with her, the body of the man, Sartre. I would suggest that these readings, with their insistent accusations, miss or obscure the political and transgressive aspects of Simone de Beauvoir's text. Their critiques imply that she is immature, not yet an adult. For if, in our culture, famous men should not be seen as incontinent and out of control, mothers are even more sacred. The most famous French women theorists of the past fifteen years – Hélène Cixous, Luce Irigaray, and Julia Kristeva – have been adding to the sacred untouchable quality of the figure of the mother within our patriarchal Judeo-Christian tradition. In their desire to explore the pre-Oedipal stage of mother–child relations neglected by official psychoanalytic discourses, in their search for a feminine specificity, they have once again magnified the mother and motherhood. Read as reading matter from their perspective, *Une mort très douce* would indeed be a naive text.

In *La Vieillesse* Simone de Beauvoir once again transgresses the boundaries of what was then permissible to write about ageing and death, about the attitudes that prevailed in nursing homes and in families towards the elderly. And once again the representatives of the official discourses on ageing were shocked and offended that a nonspecialist had been audacious enough to theorize and sermonize about their materials.

With respect to women and ageing, what characterizes Simone de Beauvoir's discourse in *La Vieillesse* is the revelation that sexism and ageism are embedded in the ideology and the language of Western culture. From the vantage point of 1985 what seems most interesting in her analyses are the ways in which sexism and ageism are intertwined. It appears, now, as if a discourse on ageing could only have developed when it was possible to write a certain discourse of the body, when a certain discourse on women's body had been elaborated. (The fact that Charcot was giving lectures at the Salpetrière in which he was putting both female hysteria and old age into discourse during the 1870s and 1880s requires further investigation.) The disgust and the fear provoked by the female body in Western discourses are related to similar effects provoked by old bodies. In both cases the reaction against contact with the woman is represented as abject, impure, and unclassifiable. Old bodies, in texts by Simone de Beauvoir, are always feminine or feminized bodies.

A detailed analysis of the paragraph in *La Cérémonie des adieux* in which 'Sartre's' incontinence is first mentioned explicitly brings together, in anecdotal form, many of the questions we have been raising:

> When we came back [to Paris from Rome] at the end of September Sartre was in great form. 'I like being back here,' he said to me. Returning to my apartment pleased him. 'As far as the rest is concerned, I don't care. But I'm glad to be in this place again.' We spent some happy evenings there, and again I almost stopped worrying.

148

But not for long. In the middle of October I once more became aware of the irreversible deterioration of old age. In Rome, I had noticed that when we went after lunch to eat Giolitti's wonderful ices, Sartre would hurry to the lavatory. One afternoon, when we were going along by the Pantheon, back toward the hotel, and he was walking very quickly ahead of us, he stopped and said, 'Cats have just pissed on me. I went close to the balustrade and I was wet on.' Sylvie believed him and laughed about it. For my part I knew what was the matter, but I said nothing. In Paris, at the beginning of October, Sartre got up to go to the bathroom – he was in my apartment – and there was a mark on his chair. The next day I told Sylvie that he had spilled some tea. 'You would say that a child had had an accident,' she observed. The next evening, in the same circumstances, there was another mark. So I spoke to Sartre about it. 'You are incontinent. You ought to tell the doctor.' To my utter astonishment he replied in a perfectly natural voice, 'I have told him. It has been going on for a long while now. It's those cells that I lost.' Sartre had always been extremely puritanical; he never referred to his natural functions, and he carried them out with the utmost discretion. That was why I asked him the next morning whether he did not find this lack of control exceedingly embarrassing. He answered with a smile, 'When you're old you can't expect too much, your claims have to be modest.' I was touched by his simplicity and by this moderation, so new in him; and at the same time his lack of aggressiveness and his resignation wounded me.[6]

In *La Volonté de savoir* (1976) Michel Foucault writes:

But there may be another reason that makes it so gratifying for us to define the relationship between sex and power in terms of repression: something that one might call the speaker's benefit. If sex is repressed, that is, condemned to prohibition, nonexistence and silence, then the mere fact that one is speaking about it has the appearance of a deliberate transgression. A person who holds forth in such language places himself to a certain extent outside the reach of power; he upsets established law; he somehow anticipates coming freedom.[7]

I should like to change Foucault's the 'speaker's benefit' to the 'narrator's benefit' and begin to read the passage from *La Cérémonie des adieux* in relation to these sentences from *La Volonté de savoir*.

The reader of *La Cérémonie des adieux* reacts both to what is happening to 'Sartre' and to the reactions of the narrator. What is happening to 'Sartre', the signs of his incontinence, are localized in Rome and in Paris and are associated with Giolitti's ices, the Pantheon, cats, and a chair in 'Simone de Beauvoir's' apartment. Perhaps, as her last name suggests, 'Simone de Beau/voir' sees signs easily, or perhaps – *elle a beau voir* – no matter how or what she sees, she sees nothing, or she does not see that which is essential. The narrator in this passage breaks the silence that surrounds 'Sartre's' incontinence. First, to her friend, 'Sylvie', whose presence in the text as an intimate friend of 'Simone de Beauvoir's' appears to balance the list of 'Sartre's' younger women friends: Arlette, Michèle, Wanda, Liliane, Melina. To 'Sylvie', who had been duped (the narrator thought) by 'Sartre's' story of the cats, the narrator lies. She lies as she lied to her mother in *Une mort très douce* and as she will lie, later on in this text, to 'Sartre' about the seriousness of his illness. 'Sylvie', whose family name is Le Bon, answers firmly but kindly, revealing that she knows. The narrator then breaks the silence a second time by confronting 'Sartre' (as if he did not know) and as if he were a child and she, his mother: 'You are incontinent. You ought to tell the doctor.' The accusatory, peremptory tone of these sentences reveals the 'narrator's benefit'. Having broken the silence, having transgressed and spoken about what one should not speak about even if one knows, she assumes a maternal position of moral superiority. I know, and because I know, I can tell you what to do. But this benefit and the feeling of superiority that accompanies it do not last long. 'Sartre' already knew; the silence had already been broken. From this point in the narrative until the end of the paragraph, 'Simone de Beauvoir' as narrator and 'Sartre' vie for the reader's attention. His puritanical behaviour seems also to apply to her. His direct reply to her question that is asked in indirect style is not the last word. His plight cannot remain the focus of our attention. The narrator's reaction: 'I was touched . . . wounded me' becomes as important as 'Sartre's' incontinence and his reactions to it. At the end of the paragraph the 'narrator's benefit' has been restored. If in 'life' the silence has already been broken and 'Sartre' has spoken to his doctor, in writing it down and showing it to the public, she comes first.

But there is something else going on in this paragraph. There is the suggestion, through the cats that piss and the strong odour associated with cats' piss, through the emphasis on 'puritanical' and the presence of 'Sylvie Le Bon', that the narrator is keeping something hidden. The secret in this text, that which the narrator does not or cannot relate, is that the discourse on 'Sartre's' incontinence is also 'Simone de Beauvoir's' discourse on sexuality, on feminine sexuality, on her feminine sexuality. The name 'Giolitti', *gît au lit*, perhaps contains the variety of possible bodily activities.

The Gods of the Pantheon eventually recall the gods of the title *La Cérémonie des ADIEUX* and the SIMONIE (simony) in 'Simone', the making of profit out of sacred things, may be read as another example of the narrator's benefit. What 'Sartre' does with the members of his female entourage, what 'Simone de Beauvoir' does with 'Sylvie Le Bon', these are the taboo subjects that the narrator's text hides and reveals. They emerge, these taboo activities, in 'Sartre's' 'lack of control', which the narrator finds 'exceedingly embarrassing'. Lack of control, we remember from other texts by 'Simone de Beauvoir' and particularly *Le Deuxième sexe*, is a sign of the feminine.

It is not my intention to enter into an analysis of the narrator's relationship to homosexuality and lesbianism. We have, in the interviews with Alice Schwarzer, her explicit and conscious remarks on this question.[8] But I am fascinated by and would like to pursue the relations between the repetition of the phrase 'Sylvie and I' in *La Cérémonie des adieux* and passages from two other texts in which what is at stake is the production of another; like herself, a double.[9]

In his 1919 essay on 'The Uncanny', Sigmund Freud wrote: 'For the "double" was originally an insurance against the destruction of the ego, an "energetic denial of the power of death" as Rank says; and probably the "immortal" soul was the first "double" of the body.'[10] We find striking examples of the 'double' in the following passages:

> I resembled her [Maggie Tulliver in George Eliot's *The Mill on the Floss*] and henceforward I saw my isolation not as a proof of infamy but as a sign of my uniqueness. I couldn't see myself dying of solitude. Through the heroine, I identified myself with the author: one day other adolescents would bathe with their tears a novel in which I would tell my own sad story.
>
> (p.140)

The narrator is describing a series of displaced identifications with Maggie Tulliver, George Eliot, and her own future adolescent readers. In this case it is through the reading and writing of literary texts that a 'double' may be produced, a double that would ensure the continuation 'of the ego'. This is one of the ways in which writing, for Simone de Beauvoir, is a means of salvation.

The notion of the 'double' who saves is particularly strong in these concluding remarks about her new friend, 'Sylvie Le Bon', in *Tout compte fait*:

> The better I knew Sylvie, the more akin I felt to her. She too was an intellectual and she too was passionately in love with life. And she was like me in many other ways: with thirty-three years of difference I recognized my qualities and my faults in her. . . .
>
> First she was posted to Le Mans and then to Rouen, in the same lycée where I had taught: when she spent the night there, she stayed in the hotel near the station where I had lived for two years, and she drank her morning coffee in the Métropole bar: all this gave me a certain feeling of being reincarnated. At present she has a post in the suburbs.
>
> This means that we can see one another every day. She is as thoroughly interwoven in my life as I am in hers. I have introduced her to my friends. We read the same books, we see shows together, and we go for long drives in the car. There is such an interchange between us that I lose the sense of my age: she draws me forwards into her future, and there are times when the present recovers a dimension that it had lost.
>
> (p.72)

The presence of the double during the years of Sartre's final illnesses, when the readers might have expected the narrator to be alone, gives further evidence of what, in the writings of Sarah Kofman and Elizabeth Berg, is referred to as the 'scandalous . . . contradictions of the affirmative woman'.[11]

I would read *Une mort très douce* and *La Cérémonie des adieux* by maintaining both a psychoanalytic and a political reading. Incontinence is certainly closely allied to sexuality and to Simone de Beauvoir's uneasiness about feminine sexuality: its odours, its wetnesses, its sounds, and in particular, the difficulties in putting it into discourse, in breaking the silences with and for others. But incontinence is not only old sexuality. It is also a new continent to be written and a new continent to be explored. But that continent lies beyond the borders, and those who move beyond run the risk of being accused of acting in violation of the law of the fathers and of the mothers. Simone de Beauvoir, unlike many of the women writing on women since the late 1960s in France and in the United States, does not move from one position to another by flying. She transgresses, that is, she steps across, she trespasses. This makes her easier to track and to follow. What her writing is up to, and this must be a major source of the critics' malaise, is the affirmation that incontinence, like death, is a great equalizer. 'Jean-Paul Sartre' with bedsores and incontinent is not very different from 'Françoise de Beauvoir' with bedsores and incontinent. Between the old man who wets his chair and the old woman who wets her bed, the readers of both sexes who await their turn ('qui attendent leur tour,' wrote Pascal) must read that, at the end, sexual difference fades and that the body that remains is the unrestrained, uncontrolled body of the old woman. It is precisely the body that Western culture and, ironically, Simone de Beauvoir herself have laboured assiduously to hide.

There is a further transgressive aspect to Simone de Beauvoir's writing. In the 'Preface' to *La Cérémonie des adieux* we read:

> I have spoken about myself a little, because the witness is part of his [*sic*] evidence, but I have done so as little as possible. In the first place because that is not what this book is about, and then because, as I replied to a friend who asked me how I was taking it, 'These things cannot be told; they cannot be put into writing; they cannot be formed in one's mind. They are experienced and that is all [ça se vit, c'est tout]. My narrative is chiefly based on the diary I kept during those ten years; and on the many testimonies I have gathered.'
>
> (p.24)

Simone de Beauvoir's project, whatever her disclaimers of false modesty, from the very beginning of her writing career and consciously assumed as the volumes of memoirs followed each other, has been precisely to put into writing what 'cannot be told . . . cannot be put into writing . . . cannot be formed in one's mind'. Writers who attempt this, whether in prose or poetry, usually turn to metaphor or to other deliberate deviations from the conventions of narrative and a commonsense language accessible to all readers.

Simone de Beauvoir has refused to abandon these conventions and the immediate entrée to the text they guarantee. She has accepted the challenge of writing what cannot be written by relying on 'the diary I kept during those ten years' and 'the many testimonies I have gathered'. The impossibility of the task is juxtaposed with the sources that made the narrative possible. The effects produced on the reader by this narrative should, in some measure, correspond to what 'cannot be put into writing'. Simone de Beauvoir succeeds admirably, I think, in replicating her position as an intimate observer and helpless witness and in providing the reader with sufficient openings for identification and distance for critical analysis. But in so doing, she transgresses what has become a ruling protocol for important writing in the 1970s and early 1980s: she revels in the referential fallacy and her writing remains readable. Having been moved herself, she attempts to move her readers.

There is a further irony. The reviewers' comments notwithstanding, references to incontinence in *La Cérémonie des adieux* are very few. If there has been so much made of them, it is because they come unexpectedly (in the text), and they are situated at a crossroads of feminist, antihumanist, and humanist discourses: sexuality, the body, sexual difference, control, dignity, public and private, subject and object, subjectivity and sociality, the Symbolic, the Imaginary, and the Real. It is as if the 'real' had overwhelmed the reviewers, as if 'pipi caca' and all the strains of toilet training had been released by Simone de Beauvoir's texts. It is as if she had made dirty, had sullied the white page. In 1954 Sartre is said, by Simone de Beauvoir, to have exclaimed: 'La littérature, c'est de la merde.' Simone de Beauvoir's example indicates how unpalatable it is to reverse the terms and exclaim: 'La merde, c'est de la littérature.'

Notes

1 A. Jardine, 'Death Sentences: Writing Couples and Ideology', *Poetics Today*, 1985, vol.6, pp.119–31.

2 A. Kolodny, 'The Lady's Not for Spurning: Kate Millett and the Critics', in E. Jelined (ed.), *Women's Autobiography*, Bloomington, Indiana University Press, 1980, p.249.

3 S. de Beauvoir, *Memoirs of a Dutiful Daughter*, translated by J. Kirkup, New York, Harper Colophon, 1974, pp.99–100. All subsequent references to this text are to the same edition and are given in brackets in the text.

4 S. de Beauvoir, *All Said and Done*, translated by P. O'Brian, New York, Warner Brothers, 1975, p.78. All subsequent references are to this edition and are given in the text.

5 S. de Beauvoir, *A Very Easy Death*, translated by P. O'Brian, New York, Penguin Books, 1983, p.89. All subsequent references are to the same edition and are given in the text.

6 S. de Beauvoir, *Adieux: A Farewell to Sartre*, translated by P. O'Brian, New York, Pantheon Books, 1984, pp.33–4. All subsequent references are to the same edition and are given in the text.

7 M. Foucault, *The History of Sexuality*, translated by Robert Hurley, New York, Vintage Books, 1980, p.6.

8 A. Schwarzer, *After The Second Sex: Conversations with Simone de Beauvoir*, translated by M. Howarth, New York, Pantheon Books, 1984, pp.35–6, 112–13. In the earliest interview, 'I Am a Feminist', Beauvoir speaks harshly about 'the sexual dogmas lesbians try to impose' (p.36). In the last interview, 'Being a Woman is Not Enough', she claims never to have had a sexual relationship with a woman but accepts homosexuality as a possibility for all women (pp.112–13).

9 Beauvoir, *Adieux*, pp.85, 94, 95, 102, 109, 115, 118.

10 S. Freud, *The Standard Edition of the Complete Psychological Works*, translated by J. Kirkup, vol.17, London, Hogarth Press, 1955, p.235.

11 E. Berg, 'The Third Woman', *Diacritics*, 1982, p.20.

READINGS OF THE FICTION

SELF-ENCOUNTER IN
SHE CAME TO STAY

Hazel Barnes

This reading of Beauvoir's first published novel, *She Came to Stay* (1943), is taken from a larger study by Hazel Barnes of the fiction of Beauvoir, Camus and Sartre published in 1961 and entitled *The Literature of Possibility. A Study in Humanistic Existentialism.*[1] Barnes describes these writers' fictions as a 'literature of possibility' because, as she puts it, they present, in the mid-twentieth-century period in which she is writing, a radically new picture of human beings which, in accordance with the existentialist view that each of us is free to determine future portraits of ourselves, is concerned above all with presenting the possibilities of what we can become. She sets out the principles of Sartre's existential psychology, his basic ontology and the account of the individual's relations with others given in *Being and Nothingness*. The fictional texts of the three writers are read largely as illustrations or in some cases developments of Sartre's basic positions; strong intertextual resonances between the fictional texts are also highlighted.

Her reading of *She Came to Stay* is prefaced by a detailed account of *Being and Nothingness*'s analysis of love – or rather its analysis of the necessary failure of love and of the concomitant descent into masochism or sadism. She also discusses the metaphysical basis of indifference and hatred. Noting that Beauvoir's novel was published in the same year as *Being and Nothingness*, Barnes presents the novel primarily as a faithful illustration of these precepts; it appears striking to today's reader that she places Beauvoir so firmly in the role of obedient disciple, and that she adopts at times a somewhat dismissive tone. I have already discussed in the general intro-duction the issue of what is at stake when a woman in academia selects Beauvoir as a subject – and Barnes should be given full credit for including Beauvoir in this major study alongside Camus and Sartre.[2] In addition, Barnes did not have available to her the letters and diaries published in the 1980s and 1990s which record Sartre's reactions to reading the novel, before he had completed *Being and Nothingness*, and she does even so emphasise in a note that she suspects Sartre's philosophical debt to Beauvoir to be considerable.[3] Setting aside the controversy over intellectual property rights, Barnes's philosophical reading of the text is both shrewd and persuasive; it offers a subtle analysis of the sado-masochistic shifts in the projects of love on which the characters embark. More reductively perhaps, the murder of Xavière is presented as an exploration of hate, the final aspect of the Sartrean theorisation of being-for-others.

As a critical mode of interpreting the novel, the existentialist approach remained dominant for at least twenty years; other later interpretations have not so much displaced this approach as opened up new areas of the text.

Notes

1 H. Barnes, *The Literature of Possibility: A Study in Humanistic Existentialism*, London, Tavistock, 1961, pp.121–36.
2 See Introduction, p.7.
3 Kate and Edward Fullbrook make the claim that 'Beauvoir was always the driving intellectual power in the joint development of the couple's most influential ideas' (p.3). They analyse *She Came to Stay* in detail to support their argument that Beauvoir developed concepts which Sartre took up in *Being and Nothingness*. See K. and E. Fullbrook, *Simone de Beauvoir and Jean-Paul Sartre. The Remaking of a Twentieth-Century Legend*, Hemel Hempstead, Harvester Wheatsheaf, 1993.

This emotional labyrinth is all faithfully illustrated for us in Simone de Beauvoir's novel, *She Came to Stay*. Although this book and *Being and Nothingness* were published in the same year (1943), the similarity between them is too striking to be coincidence. As with all of de Beauvoir's early fiction, the reader of *She Came to Stay* feels that the inspiration of the book was simply de Beauvoir's decision to show how Sartre's abstract principles could be made to work out in 'real life'.[1] This is not to say that the novel has no merit in its own right. De Beauvoir is skilful in portraying emotional moods, and she has considerable ability in delineating character, especially in whatever fictional personality she has chosen to represent herself. But she is not yet the novelist of *The Mandarins*. The basic problem is handled more like a *quod erat demonstrandum* than a life situation, and the analysis of human relationships and personalities is more philosophical than psychological. Perhaps de Beauvoir and her fictional counterpart are accustomed to think in this way about themselves and their reactions, but most people are not so metaphysically articulate.

On the frontispiece de Beauvoir gives us the theme of the novel – the same quotation from Hegel which Sartre had used as the basis of his discussion of being-for-others: 'Each consciousness pursues the death of the other.' As in *No Exit* we have a triangle consisting of a man and two women. They are Pierre, writer, director, actor, and – quite evidently – an early version of Jean-Paul Sartre; Françoise, who is clearly Simone de Beauvoir and hardly to be distinguished from Anne in *The Mandarins*, and Xavière. Who is the original of Xavière, I do not know. But there must have been an original, for Ivich in *The Age of Reason*, which appeared two years later, is obviously Sartre's portrayal of the same girl. Both Ivich and Xavière have long golden hair which they generally allow to fall over the face (apparently de Beauvoir liked the hair style and Sartre did not); both girls are selfish, egocentric, gratuitously disagreeable. Both – without being actually homosexual – like to appraise other women's sexual attractions. Both are mad about dancing and have an odd habit of ordering and drinking cocktails which they do not like. It is possible that the model for Xavière and Ivich was the Olga Kosakiewicz, to whom both books are dedicated. I am inclined to hope not.[2]

Besides Pierre, Françoise, and Xavière, there are two other important characters in *She Came to Stay*. Of these one is Elisabeth, Pierre's sister, who, chiefly from jealousy at the happy self-absorption of the other three, urges a young actor, Gerbert, to try his luck with Xavière. Gerbert's success not only destroys the self-containment of the original trio but sets up another triangle impinging upon the first. He and Françoise had always felt a certain attraction toward one another. When they finally go on a hiking trip together, their relation does not seem to bother Pierre but is disastrous in the eyes of Xavière.

Xavière is unquestionably the apex of the first triangle. But it is not a triangle of the usual sort. Pierre and Françoise have for almost ten years maintained a relation which we are obviously meant to take as a reciprocal love in good faith. They are not married and they do not maintain a common household. But they sleep together, work together, and believe with all the fervour of pre-existentialist romances that they are united by a firm bond for the rest of their lives. Each means that the other shall be entirely free. Pierre occasionally makes use of his freedom for a light affair with other women. Françoise cannot bring herself to behave in similar fashion but feels in no way threatened by such conduct on the part of Pierre. It seems quite clear that de Beauvoir intends this relationship to serve as a model of love in good faith against which is played the conflict of love in bad faith initiated when Xavière, a little girl from the provinces, comes on a visit to Paris.

Relations at the beginning are on the plane of indifference. Françoise enjoys showing Paris to the provincial, feels vaguely sorry that Xavière must return to her dreary existence at home. When Pierre proposes that Françoise might suggest to Xavière that she come to live in Paris, that they might support her until she could shift for herself, Françoise is mildly disturbed at the prospect of complicating her life, but agrees. Then as she persuades Xavière to come, Françoise herself becomes enthusiastic. But she has not actually ceased to be indifferent, for what she envisions is a picture of herself moulding Xavière's life into the image of what she thinks it ought to be. She does not see Xavière as a self-determining subject or as an Other who might in any way affect Françoise's life. She is but the material for one of Françoise's projects.

Xavière accepts the invitation. There is a bit of friction from the beginning, for Françoise finds that Xavière is not content merely to share Françoise's leisure time. That there is an actual problem becomes evident when the two women spend an evening with Pierre. Pierre takes Xavière's immature pronouncements seriously. What had seemed to Françoise selfish irritability takes on for Pierre a fascinating quality of pure emotional intensity. Horrified, she seems to see Xavière changing shape, ceasing to be a harmless sulky child and advancing in heavy menace.

> Françoise tried with all her strength to push back this precious and encumbering Xavière who had just been revealed; it was almost hostility which she felt within her. But there was nothing to do, no way of going back. Xavière existed.[3]

Xavière's emergence as a subject threatens Françoise in two ways. In the first place she forces Françoise to become aware in a new way of her self-for-others and to see her whole life in a different and dubious light. Françoise had developed through her relation with Pierre and her work a quiet contentment. She assumed that one pursued happiness; she had developed a routine to guarantee its future. She lived by a code based on complete honesty toward herself and others. While she was not unaware of a certain complacency in her outlook, nevertheless she tried to make her way of living a base of support for such changes as might come rather than an ironclad 'adjustment'. It seemed that one could do no more. Xavière challenged all this. By scorning Françoise's work programme as a regimented 'living by bells', by declaring that she hated intellectual discipline and purity, by expressing contempt for the desire to find happiness in life, she thrust upon Françoise a view of her life as being nothing but a dull subservience to the demands of the Serious World, and of herself as a combination of awkward prudery and pedantry. Although Françoise had always known, as an existentialist heroine should, that values are chosen and created, nevertheless the violent confrontation with those of Xavière seemed to undermine her own, to alter and transform them. She might refuse to accept Xavière's, but she could not close her eyes to their existence.

The second threat is to Françoise's relation to Pierre. In part this is simply the Sartrean disintegration of a dual relation under the Look of a Third. Before Xavière's lofty disdain of human bonds, their mutual dependency begins to appear ridiculous. More seriously, Françoise is forcibly reminded that she and Pierre had not really been one. Although they had scrupulously respected each other's freedom, still Françoise, at least, had come to believe that they not only shared all experiences with each other but that either one could penetrate to the unspoken thought of the other. Now the difference in their evaluation of Xavière

160

makes her see Pierre as an opaque being with whom she can no longer feel an absolute unity. A little later there inevitably arises the question as to whether either one can achieve any significant relation with Xavière without excluding the other.

Rather cold-bloodedly the two of them discuss the situation, or rather the possibility of there being a situation. Pierre inquires first whether Françoise, having discovered Xavière, would not prefer to remain the most important person in her life. Later he puts the question on another basis. Would Françoise feel that a personal bond between him and Xavière was any threat to their own relation? In each instance Françoise declines to stand in the way, though not without some misgiving. Once all have abandoned the pretence of indifference, once Xavière's being-as-subject has been recognized, the problem arises as to whether all three parties can remain subjects or whether inevitably one or more must be reduced to objects. The action develops through three stages.

During the first part where there is conflict without even a temporary resolution, the novel comes closest to following the conventional treatment of the triangle. Françoise's relation with Xavière is not primary, though she feels an occasional pang of disappointment at the thought that Pierre is becoming more important to Xavière than she had been. But the real question is whether Xavière is threatening Françoise's position in Pierre's life. From the beginning it is clear that any relation between Pierre and Xavière will not be the light sexual affair which he has had with other women. Although he explains his interest by saying that he cannot resist the idea of making a conquest and that it is always the beginning of an affair which fascinates him, yet it is plain to him as well as to Françoise that Xavière is not to be conquered without demanding a commitment in return. De Beauvoir is careful to tell us that Françoise is not at any time jealous of Xavière. But it is a little difficult to classify her reactions if they are not jealousy. She observes the difference between Pierre's gravely polite attention to what she says and his eager look toward Xavière. She feels that they have come to take each other for granted, that their love is growing stale. When she tries to discuss the matter with him, he is a little impatient. He feels that their love is beyond question and needs no constant reaffirmation. Nevertheless he offers to give up all thought of Xavière if this will reassure Françoise. But faced with this possibility she refuses. She does not want a love based on the refusal to accept the truth of Xavière's existence. She insists on their continuing in the same way and faces the inevitable risk, not with resignation, but with 'an impersonal curiosity so violent that it had all the warmth of joy'. Her fears are soon realized. Pierre begins to show signs of accepting Xavière's values. He seems to encourage her in irresponsible evasions of duty. Françoise feels that her attempts to make them think of a future for Xavière result only in spoiling their pleasure and making herself hateful in her own eyes. On a lonely midnight walk she realizes that she had allowed herself to become somewhat lost in Pierre. She could use only 'our' with respect to the future. Pierre quite obviously could still say 'my'. She feels utterly abandoned, isolated even from herself. At this point, quite understandably (since the other two had prevented her from either working or sleeping), she comes down with pneumonia.

Françoise's stay in the hospital somehow solves the problem of her relation to Pierre. His devotion and his passionate anxiety convince her finally that her relation to him is secure. Stage one is ended. But the conflict resumes. And now it is openly a struggle for Xavière. The lines are laid down before Françoise is even ready to leave the hospital. During her illness the other two had apparently concentrated wholly on serving her. But at noon on almost the first day of her convalescence, they come in together to tell her that they had decided that they were in love with each other. Françoise is disturbed. 'She was not jealous of him, but that silky little golden girl whom she had adopted early one acid morning – Françoise was not giving *her* up without a struggle' (p.209). Pierre had inadvertently given her an opening. Xavière had consented the night before to telling Françoise that she and Pierre had decided they loved each other, but she turns sullen when he actually begins to discuss their relation and leaves in a fit of temper. Later with Pierre's consent Françoise tries to pacify Xavière by proposing a three-way relationship:

> 'A closely knit couple is already beautiful, but how much richer still are three people who love one another with all their strength.'
> She hesitated a bit. Now the moment had come to commit herself also and to accept the risk.
> 'For after all there is, isn't there, a kind of love between you and me?'

Xavière admits to the bond between them, and Françoise continues:

> 'You see, if there is also a love between Labrousse and you, that makes a beautiful, perfectly balanced trio. It is not the usual way of living, but I don't believe that it is too difficult for us.'
>
> (pp.218–19)

For a time the triangle appears to be equilateral and set firmly on its base. Although to outsiders the mutual absorption of the three seems slightly ridiculous, they seem to themselves to have captured an elusive and precarious happiness. The bonds uniting them are not overtly sexual, though a hidden sexuality is certainly present. De Beauvoir's restraint is not, I think, primarily due to a fear of offending good taste. The real reason is her resolve to document Sartre's statement that, whereas all human relations are implicitly sexual, they do not have sexual intercourse as their specific goal. De Beauvoir gives full weight to both parts of this theory. There is much made of the caress (an occasional chaste kiss or a handclasp), but there is an express denial that Pierre wants to seduce Xavière or that Françoise wants a full homosexual relation. But as both agree that it seems a kind of profanation to think of Xavière as a sexual object, neither can bear the idea of her sleeping with anyone else. Their reasons are somewhat different. Pierre declares that he is not a sensualist. (As a matter of fact, he displays little real passion at any time.) His desire to establish a relation between himself and Xavière is in the beginning based almost wholly on vanity, which has taken the form of the need to dominate. He is interested in Xavière because she offers resistance; he is jealous of anyone else who might attract her because this threatens his own supremacy. Later he becomes the pure embodiment of the Sartrean project of love (love in bad faith, of course). In loving Xavière he wants to *be loved* by her. He wants her to choose him as the centre of her existence. Recognizing the intensity of her will to be the subject in any relationship, it will be the supreme conquest if she voluntarily chooses him as the limit of her freedom. This is not the same as reducing her wholly to an object, for in that case she would be no more than the women of his other affairs. (This is another reason for his not wanting the relation to become simply a sexual one.) Pierre must somehow keep Xavière wholly free and yet be assured each day that she is freely entrusting herself to him. It is a relation in bad faith, for in the name of guaranteeing her freedom he is actually trying to ensnare it.

Françoise's position is a little different. In a sense her project is also one of love, for she wants to be important in Xavière's life and she tries to guide and direct Xavière's existence. She acts in tenderness and in good will, but she is nevertheless trying to give shape to Xavière's life. In one sense she is more violently offending Xavière's freedom than is Pierre. During the consultation with Pierre at the hospital, she had taunted Pierre by saying that in his need for assuring himself of Xavière's dependency he would continue to ask for more and end up by sleeping with her. The thought is repugnant to Françoise but not because of sexual jealousy of either one of them. The picture of Xavière which she has cherished is of the little girl from the provinces; Françoise would like to arrest her at that level. She feels that if Xavière should awaken sexually in Pierre's arms she would be like all the other women Pierre had known and no longer Xavière. Yet while this reaction belongs to Françoise-subject, she begins to assume more and more of an object role toward Xavière. Sartre follows Freud in holding that all love is to a certain extent a blend of masochism and sadism – or more accurately it bears within it the seeds of both and almost inevitably collapses into one or the other. Whereas Pierre, whose subjectivity is never really in question, uses Xavière as a test of his own power and hence skirts the edges of sadism, Françoise has more at stake. Already even in her relation with Pierre she came dangerously close to accepting a dependent kind of being. She saw the world through his eyes, waited for him to give the final stamp to any mood or opinion. Even Xavière did not assume real importance until Françoise began to see her as she appeared to Pierre. Françoise had never quite accepted the status of object. In a crisis she could still judge Pierre, though it shocked her to find herself doing so. She never really became masochistic.

True masochism is represented by Pierre's sister. Elisabeth had for years let her life be made almost unbearable by an unsatisfying relation with a married man.

For a time she deceived herself into thinking that Claude would break with his wife. Then she realizes that he never will and tries to break away. She is unable to give him up, partly because she cannot resist his physical attraction but mostly because even her unhappy relation to him gives her a kind of justification for her existence which she is unable to find anywhere else. She is pathetic – as well as in bad faith – in that she is able neither to accept an irregular, subordinate position for what it is worth nor to reject it. Like all masochists she prefers to be tormented rather than to face things squarely and enter into a way of life which would necessitate a change in her choice of herself. Rather surprisingly, Françoise and Pierre seem to feel that she is incapable of such adjustment and deliberately try to keep her in bad faith.

Elisabeth's example is influential in preventing Françoise from ever giving in to the temptation to lose herself in Pierre. She is never in real danger of falling into masochism. With respect to Xavière, however, the risk is greater. This is partly because Xavière, unlike Pierre, is not willing to maintain a relation in good faith with Françoise. It is also because the whole relation with Xavière had from the beginning been in bad faith on all sides. While not as domineering as Pierre, Françoise had from her first recognition of Xavière sensed that they were involved in a conflict. The relation was never one of mutual enrichment and growth. As she becomes more closely involved with Xavière, she allows herself to become more and more dependent on her. Her mood for the day is determined by Xavière; the slightest word from her is sufficient to exalt Françoise in happiness or plunge her in misery. More important, Françoise feels herself alienated from her own life. All that she had treasured is made to seem contemptible beneath Xavière's scornful look. Even her own body seems an awkward excrescence which finds no place in Being except when Xavière 'makes her dance well' or compliments her on her appearance. Hers is a project of love in which she is almost snared in the object-state with which she has hoped to fascinate Xavière's freedom; it is love on the masochistic side. She is saved from complete reduction only by the habit of reflective thought, which never quite deserts her, and by the fact that the shifting relation among the three of them prevents any subject–object relation from being final.

So far we have seen, in terms consistent with Sartre's analysis, exemplifications of indifference, of two projects of love, and of masochism. In Xavière we see a portrayal, in very delicate terms, of sadism. There was obviously no place in this novel for the torturer-sadist whom Sartre described. Such a description de Beauvoir provided later in her study of the Marquis de Sade. But Xavière is no less a sadist because as her instruments of torture she uses cutting words and a look of helpless appeal. She is the pure form of sadist in that she wants to keep her own subjectivity supreme at all costs. She demands the enslavement of all those with whom she comes in contact, and she makes no commitment in return. For her even generosity is a form of enslavement.[4] She gives imperiously, not as an expression of tenderness but to assert her own supremacy. She enters into the triangular arrangement with Pierre and Françoise because she sees herself as its apex, which she is for a time. But all the while she is trying to break down the relation between the other two. It is significant that her efforts are directed more toward Pierre. This is in part due to sexual vanity; much as Françoise may try to deny it, Xavière is a passionate woman in spite of her sheltered virginity. In addition, Xavière realizes that Françoise is more dependent upon her than Pierre is, and she senses that in the relation of the other two, it is Pierre who is more free. Thus by winning him away from Françoise she can prove her power over them both. As with most, if not all, sadists, Xavière sometimes turns toward herself the hostility which she generally manifests toward the world. Her demands upon herself are excessive, and she punishes herself if she does not meet them. Thus, for example, after sentimentally letting herself wear a faded rose given her on the night before, she not only suddenly resolves to destroy the rose but takes a cigarette and with deep, voluptuous pleasure burns a deep hole in her hand. Mostly, though, she worships her own subjectivity and transfers allegiance back and forth between Françoise and Pierre, playing one against the other in an endeavour to use both of them for her own ends.

De Beauvoir's analysis of the emotional fluctuations of her trio is brilliant. It is done largely from Françoise's point of view. On the whole, the occasional moments of happiness she finds alone with Pierre or with Xavière are not enough to make up for the friction when all three are together – even during the weeks when she still has hope that the trio may achieve a satisfactory *modus vivendi*. She suffers alternately for Pierre and for Xavière as they hurt each other in their struggle for dominance, and she is miserable when a temporary reciprocity between them seems to shut her out. When Pierre suggests that they might all go on a holiday together, a vacation she had expected to spend with Pierre alone, Françoise can hardly bear the thought and resolves to make the trio a duo at all costs.

As I mentioned earlier, it is Elisabeth who (although actually a fourth person) functions here as a Third to upset completely the uneasy equilibrium which they had established. At her suggestion, Gerbert invites Xavière out for an evening. Xavière has been attracted to him all along. In fact her interest in Gerbert, her admiration for his good looks and boyish charm, is almost the only thing about her which makes her seem like a normal girl instead of a self-worshipping monster. One feels that if at the start she had met Gerbert and not the other couple, she might have developed some of the more graceful outgoing qualities of youth instead of merely its narcissism. As the situation develops, however, Xavière is too proud to let Gerbert see that she is interested in him. When she finally consents to go out with him, it is chiefly because she is offended that Pierre and Françoise had earlier had an appointment with Gerbert at which she was not included.

The evening which the two spend together is like a breath of spring to Xavière and Gerbert – and to the reader – but the consequences are disastrous for all concerned. Pierre is furiously jealous. When the trio meets the next evening, he so torments Xavière with insinuations about the evening that she thinks Gerbert has talked about her. The thought of having been made an object by him is so repugnant to her that she turns from him with hatred, renewing her allegiance to the trio. But Pierre goes too far. He forces Xavière to admit that her unpleasant behaviour has been motivated by jealousy of Françoise and by resentment that she cannot destroy the relation between the two of them. For the moment Xavière does nothing. It is Françoise who snaps. Ever since Xavière's arrival Françoise has felt menaced by her. Now the threat seems suddenly to take on a metaphysical character. Just as mystics in religious ecstasy experience in intensified form the reality of the God in whom they have always believed, so Françoise *feels* for the first time the perilous quality of her subjectivity before the existence of another consciousness. What she experiences now is no more like her intellectual comprehension of the existence of separate consciousness than St Teresa's trance resembles the recitation of the Creed.

> Across Xavière's mad possessive pleasure, across her hate and jealousy, the shocking scandal burst forth as monstrous, as definitive as death. Face to face with Françoise and yet apart from her there existed something which stood as a condemnation without appeal: free, absolute, irreducible, an alien consciousness was rising up. It was like death, a total negation, an eternal absence, and yet in staggering contradiction, this abyss of nothingness could render itself present to itself, could make itself exist for itself in absolute fullness; the whole Universe was swallowed up in it, and Françoise, forever dispossessed of the world, was herself dissolved in this void whose infinite circumference no word, no image could encompass.
>
> (p.301)

In this passage de Beauvoir has compressed the essence of Hegel's conflict of consciousness and of Sartre's idea that the emergence of another consciousness effects an internal haemorrhage of my world. The keyhole example soon follows.

Incensed by Pierre's accusations, Xavière not only goes out with Gerbert again but becomes his mistress. The haughty Pierre, whom Françoise on more than one occasion had gently accused of thinking that he was God the Father, this unchallenged subject, not only paces the floor above Xavière's room but is reduced to looking through the keyhole. He is not discovered there like the man in Sartre's example, but he becomes momentarily an object of shame as he confesses to Françoise what he has done and feels her half-compassionate, half-scornful appraisal. The next morning they find a note from Xavière under Françoise's door.

> I am so disgusted with myself. I ought to have thrown myself out of the window, but I will not have the courage. Do not forgive me. You yourself must kill me tomorrow morning if I have been too cowardly.
>
> (p.321)

On her door is tacked up another note with the words, 'No forgiveness.' Xavière's reaction is not simply that of a girl frightened or disillusioned by her first sexual experience. Once again she hates herself for having given in response to a demand, for having for the moment lost her subject-being. It is not enough to punish herself afterwards. She also turns against Gerbert and throws him out. Her insistence that she must not be forgiven is in itself a defence of her being-as-subject, for forgiveness as much as judgement throws the weight of Being over upon the one who makes the decision. Later in the same day Xavière withdraws even more completely by disclaiming all responsibility for the note, pleading intoxication and pretending that nothing of significance has taken place.

Xavière's night with Gerbert brings to an end the second stage of the story. She continues to see Gerbert occasionally, but he no longer has any real interest in her. Pierre, after first breaking with her completely, consents to a sort of truce and secretly hopes to make her give up Gerbert. The two of them fall into a sort of complicity which Françoise feels excludes her. This time she neither tries to win back Xavière nor takes steps to ensure that her own relation with Pierre will not suffer. Utterly disgusted with Xavière's egoistic duplicity and Pierre's blindness toward Xavière and lack of consideration for herself, Françoise at last refuses to be an object before either of them. Toward Pierre she feels almost indifference.

> Facing Xavière she felt with a kind of joy the upsurge within her of something black and bitter which she did not yet recognize, something which was almost a deliverance: powerful, free, bursting forth in full bloom – it was hate.
>
> (p.369)

Rejecting all hope of reciprocity with Xavière, unable to make her an object and unwilling to give up her own subjectivity, Françoise finds recourse in the one attitude untried. For the moment she does not pursue the emotion to its logical outcome; since she is leaving Paris for a vacation, she can pretend that Xavière does not exist. She is not forced to recognize hate for what it really is: the will to annihilate the Other.

In the last and decisive phase of the novel events move swiftly. Françoise and Gerbert have set off alone on a hiking trip. Although the arrangement was intended to be a platonic one, she eventually becomes his mistress and they live a summertime idyll based partly on sexual attraction and partly on tender friendship. De Beauvoir's intention is apparently merely to show that Françoise is finally able to live for herself again, that there are other interests in life besides Xavière and Pierre. Though the thought is perhaps unjust, I cannot myself refrain from thinking that there is a bit of sadism in Françoise's action. Although she does not recognize in the love affair any connection with those left behind in Paris, the fact remains that by sleeping with Gerbert she is both hurting Xavière (who had never wholly relinquished her claim to him) and rather forcefully asserting her subjective independence of Pierre.

167

Upon returning to Paris, Françoise learns that Pierre has given up all but politely casual relations with Xavière. Rather inconsistently he explains his decision by accusing Xavière of bad faith. Xavière had suddenly lost all importance to him, he says, precisely when she became all repentance and tenderness.

> If she had thrown herself unreservedly into my arms, I would have been really moved; perhaps too if she had remained on the defensive, I would have been challenged by her resistance. But when I saw how greedy she was to get me back and how anxious she was to sacrifice nothing for me, I felt only a faintly disgusted pity.
>
> (pp.386–7)

Françoise allows herself to gloat just a bit over her victory. In her eyes it is the old-fashioned virtues which have won out over obstinacy, egoistic caprice, and deceit. Defeated, Xavière is no longer a threat. Françoise 'once again existed alone, without an obstacle, at the heart of her destiny'.

I am inclined to think that it would have been better from a strictly literary point of view if the novel had stopped at this point. But de Beauvoir has not examined quite all of the philosophical implications of being-for-others. There still remains the exploration of hate. Now we are thrust into the midst of World War Two. Pierre and Gerbert both go off to the army. Françoise continues to see Xavière. Suddenly the conflict is on again between the two of them more violently than ever. First, Françoise discovers that Xavière has been telling Gerbert a false version of the story of her relation to Pierre and that she is trying to build up even yet a picture in which she and Françoise play respectively a sort of Mary and Martha role with regard to him. This is bad enough, for Françoise's knowledge of how things really have been cannot prevent her from being aware of a possible different interpretation. But the decisive engagement takes place when Xavière breaks open Françoise's desk and reads letters she has had from Pierre and Gerbert. Françoise, confronting her, now sees the story of recent events as they appear to Xavière: she sees herself jealous of Pierre's love for Xavière and getting revenge by taking Gerbert from her. It does not seem to Françoise that this is exactly how things were and she feels that somehow innocent love has been tortured into sordid betrayal; but she is horrified at the picture of herself which she sees in Xavière's eyes. She begs for forgiveness, for the chance to make it up somehow to Xavière. Xavière refuses. Now it seems to Françoise that she and Xavière cannot both go on living.

> *There* was Xavière, existing only for herself, entirely self-devoted, reducing to nothingness everything which she excluded. She enclosed the whole world in her own triumphant solitude, she expanded without limit – infinite, unique. Everything which she was she drew out of herself. One could get no hold upon her. She was absolute separation.
>
> (p.418)

'It is she or I,' thinks Françoise. And arranging things to look like suicide, she turns on the gas to kill Xavière while she sleeps. Françoise has 'chosen herself'.

Strictly speaking, de Beauvoir has not gone quite to the bitter limit of Sartre's analysis. As we have seen, hatred of one Other is hatred directed toward all Others. There is no reason to think that Françoise will never encounter another Xavière. Moreover, she can never erase the memory of Xavière's Look. She will never be able to think of herself and Gerbert without taking Xavière's view of things into account. But of all this de Beauvoir tells us nothing.

I think we should not be afraid to say that this is a shocking book. There are, of course, allowances which must be made. In all fairness we must grant that the denouement is a metaphysical murder rather than a real one. There is no sign in the rest of her work that de Beauvoir actually believes it justifiable to kill anyone blocking the way to one's self-realization. In essence Françoise's decision to kill Xavière is but the dramatic conclusion of a philosophical proposition: if one insists on choosing bad faith as the mode of living one's human relationships, then only one's own death or that of the Other will end the conflict. To the extent to which the emotional involvements of the characters in *She Came to Stay* are intended as an illustration of bad faith, the novel is an exposé of the way in which many people use love and friendship as a cloak for their exploitation of others. It attacks the notion that through love one is justified either in living another's life for him or in letting one's own life be determined wholly by another. In these respects, and in its denunciation of egotism, selfishness, and deceit, the book is as moral as a sermon by Billy Graham.

But difficulties arise when we try to find the other side of the picture. Is there anywhere in the novel a standard for human relations in good faith? Abstractly this is easy to find. Pierre defines it when he points out how his relation with Françoise is different from any they have been able to establish with Xavière. 'Between us there is reciprocity. . . . The moment that you recognize me as a consciousness you know that I recognize you as a consciousness too' (p.312). The trouble is that this recognition on Pierre's part seems to be restricted to Françoise, and even in her case it is sometimes a little myopic. Pierre acknowledges a need for frequent light affairs with women, 'conquests' which are not even in answer to sexual needs but rather the result of his compulsion to dominate. He and Françoise profess a strict code of honesty, but it does not prevent them from lying to Gerbert when they want to have Xavière to themselves. Moreover, their demands upon Xavière are no more justified than hers upon them. To ask that this impulsive, highly emotional girl, who loathes nothing so much as introspection, should conform to their continual demands for reflective self-analysis and consistency is doing violence to her right at the start. Of course we may say that Pierre's and Françoise's defections are the result of their having forsaken their usual life in good faith and that it is Xavière's peculiar character which has seduced them into the way of bad faith. They have 'backslid', as it were, and return to the fold when the evil of sin is made manifest. But Françoise's choice of herself through murder is not an act in good faith. By existentialist standards she should have had the courage to accept the consequences of her own acts and to live with her own view of things no matter how Xavière tried to picture them. Perhaps we are to assume that de Beauvoir recognized this, that she meant to represent Françoise as so utterly destroyed by having entered into the wrong kind of relation with Xavière that redemption is impossible. In that case the novel is an unrelieved tragedy, and Françoise's choice of herself is as much a defeat for her as death is for Xavière. But then what becomes of the existentialist theory of the unity of the personality? Sartre maintained that a man could not be an anti-Semite and in other respects a good citizen. Hatred of any one Other, as we have seen, is hatred of all Others. Françoise herself recognized the universal nature of her first perception of Xavière as an alien consciousness confronting her. Is it possible for Pierre and Françoise to be in good faith with respect to each other and in bad faith toward most of the rest of their world? It seems to me that there are only two possibilities: either all of the novel's characters are in bad faith and no one has been able to maintain a true reciprocity – or else de Beauvoir's picture of human relations in good faith is such that there is little reason for anyone to choose good faith rather than its opposite.

Notes

1 I do not at all preclude the possibility that de Beauvoir has contributed to the formation of Sartre's philosophy. I suspect that his debt to her is considerable. All I mean in the present instance is that the novel serves as documentation for the theory, regardless of who had which idea first.
2 The model for Xavière was in fact Olga (ed.).
3 S. de Beauvoir, *She Came to Stay*, p.69. Page references are to the French edition (*L'Invitée*, Paris, Gallimard, 1943), translated by Barnes. Subsequent references are given in brackets in the text.
4 Sartre discusses generosity as a combination of destruction and enslavement in *Being and Nothingness*, translated by H. Barnes, New York, Philosophical Library, 1956, pp.594–5.

SHE CAME TO STAY:
THE PHALLUS STRIKES BACK

Jane Heath

A novelist as well as critic, Jane Heath published her stimulating study of Beauvoir's fictional and autobiographical writing in 1989, nearly thirty years after Hazel Barnes's readings of Beauvoir's fiction in the light of Sartrean existentialism.[1] Heath adopts a very different theoretical framework: writing in the wake of developments in psychoanalysis and of the 'new' French feminisms of the 1970s, she focuses on what she sees as the censorship and repression of the feminine in Beauvoir's texts. Drawing on Lacan and Kristeva in particular, she takes as axiomatic that gender identity is not fixed at birth but produced in language. The terms 'masculine' and 'feminine' are taken to describe a subject relation to the Lacanian phallus (as distinct from the penis) in which the masculine becomes the unifying, conceptual discourse of repression whilst the feminine is identified with the unconscious and the disruptive.[2]

Noting the fact that Beauvoir was able to produce *The Second Sex* without apparently identifying with women as a group or even identifying herself particularly as a woman, Heath proposes that many of Beauvoir's texts identify with the masculine. This does not necessarily have to be taken as a root and branch criticism of Beauvoir's position – Heath herself notes that Beauvoir's identification with a particular elite group of Parisian male intellectuals was probably a crucial enabling factor for the writing of *The Second Sex*. However, the argument that Beauvoir's writing is aligned with a repressive masculine echoes the position taken up by one of the tendencies in French feminism which emerged in the early 1970s.[3]

Be this as it may, the reading of *She Came to Stay* which Jane Heath produces from this perspective offers an innovatory and stimulating approach to the novel. Xavière is identified as the locus of the threatening and destabilising feminine within the text, undermining the masculine economy represented by Pierre and Françoise. The murder of Xavière, which is explained by Barnes as a completion of Beauvoir's philosophical exploration of being-for-others, becomes a phallic backlash, an act of repression of the hysterical feminine undertaken by the masculine-identified Françoise, in the interests of maintaining the phallic order.

Notes

1 The following extract is taken from J. Heath, *Simone de Beauvoir*, Brighton, Harvester, 1989, pp.29–43. Her novel is published under the name of Jane Ellory, *Maidenhope*, Weeley, Essex, Vinca Books, 1995.
2 Whereas the penis is the organ, the phallus is the supreme signifier in Lacan's system. See Malcolm Bowie, *Lacan*, London, Fontana, 1991, pp.122–57 for further elaboration.
3 The 'psych et po' tendency in French feminism with which the name of Hélène Cixous is closely associated. See E. Fallaize, *French Women's Writing: Recent Fiction*, Basingstoke, Macmillan, 1993, pp.8–12 for further details.

In what ways is Xavière a destabilising force undermining the status quo, the masculine economy represented by Pierre and Françoise? Xavière is dismissive of all forms of art which involve the labour of production. She despises Elisabeth who wants to be a great painter because she disciplines herself, works to a programme. Xavière considers that artists, with the exception of Baudelaire and Rimbaud, are like bureaucrats. Pierre and Françoise, who is herself working on a novel, are subsumed in this category of artists or putative artists who lead tidy, well-regulated lives. Xavière lives in and for the present. She is contradictory, unpredictable and resists the judgement of others. She is both literally and metaphorically disorderly. Her room is a slum. She would happily be a *ratée*, a failure (p.49: p.69).[1] She seeks and values an unmediated relationship to the world around her. She takes her pleasure neat, or as Françoise remarks, " 'You happen to be a little aesthete. You want unadulterated beauty" ' (p.96: p.123).[2] Xavière is not interested in whether music is good or bad, " 'I like the notes for themselves; the sound alone is enough for me" ' (p.94: p.121). She has a similar relationship with words: for her they are voluptuous (p.97: pp.124–5). However, she scorns sitting down at a table and working with them. Françoise sums up Xavière's effect on her when she tells Gerbert that Xavière is a living question mark (p.123: p.156).

Xavière's interrogatory stance has dramatic consequences for Françoise who begins to recognise words as ambiguous signs: 'when Pierre's words and smiles were directed to her, that was Pierre himself. Suddenly, she felt as if they were ambiguous symbols' (pp.126–7: p.160). It is as if initially, for Françoise, the signifier (Pierre's words and smiles) had coalesced with the signified (Pierre himself) producing the reassuring certainties of the Imaginary.[3] Now, however, the signifiers have been barred off and Françoise begins to glimpse her alienation as a subject in language. Xavière's function is to force Françoise into a confrontation with herself as split subject. This is achieved, in general terms, by Xavière's attitudes, and in particular through her relationship with Pierre who becomes so involved with Xavière that he can no longer function as Françoise's alter ego. He has to disown 'we are as one', and instead assert that he and Françoise are 'two distinct individuals' (p.57: p.78). Thus Françoise loses the sense of herself as a sovereign subject, 'je suis là', 'I am here' (p.1: p.11) with which the text began. By Chapter 7 she is completely undermined; she asks the question 'What am I?', and answers, 'I am no one' (p.146: pp.183–4). Françoise has reached a crisis concerning her subjectivity. Deprived of Pierre as a prop to her (fixed) identity, she seems unable to recognise her radical alienation ('je est un autre') which is a precondition of 'true' intersubjectivity. A similar crisis of subjectivity occurs in *Les Mandarins.*

My reading of Xavière as a destabilising force in Françoise's orderly life is so far reductive in that I have not emphasised the importance of Xavière as the locus of the feminine within the text, the feminine being defined as that which is problematic to a phallic economy and which always exceeds any attempt at containment. I am arguing that the case of Xavière exceeds both her construction within the text as a rebellious contestatory child and as 'other' with a small 'o', Françoise's adversary in a Hegelian confrontation.

In the second part of the novel, Françoise, Pierre, Xavière and Paule visit a Spanish night club. On the way Françoise calls for Xavière who is staying in the same hotel as Françoise. For Françoise, an atmosphere of evil exoticism and unassuaged desire suffuses Xavière's hotel room, which is described not only as a 'sanctuary where Xavière celebrated her own worship' but a 'hothouse in which flourished a luxuriant and poisonous vegetation; it was the cell of a bedlamite, in which the dank atmosphere adhered to the body' (p.274: p.342). Note here the emphasis on madness, the body, a different religion (another economy?).

At the night club, there are two women performers. One is a dancer and the other recites a poem. During their performances, Xavière goes into a sort of trance and deliberately burns herself with a cigarette. These feminine performances are characteristic of the Kristevan semiotic. First, a woman, 'plump and mature', elderly even, is completely transformed by her dance (pp.283–4: pp.353–4). What the text emphasises, and what Xavière watches so intently, is the *movement* of the woman s body. The performance is kinetic, transitory, its product ephemeral. (This compares with Xavière's scorn for works of art, static representations which become objects of exchange.) In the second performance (pp.291–2: pp.362–3) the text makes it clear that the effect of the poetry has little to do with the meaning of the words: 'Even without full knowledge of the meaning of the words, her impassioned accent, and her face illuminated by emotional fervour were deeply moving' (p.291: p.363).[4] The audience responds to something (the semiotic) that 'comes through', traverses the words, and which has to do with a quality of the voice, its 'accent passionné', its 'sursauts' (rhythm and movement again), its 'plaintes', a vocal expression of pain, its 'mystérieuses sonorités'.

Let us examine now Xavière's response to the performances and Françoise's reaction to it. During the dance Françoise turns to look at Xavière who 'was pressing the glowing brand against her skin with a bitter smile curling her lips. It was an intimate, solitary smile, like the smile of a half-wit; the voluptuous tortured smile of a woman possessed by secret pleasure. The sight of it was almost unbearable, it concealed something horrible' (p.284: p.354).[5]

After the performance, Xavière burns herself again:

> Behind that maniacal grin was the threat of a danger more positive than any she had ever imagined. Something was there that hungrily hugged itself, that unquestionably existed on its own account. Approach to it was impossible even in thought. Just as she seemed to be getting near it the thought dissolved. This was no tangible object, but an incessant flux, a never-ending escape, only comprehensible to itself, and for ever occult. Eternally shut out she could only continue to circle round it.
>
> (p.285: pp.354–5)[6]

Xavière burns herself a third time while the poem is being recited:

> Xavière was no longer watching the woman: she was staring into space. A cigarette was alight between her fingers and the glowing end was beginning to touch her flesh without her seeming to be aware of it, she seemed to be in the grip of hysterical ecstasy. . . . This hostile presence, which earlier had betrayed itself in a lunatic's smile, was approaching closer and closer: there was now no way of avoiding its terrifying disclosure. Day after day, minute after minute, Françoise had fled the danger; but the worst had happened, and she had at last come face to face with this insurmountable obstacle which she had sensed behind a shadowy outline, since her earliest childhood. At the back of Xavière's maniacal pleasure, at the back of her hatred and jealousy, the abomination loomed, as monstrous and definite as death. Before Françoise's very eyes, and yet apart from her, something existed like a sentence without an appeal: detached, absolute, unalterable, an alien conscience was taking up its position. It was like death, a total negation, an eternal absence, and yet, by a staggering contradiction, this abyss of nothingness could make itself present to itself and make itself fully exist for itself. The entire universe was engulfed in it, and Françoise, for ever excluded from the world, was herself dissolved in this void, of which the infinite contour no word, no image could encompass.
>
> (p.292: pp.363–4)[7]

Xavière is surely more here than the Hegelian other, an 'alien consciousness'. Françoise, positioned on the side of a phallic economy, constructs her as a mad-woman, an hysteric. Feminists have already noted the way in which phallo-centrism relegates 'woman' as hysteric to the margins. The text, however, effects a reversal which places Xavière at the centre and consigns Françoise to the peri-phery. 'All you could do was go round it in circles for ever excluded.' Françoise, whose position is similar to that of Lacan when he looks at Bernini's statue of St Teresa, can only gaze in horrified and confused amazement at the 'extase hystérique'. For there is no mistaking the sexual nature of Xavière's pleasure, its excessive *jouissance*. Whatever Xavière stands for, or is, is beyond representation. In the first passage this unrepresentability is conveyed by a metaphor of fluidity – the semiotic again.

There is a slippage from Xavière as 'hostile présence', other with a small 'o', to Xavière in the place of the Other, capital 'O'. In the second passage Xavière as presence is unveiled to reveal absence, a massive lack, death, which no word or image can fill. (This is the crux of the problem for Françoise.) Xavière comes thus to represent the death instinct, a crucial component in the castration complex.

The following quotation from Laplanche and Leclaire can be read in conjunc-tion with the passage above, in particular the notions of 'death' ('the death instinct'), 'hysterical ecstasy' ('ecstatic instant', 'a swoon or ecstasy'), 'that no word or image could circumscribe' ('screaming out its appeal for a word'), 'dévoilement' ('to veil and sustain it'):

> The death instinct is that radical force which surfaces in the catastrophic
> or ecstatic instant when the organic coherence of the body appears as
> though unnamed and unnameable, a swoon or ecstasy, screaming out its
> appeal for a word to veil and sustain it. It constitutes the basis of the
> castration complex and allows the development of language, together
> with the possibility of desire and the development of the sexual
> instincts.[8]

With Xavière, the text stages a representation of the moment/possibility of desire and Françoise's traumatised reaction to it.

I suggested earlier that the text, at one level, inscribes Pierre, Françoise and Xavière in a familial/Oedipal triangle with its attendant loves, prohibitions and rivalries. This triangle can be mapped on to another one that is free of familial interdictions. It is on the text as a version of the 'eternal triangle' that the recent interpretations I referred to earlier have depended. In this scheme Françoise has been seen as the typical jealous heterosexual woman who directs her murderous aggressivity against her rival, Xavière, rather than against her beloved, Pierre. Lest there be any doubt about the inappropriateness of such an interpretation, the text proposes just such a banal eternal triangle in the case of Elisabeth/Claude/Suzanne which functions as a counterpoint to Pierre/Françoise/Xavière. The text does make a connection between this sort of heterosexual jealousy and murder. Elisabeth recounts the violent attack of Moreau, a man who would like to be her lover: ' "Just imagine, he pinned me against a lamp-post, grabbed me by the throat, while he shouted dramatically: 'I'll have you Elisabeth, or I'll kill you'." ' (p.222: p.281).

My argument is twofold. First, that the text exceeds the possibility of containment within the familial; and second, that we do have another triangle (but *not* a banal 'eternal triangle') the nature of which I shall try to trace. What is important here is the textual ambivalence, the way in which the familial/Oedipal can be invoked and exceeded. The text seems to evade any attempt to pin it down to one scenario or the other, such is its irreducibility.

Where are the Oedipal interdictions? They arise first in the case of Françoise who has 'a maternal feeling towards Gerbert – maternal with a faintly incestuous touch' (p.36: pp.51–2). When Xavière is going through a moment of deep depression, Pierre turns to Françoise and angrily asks her to calm Xavière:

'You ought to have put your arms around her a long time ago and said – said something to her,' he added lamely.

Mentally, Pierre enfolded Xavière in his arms and rocked her soothingly, but respect, decency, and strict convention paralysed them, his warm compassion could be embodied only in Françoise.

(p.103: p.132)

Pierre here is cast in the paternal role in the same way that Françoise is cast in a maternal role in relation to Gerbert. Note also the way in which physical tenderness between Françoise and Xavière as mother and daughter is here legitimised.

As Pierre's attachment to Xavière grows stronger, so his role as putative lover develops. The text maintains a delicate equilibrium (ambivalence?) between the roles of father and lover: 'Their relationship was virtually chaste, and yet, through a few kisses and light caresses, he had established between them a sensual understanding, which was clearly visible beneath their reserve' (p.238: p.299). It seems that Pierre's transition from the role of father to that of lover can be accomplished with relative ease. This must have to do with the fact that the relationship is in both cases heterosexual. The same can be said for Françoise and Gerbert whose relation to Pierre and Françoise is similar to that of Xavière. Both are like children to Pierre and Françoise. Françoise can make love with Gerbert because that too is a heterosexual relationship. However, in the case of Françoise and Xavière, the relationship is homosexual and, though physical contact between mother and daughter is socially acceptable, Xavière as a love-object for Françoise is not.

It remains now to examine that relationship.

Just as Pierre initially plays father to Xavière, so Françoise plays mother. That relationship plays out a mother/daughter rivalry for the father so that, for example, Françoise is shocked to see Xavière's coquettishness towards Pierre. Pierre's increasing involvement with Xavière is presented first of all as a potential threat to the 'we are as one' mythical couple. Indeed the reality of this threat and the structural impossibility of the trio as some new sort of sustainable interpersonal relationship is made evident when Pierre says ' "When I look at her I don't look at you" ' (p.164: p.206). In other words, he can't look two ways at once. The first effect of Pierre's involvement is a split in the 'unity' of the couple involving an outflow of content: 'Pierre still repeated: "We are but one," but now she had discovered that he lived for himself. Without losing its perfect form their love, their life was slowly losing its substance' (p.154: p.194).

This rupture produces Françoise's crisis of subjectivity and her flight into illness. By the end of Part I, Pierre, in Xavière's presence, has declared to Françoise that he and Xavière love each other. Pierre's passion has been increased by his fear that Xavière might be in love with Gerbert. This masculine rivalry urges Pierre on so that his earlier reluctance to make physical contact with Xavière evaporates:

'When I said the word "love", she trembled a little, but her face gave immediate consent. I took her home.' . . .
'When I was about to leave her, I took her in my arms and she held her lips up to me. It was a completely chaste kiss, but there was so much tenderness in her gesture.'

(p.207: p.258)

This is another example of the text sustaining both the purity (observing Oedipal interdictions) and the sensuality (defying them) of Pierre's relationship with Xavière.

It is at this mid-point in the text that Françoise, if she is to be read as the archetypal jealous woman, will manifest that jealousy. Before examining the text closely, it should be noted that the text has made it clear that Pierre has had a series of affairs (comparisons can be made with Sartre here) but that none of these seems to have caused Françoise any anguish. The reader must therefore ask what is special about Xavière. After all, on several occasions Pierre offers to end his relationship with Xavière. At a banal level, Françoise is never in danger of 'losing' him.

When Pierre declares that he and Xavière love each other, Françoise is deeply upset because of the threat he poses to Françoise's relationship with Xavière. 'She [Françoise] was not jealous of him, but not without a fight would she lose this little sleek, golden girl whom she had adopted one chilly morning' (p.201: p.252). Later, when Pierre and Françoise are alone, Pierre recounts the end of his successful evening with Xavière and again we have Françoise's reactions: 'The picture seared Françoise like a burn. Xavière – her black suit, her plaid blouse and her white neck; Xavière – supple and warm in Pierre's arms, her eyes half closed, her mouth proffered. Never would she see that face' (p.207: p.258). This is a textual reversal. Previously it was Pierre who was prohibited from physical contact and who now enjoys it. The interdiction has fallen on Françoise: 'She would never see that face.' Françoise's disarray is compounded by the thought that

'Pierre, with his caressing masculine hands, would turn this black pearl, this austere angel, into a rapturous woman'. And further, Françoise adds, ' "It always seems a sacrilege to me . . . to think of Xavière as a sexual woman" ' (p.208: p.260). Is this the jealousy of the mother who recognises but would seek to deny the sexual maturity of her daughter? Or does it indicate another difficulty – that of Xavière as a desiring woman with whom Françoise could have a sexual relationship?

Pierre's visit to Françoise (who is in hospital) is followed by one from Xavière. In a moment of sublime textual ambiguity Françoise looks at Xavière, the woman Pierre loves, 'avec des yeux d'amoureuse' (p.210: p.263). The ambiguity turns on the word 'amoureuse' – Françoise in love, but with whom? Pierre tries to reassure Françoise that Xavière loves her as much as him. And yet, for Françoise, her relationship with Xavière is submerged, devalued by Xavière's (heterosexual) relationship with Pierre who 'deliberately behaved as if this feminine relationship seemed unimportant to him' (p.238: p.300).

Later, when Françoise is well again, she goes walking with Xavière in Paris. Xavière takes the initiative, making a point of taking Françoise's arm in hers. As they enter a 'bal colonial', a sort of night club, they see a group of friends: 'she [Xavière] had not let go of Françoise's arm, for she did not dislike having people take them for a couple when they entered a place: it was the kind of provocation that gave her amusement' (pp.245–6: p.309). The two women dance, Xavière authoritatively taking Françoise in her arms:

> She felt Xavière's beautiful warm breasts against her, she inhaled her sweet breath. Was this desire? But what did she desire? Her lips against hers? Her body surrendered in her arms? She could think of nothing. It was only a confused need to keep for ever this lover's face turned towards hers, and to be able to say with passion: 'She is mine.'
>
> (p.246: p.310)

Françoise adopts a masculine, possessive attitude towards Xavière, displaying the features of 'amour captatif' described by Toril Moi in her article on jealousy and sexual difference. The characteristics of this type of love, which Moi takes from the work of Daniel Lagache, are a desire 'to possess the object totally and exclusively'; the 'loved object is seen as a thing; not as an independent conscious-ness: the possessive lover refuses to acknowledge the alterity of the Other, of the beloved.' Moi goes on: 'For Lagache, jealousy can only exist within the limits of the *amour captatif*, and therefore the death of the beloved is the extreme but logical outcome of this kind of love'.[9] The implication is that this type of love is typically masculine.

Françoise and Xavière leave the night club, and as they get into a taxi, Françoise feels convinced that she has 'repossessed' Xavière. Back at their hotel, Françoise goes into Xavière's room. But her composure is threatened, she is unable to act: 'paralysed by the frightening grace of this beautiful body that she could not even desire, Françoise was at a loss for a gesture' (p.251: pp.315–16).[10] Awkward moments follow and just as she is about to leave, Françoise takes Xavière in her arms, 'Xavière yielded, and for a moment she was light and taut against her shoulder. What was she waiting for?' (p.251: p.316).[11] But Françoise cannot handle her desire. At the very moment she becomes aware of it, it is blocked by a mental and physical paralysis.

The case of Gerbert and his relationship with Françoise provides further evidence of Françoise's masculinity and, to a certain extent, places a question mark over Gerbert's own sexual identity. I have already pointed out that Gerbert occupies a structurally homologous position to that of Xavière in relation to Pierre and Françoise – another Oedipal triangle. At the beginning of the narrative Gerbert is not only childlike for Françoise he is also feminised, with his long girlish eyelashes and his childlike eyelids (p.8: p.20). In Part II, Chapter 3, written from Gerbert's point of view, we learn that he finds women boring, 'if he had had the good fortune to be a homosexual, he would have associated only with men' (p.269: p.337). Towards the end of the novel, when Gerbert and Françoise are on a walking holiday, he declares that he will never love a woman (p.366: p.451). He repeats his distaste for the company of women, a category from which, significantly, Françoise is excluded. ' "You're like a man!" ' he tells her (p.366: p.452). Françoise finds herself in some difficulty at this stage. She wants to sleep with Gerbert but, given the air of masculine camaraderie that has been established between them (' "I know you think of me as a man," ' says Françoise: (p.372: p.459), she is unable to deploy what she considers to be feminine strategies. There are other impediments. The text emphasises Gerbert's respect (filial love?) for Pierre. 'He was thinking of Pierre. He was thinking that it was impossible to be fonder of anyone than he was of Pierre' (pp.367–8: p.453). Gerbert hesitates also because he does not want to occupy the same position in Françoise's life as that of the 'other women' in Pierre's life. Gerbert here places himself in a feminine position in relation to Françoise – *he* does not want to be *her* 'bit on the side'. Eventually all these difficulties are overcome and Françoise and Gerbert do make love. It is notable, however, that in order to do so they have to leave the city for the hills, a natural rather than a man-made (cultural) environment.

If we read *L'Invitée* as a family romance, the text stages the Oedipal scenario in its positive (heterosexual) form: the son (Gerbert) sleeps with the mother (Françoise), and the father (Pierre) comes close to sleeping with the daughter (Xavière). While this scenario breaks the incest taboo, the heterosexual injunction remains intact. Thus what remains as a stumbling-block, unresolved, is the question of female homosexuality, the Oedipus complex in its negative form, love for the parent of the same sex (in this case, between mother and daughter). That relationship is present in the form of an absence when Françoise considers the trio: 'She looked at Xavière, then at Pierre – she loved them, they loved each other, they loved her' (p.229: p.289). What is missing here is that Françoise and Xavière loved each other.

Pierre and Françoise are inscribed within the phallic economy. They are both masculine. The fantasy of unity, the 'we are as one', that initially characterises their arid liaison belongs within the Imaginary. It is a fiction which is shown, ultimately, as just that. Pierre's 'Don Juanism' is a symptom of his entrapment in the Imaginary as he goes from conquest to conquest in his search for the self in the other.[12] But the drama centres on Françoise. She is problematically inscribed on the side of the masculine because, as a woman who desires another woman, she faces an interdiction on homosexuality. (A similar interdiction fell on Dora in Freud's case-history, 'Dora'.) The Hegelian problematic, Françoise's 'either/or', 'her or me' oppositional attitude towards Xavière, is both phallocentric and Imaginary. Within that problematic, Xavière's murder is a dead end since the text proposes no transcendence of the appositional relation. As Anthony Wilden puts it:

> If one interprets the Imaginary relationship as a Hegelian struggle for recognition, as Lacan does, then one understands that the 'struggle for pure prestige' in the Imaginary cannot depend on any kind of real death. It is in effect dependent on an implicit or unconscious pact between the participants: that they shall both survive, for one cannot be recognized alone. The dialectic must depend therefore on IMAGINED DEATH.[13]

The radical and political importance of the text is that, in Xavière, it represents a dynamic and subversive femininity which exceeds all masculine efforts at containment and control. It is so threatening that it must, ultimately, be eradicated, killed off. It is thus no accident that the first title of the novel was 'Légitime défense', suggesting that Xavière's murder was the justifiable and legitimate act of the forces of law and order – a fatal phallic backlash.

Notes

1 Each quotation from *She Came to Stay* is followed in the text by two references: the first is to the English translation, *She Came to Stay*, London, Fontana, 1975; the second is to the French text, *L'Invitée*, Paris, Gallimard, 1943.
2 The published translation gives 'unadulterated' for the French 'cru': 'raw' would be preferable as it is closer to the French and not value-laden.
3 Since the concepts of the Imaginary and the Symbolic recur throughout this study, I have tried, at the risk of crude simplification, to offer some notes which may help the reader.

   The Imaginary, as the name suggests, is concerned with ideal and therefore pleasurable images of the self. Such images are not a true reflection of the self, they are fictive. This means that in our relations with other people we may see only what we want to see, i.e. *resemblance*, For example, I might say, in relation to another person, 'Yes, that's me. I'm like that!' This is also the domain of the double, the *doppelgänger*. Something similar occurs in the case of advertising images. I may identify with a flattering representation and, as a consequence, buy the perfume, clothes, newspaper or whatever, presented as integral to the image.

In the Symbolic, the two-way short-circuit between self and other is broken. In the Symbolic, I have to recognise that other people are different and that in my relations with them I am in some way divided from myself, certainly *not* together!, positioned 'out there' in a variety of ways (as 'she', 'you', part of 'we', or 'they'). It is because of this split that I have to say that as far as intersubjectivity is concerned, 'I am not myself – I am another'.

The following notes relate more closely to Lacanian psychoanalysis:

The mirror phase (the Imaginary register) opens up a first and *necessary* division between self and other. It is an enclosed, two-way *immediate* relation which involves a blurring or merging of self and other. (An example of this would be the situation in which child (a) on seeing child (b) being hit would state that it is she/he, child (a), that is being struck.)

The Symbolic is a three-way, *mediated* relation. During Oedipus and its resolution, the dual relation of the Imaginary is broken by the intervention of a third term, the Law of the Father (threat of castration/absence/loss/death). Entry into the Symbolic order, into language, involves the loss of Imaginary plenitude (of the 'Yes, that's me, together, all there!' variety). I am not fully present in language, I am only represented there. The subject as split is dramatised in the utterance 'I am lying'. At first, there seems to be a single homogeneous subject present. However, on closer examination we realise that there must be two subjects, two 'I's: one of which is lying and one of which is not. (The terms used to designate these two 'I's are the 'I' of the statement ('énoncé') and the 'I' of the utterance (énonciation). Finally, it is at the moment of entry into the Symbolic, out of that necessary splitting, that the unconscious and desire (for lost Imaginary plenitude) are produced. There is no desire in the Imaginary.

For further elaboration of these points see the chapter on psychoanalysis in T. Eagleton, *Literary Theory: An Introduction*, Oxford, Blackwell, 1983 and C. Belsey, *Critical Practice*, London, Methuen, 1980, Chapters 3 and 4.

4 The published translation is weak here: the original text insists on the fact that the *effect* of the performance is totally independent of an understanding of the meaning of words. Further, the original speaks of a 'visceral' reaction to the performance (i.e. of the body) rather than its being just 'deeply moving'.

5 'Half-wit' (so pejorative) should be translated 'madwoman' (we know something of her history).

6 The published translation does not adequately represent the words of the original, which suggest fluidity. I cannot see any justification for the use of 'occult' in the penultimate sentence. The French uses 'impénétrable' which is of course the same in English. This is important, for surely impenetrability is a feminine/feminist response.

7 For the same reason as that given above, 'madwoman' would be preferable to 'lunatic' (line 6). The translation gives 'pleasure' for the original 'jouissance', which is surely to diminish Xavière's experience.

8 Quoted in S. Leclaire, 'Sexuality: A Fact of Discourse', in *Homosexualities and French Literature*, ed. G. Stambolian and E. Marks, Ithaca and London, Cornell University Press, 1979, p.167.

9 T. Moi, 'Jealousy and Sexual Difference', *Feminist Review*, June 1982, p.64.

10 The words 'could not' do not convey the force of 'ne savait même pas', which suggests that Françoise *did not know how to* proceed.

11 'Taut' is incorrect. The original word is 'souple' which suggests pliancy. Also the French has 'immobile', 'motionless', where the published translation has 'light'.

12 See A.Wilden, *Speech and Language in Psychoanalysis*, Baltimore, Johns Hopkins University Press, 1981, p.165.

13 A. Wilden, *System and Structure*, London, Tavistock, 1980, pp.468–9.

MYTHICAL DISCOURSE IN 'THE WOMAN DESTROYED'

Anne Ophir

In the introduction to her 1976 study of the way in which women writers portray contemporary French society, and the role of women within it, Anne Ophir writes that she would have found it inconceivable to use the fiction of anyone other than Simone de Beauvoir as her starting point.[1] Interested by the role of men as well as women in contemporary France, conscious of a crisis in relations between the sexes, Ophir is struck by the fear which *The Second Sex* had aroused in those men and women who find safety in fixed gender roles, and sets out to explore fictional responses to these issues which go beyond such fixities. Reading the three short stories which Beauvoir published in 1967 under the collective title of *The Woman Destroyed* alongside novels by Christiane Rochefort and Claire Etcherelli written in the same period, Ophir thus focuses on questions of gender and language within a tightly prescribed historical framework.[2]

   The piece which follows is taken from her reading of the fictional diary which forms the title story of Beauvoir's collection, 'The Woman Destroyed'. Opening with the question 'Who is Maurice?', Ophir's project here is to draw out from Monique's first-person account of the breakdown of her marriage the shadowy figure of the husband. Can Maurice be fitted into the stereotype of the faithless husband, tiring of his wife when she has brought up the children and trading her in for a younger model? Or perhaps husband and wife are both victims of an unsustainable social discourse on marriage? Examining such discourses, deploying an irony and verve which spring from a deliberate decision to avoid conservative academic language, Ophir focuses minutely on Monique's own use of mythical language and the ways in which she uses writing to create a protective shell against reality. This aspect of Ophir's analysis coincides with the emphasis which Beauvoir places on Monique's bad faith in her preface to Ophir's book; however, Beauvoir goes on to underline the way in which Ophir also draws attention to a social context established in the narrative of which Beauvoir herself was barely conscious.[3]

Notes

1 A. Ophir, *Regards féminins. Condition féminine et création littéraire*, Paris, Denoël, 1976, p.9. The extract which follows here is taken from *Regards féminins*, pp.77–87, translated by Elizabeth Fallaize.
2 The texts in question are Claire Etcherelli, *Elise ou la vraie vie*, Paris, Denoël, 1967 and C. Rochefort, *Les Stances à Sophie*, Paris, Grasset, 1963. Beauvoir praised this first novel by Etcherelli warmly and the latter subsequently became a collaborator with Beauvoir on *Les Temps modernes*.
3 'Anne Ophir shows that consumer society, which I explicitly evoke in *Les Belles Images*, is also the implicit context in which each of my three stories take place'. S. de Beauvoir in A. Ophir, *Regards féminins*, p.12.

Who exactly is Maurice? Monique questions her close friends, questions herself. And, on the basis of her diary, what do we, the readers, think? That Maurice and Monique walked blindly into the trap of a concept of marriage elaborated by a male-run society, against the interests of human beings and, therefore, also against the interests of men. For Maurice is not happy. As a male he has all the rights, he claims them, but he does not really benefit from them. He played society's game – he thought it natural that his wife should sacrifice herself – let him play it to the end! He *must* pay attention to his faithful wife, perfect house-wife and attentive mother. Who is 'castrating'? Monique? Society? His brilliant and demanding Mistress? (She is part status symbol: the successful doctor leaves the humble nurse for a fashionable female lawyer – no doubt he changed his car as well ...). A couple in which each partner is both victim and persecutor; a couple for whom only petty revenge is left, followed by complete indifference?

Maurice stayed silent for years. Why? To protect his wife? An easy excuse, perhaps. But what if he is telling the truth? What if he feels the remains of real affection for her, the embers of the passion of their youth? A self-centred affec-tion, offering security? After the discussions which she has with her friends, Monique eventually recognises her 'worst mistake': she had failed to understand that 'time goes by', she had remained 'set in the attitude of the ideal wife of an ideal husband' (p.183).[1] As she had 'stopped time' (p.184), she had not been able to cope with changing reality. 'Is there still time?' (p.184) she asks herself.

At the end of December, Maurice takes her to the Club 46 again. The time for speech is over. This second outing to the Club 46 marks an irrevocable passage from speech to sight. All the couples look to Monique like expensive, mechanical dolls, going through their well-regulated paces at the distance where they have been set down.

All those couples ... The women, well-dressed, bejewelled, perfectly coiffed and made up, all laughing and showing their teeth tended by

excellent dentists. The men lit their cigarettes for them, poured them
out champagne . . .

(p.189, TA)

The eyes slide over the surface of an advertising image. The figures perceived are
arrayed for a celebration and yet their appearance has something of the phantas-
magorical about it. Are there living beings, flesh and blood, behind the moving
images? They resemble mortuary masks, Egyptian mummies. The death's heads
laugh, all their teeth showing. Is Monique watching a Dance of Death? She sees
docile women, expensive dolls, barely animate, serving as a backdrop to Man, for
there is only one man. (Monique sees only one Man.) And the man is the only
active being, but his actions consist of gestures which are offerings made to the
doll idols. The man is not really active, he is not in his usual habitat. Gallant
gestures, insignificant offerings made to nebulous idols whom he likes to regard
as frivolous. Curls of smoke rising in blue spirals, golden champagne bubbles
turning pretty heads. The camera's eye: insubstantial, inconsistent, random.
Nothing solid or necessary. The fleeting vision of a magic lantern. The camera's
eye or the projector?

> Other years it had seemed to me that the bond which joined each
> woman to *her* particular man, each man to *his* particular woman was
> positively tangible. I believed in their unions, because I believed in
> ours. Now what I saw was individuals set down by chance opposite one
> another. I felt like shouting 'It's all fake, it's all play-acting, it's all a
> farce – drinking champagne together does not mean taking
> communion'.

(p.189, TA)

The admission of an irredeemable failure? Monique has certainly become
strangely lucid. But is she being entirely honest, has she completely left behind
her mythical mode of discourse? She notes that she and Maurice are 'strangers',
that there is no communication between them. Has she *finally* established the
causal chain corresponding to the reality of human relations? (She and Maurice
have become strangers because they have not been able to maintain a real dialogue.) This is not exactly what Monique sees. She projects the failure of *their*
couple on to *all* the couples. Her generalisation becomes a universal affirmation:
'It's all fake'. The wearily familiar mechanism of inversion comes into play, 'all or
nothing'. Monique does not simply generalise on the basis of her relationship but
also on the temporal level. She prejudges the lives of the couples, as if the partners in all the couples spent their lives drinking champagne together. However,
this particular generalisation is useful in revealing something that Monique herself will shortly be able to formulate. She recognises here that there has been no
communication between herself and Maurice because she has wanted to live her
life with him as a series of exceptional moments, each held out to her as easily as

185

the glass of champagne so freely offered? Now, she no longer lays claim to gifts which are always exceptional and always considered to be her due. Monique is willing to compromise, declares herself ready to make a sacrifice, and the couple now again seems to her to be possible:

> I ought not to be delighted at Maurice's good temper: the real reason for it is that he is going away for ten days with Noëllie. But if at the cost of a sacrifice I rediscover his affection and cheerfulness . . ., why then I gain by it. We were a couple once again when we arrived at Isabelle's. Other couples, more or less limping, more or less patched up, but together nevertheless, surrounded us.
>
> (p.190, TA)

Monique no longer lays claim to a champagne existence. Now she sees what lies between the toasts. This is less of a welcome development than an attempt at adapting to reality, and a limited attempt at that. As events progress, Monique allows reality to break through in strict proportion to the benefits it brings her. A sadly narrow calculation which tolerates Maurice's pleasure weighed up against her own lack of suffering. An attitude of resignation and 'fair's fair', with no reciprocal element. Not drinking champagne together does not mean communion either. The word communion has never been learned and put into practice – it does not exist. In its place is Monique's elusive, disembodying mirror gaze, aloof, separating, creating gulfs, making what it observes unrecognisable. Monique begins talking about the Salines de Ledoux:

> They listened to me and asked me questions, but suddenly I wondered whether it did not look as though I were imitating Noëllie, trying to shine as she does, and whether Maurice would not think me ridiculous again. He seemed rather tense.
>
> (p.190)

Where is the real self? And where the appearance? A woman friend tries to reassure Monique: 'What you said was interesting!' The description of an abandoned town is undermined by an ulterior motive. In Maurice's presence even a narrative addressed to third parties is no longer possible. Or is Monique imagining things? Ulterior motives destroy ordinary speech. Friendly interchange is really no longer possible between Maurice and Monique. Each word is a weapon, a trap, a source of pain.

Maurice goes away with his mistress, Monique shuts herself up in their flat. Like Murielle, she cuts herself off from the world: no visits, no telephone conversations, except the calls from Maurice in which she recounts imaginary outings. No dialogue. Only writing remains, reduced to the function of 'occupation'. Monique prefers it to knitting – which no longer offers her protection – because it allows her to escape from the endless round of her thoughts.

'If I write, it fills up my time, it lets me escape' (p.192). Words written down, non-thought, non-communication. Useless words?

For a fortnight Monique writes nothing, because she has re-read her diary: 'I saw that words say nothing. Rage, nightmares, horror, words cannot encompass them' (p.194). On top of this, the pages she re-reads are full of lies and errors. Every line calls for 'a correction or a denial' (p.194). Monique is not used to handling words on a daily basis – twenty years of mythical discourse paralyse and deform expression – just as she is not used to seeking out reality day by day. Her criticism of the pages she has re-read shows that she is still seeking an atemporal truth. The notion of change is so alien to her way of thinking that she cannot even conceive that a 'truth of the now' might exist. Something she once thought was true turns out to be false? She must have been deceiving herself (Monique has certainly deceived herself frequently, but surely not always). All or nothing, truth or lies, affirmation or negation. Words do not relate to objects, objects escape words. Words which are definitively useless? Why does Monique start keeping a diary?

> The reason why I began to keep it, at Les Salines, was not that I had suddenly recovered my youth nor that I wanted to fill my loneliness with people, but because I had to exorcise a certain anxiety that would not admit its own existence.
>
> (p.194)

Words were intended to protect her against a troublesome reality. Why does knitting no longer suffice? Is it not because a twenty-year silence, hidden beneath a carapace of empty formulae, has become impossible since the house has become empty, just as the role of wife-and-mother has become empty? The role and mythical discourse had provided Monique with a precise contour. Deprived of her shell, Monique is barely conscious of her own existence as nothing separates the external void from her internal void:

> I have taken to my pen again not to go back over the same ground but because the emptiness within me, around me, is so vast that this movement of my hand is necessary to tell myself that I am still alive.
>
> (p.194)

Is writing thus no more than an ersatz, a substitute safeguarding her against anxiety? Perhaps so, but why has Monique never managed to go beyond the stage of writing as a defence? What has prevented her from going on from a utilitarian practice to a kind of writing which would be at least more intimate, if not more liberating? In her diary there is no trace of pleasure in playing with words, no sign of satisfaction in an intimate activity. Monique writes to escape and to protect herself, as we know, but why does she not go on? When she begins to keep her diary, she speaks of 'happiness' and 'freedom': 'I began writing just for myself, as I did when I was twenty' (p.105). At the beginning, Monique does not see her diary as a quest for lost time (since she denies the passage of time), nor as a depository of events which might slip from her memory (again for the same reason), nor as a space for investigating the present, or at least taking stock (her mythical affirmation of the couple excludes problems with a temporal dimension). If she becomes aware of a possible danger, she literally changes the subject by creating a specious causal link.

Writing is, from the beginning, a defence, a talisman. This function is accentu-ated after Maurice's confession. Monique writes to fight for her survival. How then would she write for pleasure? She could emphasise reality negatively – her diary would then have an emetic, cathartic function. She could equally try to disaggregate the ambiguous stuff of daily life in order to analyse, if possible, its various elements, understand where her errors lay and try to do better. She could also select particular elements and deliberately rearrange them in a way not corresponding to the reality experienced, thus creating if not a work of art, at least an imaginary universe.

Monique's diary has some of the features of each of the three modes described above, but they are employed to a particular end: the affirmation that the desired reality is indeed reality itself. Penelope would have waited as long and faithfully for Ulysses in order to demonstrate to him the joys of homecoming. But the Ulysses of this world are cunning people. They are suspicious of the return of the prodigal child routine. What if Penelope had poisoned the exquisite dishes she serves him? Ulysses is suspicious, especially as his conscience is not clear. After all, Penelope has probably grown old and bitter. Better not to go home at all. Penelope, meanwhile, has been thinking. Nothing has disturbed her thoughts over the long years of solitude. Weaving-knitting-writing has kept her hands busy, and occupied her thoughts, her moods. Thoughtfully she looks at her hands. Threads can make nets. No! She will not lower herself to fishing of that kind. And in any case, her irreproachable past has earned her the right to this return. She continues weaving-knitting-writing. Above all, she writes. The magical power of words. Penelope dreams of remodelling the real. Isn't her handiwork real – isn't it reality? The three Fates turn up. She cuts off threads but gets more of them crossed. 'You should have . . . ' 'Why haven't you . . .?' Penelope becomes irritated, she suspects the Fates of wanting to trap her in the entangled threads. What have they done to her lovely handiwork? That of course is when Ulysses comes home. The general air of chaos and Penelope's white hair give him an excuse to pick up his bags. Penelope tries to hold out her arms to him, the threads prevent her, she falls and the door has already slammed shut behind Ulysses. Penelope lies stretched out on the kitchen floor, then painfully gets back on her feet. Rage and the survival instinct have brought her back to life.

As Penelope-Monique is clearing up one day, she finds some old threads, forgotten letters:

I re-read them, and the feeling of uneasiness is still with me. The early letters are in tune with Maurice's, eager, loving and happy. Later they give an odd sort of a ring, vaguely whining, almost querulous. I assert with altogether too much rapture that we love one another as we did the first day; I insist upon his assuring me of this; I ask questions that call for given replies – how can I have been satisfied by them, knowing I had wrenched them out of him? But I did not realize. I forgot. I have forgotten a great deal.

(p.196)

In her boredom, Penelope-Monique dreams up demands which exasperate Ulysses-Maurice. Boredom atrophies intelligence and memory. The woman forgets. The man encourages her to forget.

What was that letter he sent me and I tell him I burnt it after our talk on the telephone? I can only remember it vaguely: I was at Mougins with the children; he was finishing his preparation for an examination; I reproached him for not writing often enough; he answered roughly. Very roughly. Distraught, I sprang to the telephone; he said he was sorry, he begged me to burn his letter. Are there other occurrences that I have buried?

(p.196)

The man encourages her to forget, because it is also in his interests that their life continues. What life? Their conjugal life, of course, a life of one little burial after another. Monique and Maurice will, however, separate before the final burial. They have no home left. They both know this perfectly well. But they do not separate 'amicably'.

Husband and wife are separated most of the time. Monique eventually agrees to see a 'specialist', of whom she is suspicious from the start. He advises her to start writing her diary again. 'I see the gimmick perfectly well – he is trying to give me back an interest in myself, to reconstruct an identity for me' (p.208). Yet she obeys him. She takes a job which consists of combing through the back numbers of medical magazines for some man. Maurice could not have chosen better. . . .

'Ergotherapy – what a joke!' (p.210, TA). When the two are at home in their flat at the same time, each withdraws to their own corner. Monique spends most of her time going round in circles, full of dark thoughts, poisoned by suspicion of everyone who tries to approach her. The atmosphere is made worse when she sinks into alcoholism and neglects her body. Does she want Maurice to feel sorry for her? Or does she want to create revenge – Ah! You're leaving me for an elegantly presented beauty! At least you'll be leaving me on good grounds! Monique has often claimed to be 'manoeuvred' yet she herself excels at blocking Maurice into corners, pushing him into saying or doing something which she fears, but which she can reproach him for afterwards.

The atmosphere is heavy with unspoken calculations and suspicion. Like Murielle, Monique now considers others as 'they': 'What's happening? What do they know? They are not the same with me any more. . . . What are the words they have on the tip of their tongue, and that they do not bring out?' (pp.200–1).

Maurice has taken a flat. Monique takes a plane to go and seek out the truth elsewhere. She gets the truth, from her daughter, an unwilling pythoness. 'I shall force her to explain everything to me. I shall know why I have been condemned' (p.213). Her daughter tries to play down the failure of the couple: 'after fifteen years of marriage it is perfectly natural that people stop loving each other' (p.214, TA). Monique interrupts and commands that Lucienne stops answering her 'with generalities, like everybody else' (p.214). Monique has not crossed the ocean to listen to banalities. She doesn't want statistics – her story is unique. Her daughter, who seems to have worked hard to turn herself into the exact opposite of her mother, tries to combat as neutrally as possible the picture book image of 'marriages that last'. Placing all your bets on a happy marriage is a sort of tombola. If you want to play, you have to accept the risk of losing! Monique does not appreciate the game. She isn't a good player. She insists that this game, the only one she plays, occupy her partner fully. If he wearies of it, she accuses him of breaking the rules he himself set up (the famous promise!).

A lack of imagination? Monique only displays imagination once . . . in starting to play. Since then, she has never stopped playing the same hand. It has become her life, reality itself. Everything else – other people's reality – is a puerile game. If other people tire of the endless game, Monique is thrown. She can't understand, can't 'disentangle the true from the false' (p.163). In a moment of euphoria, 'true and false merged in an iridescence of converging shades' (p.180). Monique's game, other people's reality fuse into a glistening liquid mass. 'Fundamentally, nothing had happened. I ended up by believing that Noellie did not exist. . . . Illusions, sleight of hand' (p.180). A magical confusion of the imaginary and the real which will henceforth be impossible. The others have brutally redrawn the lines. This re-establishment of clear limits acts like a bruising boundary which Monique constantly runs up against. For Monique is now pure palpitating flesh, cut to the quick, a sort of mollusc deprived of its protective shell. In putting the imaginary and the real back where they belong, the others have taken away all Monique's previous means of existence. Even the external reference points are disappearing. Now the process of confusion is terrifying; not just the true and the false but Monique herself is drowning.

> 'How do you see yourself?'
> 'As a marshland. Everything is buried in the mud.'
> 'You'll find yourself again.'
> No: and perhaps that is the worst side of it all. . . . I no longer know anything. Not only do I not know what kind of a person I am but also I do not know what kind of a person I ought to be.
>
> (pp.218–19)

Monique is only too aware that she has become a species of amorphous larva, lost in a magmatic universe. She also knows why she turned into one. She has lived her life as an inessential being, entirely dependent on Maurice for providing a protective shell and radar direction. Does she recognise this? Yes and no, since she gives her 'explanation' a particular connotation. She does not say: I have behaved like a dependent being while using Maurice like a hermit crab uses the shell of another animal. Monique presents things in a different way. Here is the passage deliberately omitted from the previous quotation:

> It is only now that I realize how much I valued myself, fundamentally. But Maurice has murdered all the words by which I might try to justify that valuation: he has repudiated the standards by which I measured others and myself. I had never dreamt of challenging them – that is to say, of challenging myself. And now what I wonder is this: why on earth prefer the inner life to the social whirl, contemplation to trifling amusements, self-sacrifice to ambition? My only ambition was to create happiness around me. I have not made Maurice happy. And my daughters are not happy either. So what then? I no longer know anything.
>
> (pp.218–19, TA)

Maurice is obviously the main guilty party. . . (far be it from us to want to relieve Maurice of blame, Maurice is merely a man). Monique does not explicitly accuse Maurice of having murdered her. In taking back his individuality, in refusing to remain an object, Maurice has apparently shown himself to be ungrateful towards the woman whose only ambition was to 'create happiness'. In a nutshell, the whole failure is made to result from Maurice's obstinate and ungrateful refusal to allow himself to be made happy. Monique is unhappy, lost, but innocent. Maurice has disowned her, the sole embodiment of true values (inner life/contemplation/self-sacrifice) in favour of the Other, her negative opposite (social whirl/trifling amusements/ambition). In short, Monique has been obliged by force of circumstance to recognise failure, but she has not really let go. Despite her doubts she continues to play her hand, even if the game is lost, as if it were the only reality. Her question 'Why on earth . . .?' is more indicative of a feeling of frustration approaching a 'What's the point' than of a genuine inner conviction. The whole story of Maurice then becomes nothing other than a pernicious game, instigated by the Other, by Satan.

Monique's situation is tragic: she sees the failure clearly but insists on blinding herself to the reasons for it. An encystment caused by twenty years of domestic bliss? What purpose does her new lucidity serve? It increasingly bores those around her and makes her unhappy – more dead than alive. 'A dead woman who still has years to drag out – how many?' (p.219). A dead woman who will live in future in a 'night all round me as dark as ever' (p.219).

Monique returns home to France. 'The window was dark: it will always be dark' (p.220). Monique wishes to be alone. What is the point of being with other people? The era of mythical discourse is over and Monique knows no other language. What would be the point of her daughter, her lacklustre double, staying over? Solitude. Her glance meets the resistance of the surface of objects. The dead woman with the motionless stare is afraid. What is hiding behind the surface-screen? The dead woman freezes. If death is where she is, is life hiding on the other side? Should she remain still? Perhaps she can forget the thing which is stalking her. Make herself an object amongst other objects. Play dead. Life will be taken in. Will not leap on her.

The motionless stare becomes more and more fascinated. By what is behind the screen. A stare hypnotised by the pull of life. Fear. Life is for sharing. Solitude. The desire to call out. How can she bear life? Solitude. Fear.

> And I look at those two doors – Maurice's study, our bedroom. Closed. A closed door: something is watching behind it. It will not open if I do not stir. Do not stir: ever. Stop the flow of time and of life.
>
> But I know that I shall move. The door will open slowly and I shall see what there is behind the door. It is the future. The door to the future will open. Slowly. Unrelentingly. I am on the threshold. There is only this door and what is watching behind it. I am afraid. And I cannot call to anyone for help.
>
> I am afraid.
>
> (p.220)

'Harmony between two individuals is never automatic; it must be worked for continually.'[2]

Notes

1 All page references are to S. de Beauvoir, *The Woman Destroyed*, translated by P. O'Brian, London, Flamingo, 1971.
2 S. de Beauvoir, *The Prime of Life*, translated by Peter Green, Harmondsworth, Penguin, 1986, p.260 (TA).

NARRATIVE STRATEGIES AND SEXUAL POLITICS IN BEAUVOIR'S FICTION

Elizabeth Fallaize

The extract which follows forms the concluding chapter in a study of Beauvoir's five published novels and two collections of short stories entitled *The Novels of Simone de Beauvoir* (1988).[1] Arguing that a focus on theme and content in the critical literature had led to a relative neglect of the formal literary properties of her fiction, and drawing on the theoretical work of narratologist Gérard Genette, the study focuses on Beauvoir's choice of narrative strategies and on the way in which they operate in relation to the sexual politics of her writing. Beauvoir's interest in the American writers of the 1930s – Dos Passos, Hemingway and Faulkner in particular – led her to pay close attention to the problem of narrative voice and perspective, that is to say to the question of who speaks a narrative, and what powers are allocated to the narrator. The principle of subordinating the external narrator's voice (where there is one) to the perceptions of the character(s) is one which Beauvoir adopted throughout her fiction, but there are marked developments in the number of narrative voices deployed, the powers allocated to them, the hierarchy of voices established and the degree of trust or mistrust established between narrator and reader.

The conclusion to the study shows that there is a steady reduction in the plurality of voices employed. Gradually the external narrator fades, the binary narrative device which allows a male and female voice to simultaneously take the narrative stage disappears, and a single fragile first-person female voice emerges. As this voice comes to the fore, the authority previously allotted to the narrative voice comes into question: her discourse becomes a web of mystifications and the role of the reader becomes that of the detective tracking down the criminal woman speaker.

The association thus created between women, madness and discourse is argued to reflect Beauvoir's own anxieties about her right to speak – and, more importantly, write – as a woman. Interesting parallels can be seen to operate between this view, arrived at via an analysis of formal structures, and that of Jane Heath, who discusses Beauvoir's alignment with the masculine from a quite different theoretical perspective.

Note

1 The following extract is taken from E. Fallaize, *The Novels of Simone de Beauvoir*, London, Routledge, 1988, pp.175–85.

From the point of view of narrative structure and voice, Beauvoir's fictional narratives fall into a number of distinct groups. *When Things of the Spirit Come First*, the earliest text as far as composition goes and which has an experimental quality, produces the widest range of approaches. Four of the text's five stories are spoken (in total or in part) by an external narrative voice whose stance varies from the overtly judgemental and ironic to the discreetly covert silent. The number of characters acting as narrator or as focus of narration varies between one (as in 'Marcelle'), two (as in 'Chantal') and three (as in 'Anne'). Of the nine characters who play this role, eight are women. Three women accede to a narrative voice: Madame Vignon in her long prayer, Chantal in her diary, Marguerite in her more formal past-tense narrative of her life. The female voice is thus largely dominant, and does at times escape the control of the external narrator – most notably in the case of the positively coded Marguerite.

The story of the rest of Beauvoir's fictional writing is the story of an ever increasing reduction of this plurality of voice, and a loss of the authority conceded to the female voice. In the first published novel, *She Came to Stay*, the external narrator remains as the main voice of the text, but gives up the irony and judgement sometimes exercised in *When Things of the Spirit Come First* to adopt the covert stance which remains the lot of the external narrator throughout both this and the next four texts, before disappearing altogether. Three characters act as focus of narration in *She Came to Stay*, of which two are female and one male. The dominance of the female character noted in *When Things of the Spirit Come First* remains, since Françoise's narrative is by far the most important of the text, and the male character's contribution amounts only to a few pages. No character narrates in the first person, though their 'I' enters the text through the long dialogues and through frequent direct transcription of the characters' thoughts.

In terms of narrative organisation, *She Came to Stay* can be seen as a transitional work, since it begins a refining process of a basic structure which is used with only minor variations in each of the following three novels. In *The Blood of Others, All Men Are Mortal*, and *The Mandarins*, the number of narratives is reduced from three to two; in each novel one of the narratives is voiced by a character-narrator in the first person (Blomart, Fosca and Anne respectively), and one is voiced in the third person by a covert external narrator focusing through a single character (Hélène, Régine and Henri respectively). The strong balance towards the male narrative in *The Blood of Others* and *All Men Are Mortal*, in which the first-person male narrative dominates the text as a whole, becomes an equal balance between male and female in *The Mandarins*, the text in which a female character is entrusted with a first-person narrative for the first time since the early short stories.

A further structural element common to these three novels is the pattern of the argument which they dramatise: the structure of 'preference', in which characters take up an absolute position, then abandon it in the face of its drawbacks before returning to their starting point and re-adopting their initial position in the full knowledge of all its difficulties, is enacted in all three texts. In the first two, *The Blood of Others* and *All Men Are Mortal*, this enactment is carried out by the figure who is also the dominant narrative power in the text, the male character whose narrative is voiced in the first person. To the extent that these characters not only voice their narratives (using the authoritative past historic as well as the more personal perfect tense), but themselves enact the structure of preference and articulate its meaning to the reader, they become figures of considerable power and authority in the text. Reinforcing this authority is the time structure of their narratives; the flashback structure, enclosed in the narrative time of a single night in which the character narrates his life story in order to draw a message from his experience, is an important channel of meaning in the text.

When we come to *The Mandarins*, in which the character who escapes the control of an external narrator and voices the narrative in the first person is a woman, we find that this authority has been removed. Though part of Anne's narrative is narrative of the past, expressed in the past historic tense just as if she shared the status of her predecessors, this narrative of the past is constantly invaded by a present-tense monologue which does not so much narrate events as raise perspectives of suffering and death. The structure of preference is articulated not by character-narrator Anne but by Robert, and is supported not by a flashback structure but by the general invasion of the structure into all the diverse strands of the text.

Despite this loss of authority by the character-narrator in *The Mandarins*, all three of these novels are clearly organised to allow the channelling of meaning either through the character's voice, or through the patterning of themes and events, or through the time structure, or through all three. *The Mandarins*, already a deviant in the pattern with its diminution of the character-narrator's power, closes this structural pattern and a new one emerges in the final two texts, *Les Belles Images* and *The Woman Destroyed*. The most obvious change is again the element of reduction. The thick volumes of the earlier novels are reduced first to the brief narrative of *Les Belles Images*, and then to the short stories of *The Woman Destroyed*. The double narrative of the previous three texts is replaced by a single focus: first that of Laurence of *Les Belles Images*, with her fragmented first-person voice which fades for long stretches of the narrative behind that of the external narrator each time that Laurence retrenches into her social persona.

Then the three women of the short stories, the unnamed woman of 'The Age of Discretion', Murielle of 'Monologue' and Monique of 'The Woman Destroyed', each in turn take the narrative stage with their uninterrupted monologues. The external narrator vanishes. The past historic tense, dominant in all of the other novels, also disappears completely in the final two texts, replaced by the perfect and, above all, by the uncertainties of the present tense. The character-narrators or centres of narrative focus no longer bestow meaning, no longer act as the reader's guide. Instead, they are offered up to us for investigation and, ultimately, disapproval. The reader becomes the detective, the character-narrator the criminal.

Why does the authority of the character-narrator or centre of narrative focus fade in this way? Is there a connection with the fact that this role is increasingly played by women? From *The Mandarins* onwards, where Anne accedes to the first-person voice, power and authority no longer reside automatically in the character-narrator. But what about Françoise of *She Came to Stay*? She imposes meaning, even if she does not have the first-person voice; she achieves a powerful act and interprets it for us. The question then, is not so much is the character-narrator or focus of the narrative a woman but, rather, what kind of woman is she?

Françoise and Hélène, who act as narrative focus in *She Came to Stay* and *The Blood of Others*, are in both cases partly defined by what they are not. Thus Françoise is *not* Elisabeth (negative, failed artist, overwhelmed by her sexuality – Elisabeth). Hélène is *not* Denise (negative, failed writer, victim of breakdown – Denise), though Hélène does inherit the troubled sexuality of the negative woman, and is subjected to an abortion which reveals her body as obscene and grotesque. Anne of *The Mandarins* is a turning point. She has charge of her own narrative (which Françoise and Hélène do not) and uses monologue to express her suffering as well as offering an account of recent events in the past historic. Anne also has a negative double in the suffering Paule who, like Denise, fails when she tries to write and is driven into temporary insanity. But Anne is both not Paule and at the same time *is* like Paule; Anne remains a reliable narrator, using words in a way the reader is expected to trust and not the myth-making language of Paule. But Anne approaches the breakdown which Paule experiences, and comes to the brink of carrying out the suicide which Paule had planned. The character-narrator woman is, in other words, coming more and more to resemble the negative woman, the madwoman who misuses words.

With *Les Belles Images*, the merger is complete. The negative woman with her mythical language emerges in the foreground and invades the narrative. Laurence's use of carbon-copy echoes of the reassuring slogans of her class and her profession is coupled with her breakdowns and her anorexia; all three women of *The Woman Destroyed* elaborate a self-deceiving discourse and are plunged into a crisis of suffering; one is despatched to the psychiatrist and another passes over the line between suffering and paranoia. In both texts, folly and the misuse of words replace the reliable powerful narrator. Power passes to the reader, whose status has been gradually rising whilst that of the character-narrator has been falling. The delusions of the suffering woman, hitherto contained in the failed writing and painting of an Elisabeth, a Denise, a Maria and a Paule, now constitute the narrative. In the last short stories, the function of this narrative for the woman – that is, the creation of a mythical discourse intended to protect the woman from the truth – is clearly the same function as writing held for Paule and Denise. Murielle uses the monologue in place of the book she dreams of writing which would be a complete self-justification. Monique's diary is in a way the complete emblem of everything that these women have wished to do.

How can this connection between women, folly and the abuse of words be accounted for? Why is the monologue form, the use of 'I' by women so consistently linked with suffering and delusions, from Chantal in *When Things of the Spirit Come First* to Murielle of *The Woman Destroyed*? Must women fail when they write – must they be mad to write? It has become almost a routine observation to point to the splitting of the female character so often observable in women's writing. Gilbert and Gubar, noting the dichotomy often set up in the nineteenth-century women's novel between monster woman and angel woman, interpret this splitting process as dramatising the anxiety felt by the woman author about entering through writing what she perceives as a male-dominated domain. Thus, they argue, through the twin faces of the mad and violent Mrs Rochester and the conformist angel-figure Jane Eyre, the woman writer expresses her anxiety about engaging in the subversive activity of writing as a woman, by both embodying her revolt in the madwoman and by punishing it. There is a reductionist tendency in this kind of analysis, especially in the danger of identifying character and author, as Toril Moi has pointed out.[1]

Nevertheless, the point that women writers have to engage with a largely male tradition in writing at all is an important one. When we turn back to Beauvoir's fiction, the evidence that she shared the perception of fiction as a male domain and that she had little sense of connection to a female tradition of writing is unmistakable. We have seen that in the early stages of Beauvoir's writing before she published anything she admired a number of writers who served in different ways as models: Dostoevsky, Hemingway, Dos Passos, Faulkner. All are male. In her autobiographies, Beauvoir draws attention to these influences, creating an implicit context for her own writing. *She Came to Stay*, *The Blood of Others* and 'Monologue' formalise this process a step further by carrying epigraphs from, respectively, Hegel, Dostoevsky and Flaubert, which not only serve to place her texts in a tradition but act, ultimately, as a kind of guarantor for the text, as Gérard Genette suggests.[2] Here we are dealing with writers whom Beauvoir admired, but another manifestation of the desire to situate her work is the way in which her texts sometimes take as reference point writers she did not admire, writers who, precisely, she wished to contest through her own writing. Thus the title of *When Things of the Spirit Come First* is borrowed from Jacques Maritain with ironic intent (as Beauvoir is careful to stress in the French preface to the stories) and the text of *Les Belles Images* parodies Foucault (as well as borrowing in a more positive spirit an image from Alain Badiou's *Almagestes*). Beauvoir stresses all these influences, borrowings and contestations with care. It is plain that she did see writing as a male tradition, and that she sought to place her work within it. Does this imply an anxiety about writing as a woman?

Beauvoir was perfectly well aware of the factors which conspire to stop women writing and discussed them herself both in *The Second Sex* and elsewhere.[3] When writing or speaking about her own fiction, Beauvoir often insisted upon what she calls the 'universal' aspect of fiction – the aspect which, for her, prevents writing from being simply 'anecdotal'. In 'My Experience as a Writer', a lecture given in Japan in 1966, she took the writing of her first novel *She Came to Stay* as an example. The text, she explained, was first and foremost the result of a 'concrete psychological experience' (in other words of the trio she had participated in with Sartre and Olga); but she could not write her novel, she said, until she had 'found a way to pass, from this particular experience to a universal level'. She achieved this when she 'realised that it was the relationship to the consciousness of others which was tormenting me'.[4] Beauvoir then repeats several times with evident satisfaction how pleased she was to have found this 'universal' aspect. Here we have the explanation of Hegel and the whole philosophical superstructure of the text: Beauvoir only felt able – only dared – to dramatise her own experience when she had found a way of making it acceptable to herself as writing. What this actually meant was that she had found in philosophy and in Hegel a way of placing her work in an authorised, male, tradition.

There are other aspects of Beauvoir's fiction which express an anxiety of authorship. Amongst the most evident are the puzzlingly ironic ring of so many of Beauvoir's novel titles (most notably *The Mandarins* and *The Woman Destroyed*), betraying her fear of identifying fully with her works, and the extraordinary eagerness with which she criticises her own work in her autobiographies, as if to ward off the inevitable criticism from others. One might also note her attribution of her own writing in *The Mandarins* to a male character, and the insistence with which Beauvoir constantly attacked the narrowness of the 'housewife' writing which she seemed so anxious to avoid.[5] However, the question should also be posed of whether Beauvoir was not right to fear that if she did not take care to place her work in this specifically male tradition, it would be much more difficult to get it taken seriously. When she changed tack and wrote about women's experience of pain without a philosophical lens in *The Woman Destroyed*, her text was greeted by newspaper critics in France with dismissive glee. The subtleties of the text were overlooked in the rush to condemn this woman writer whose pretensions to a 'universal' writing had been at last unmasked – the comparisons with Françoise Sagan are instructive.

The development – one might almost say the dissolution – of narrative structure in Beauvoir's fiction, and the loss of authority of the narrator-character or character focus of narration, can be seen to be closely associated with the gradual emergence of the figure of the 'negative' madwoman, who moves in stages from the background to the foreground of the texts, eventually taking over the narrative voice completely. The figure of Murielle of *The Woman Destroyed*, with her violent and powerful monologue, heavily marked by folly and by sexuality, is the extreme point of this process. As this woman moves into prominence, so the narrative forms change and dissolve. The tone and form of Anne's monologue is inherited by the later women; even its ending – 'Who knows? Perhaps one day I'll be happy again. Who knows?' (*The Mandarins*, p.763) – is echoed in the final words of Laurence of *Les Belles Images* and the woman of 'The Age of Discretion'.[6] The origin of this association, I have suggested, can be sought in Beauvoir's own attitude to writing as a woman. But we still have to try to account for why this woman and her narrative forms are increasingly allowed to take the stage. One factor that could well be significant is the writing of the autobiographical texts which took place in the long gap in Beauvoir's fictional production, between 1945 and 1966 (between the production of *The Mandarins* and *Les Belles Images*). Writing about her life in this direct way not only allowed Beauvoir to focus on the individual without the same degree of concern for the 'universal' (though she still defended the 'narcissistic' practice of writing about herself in terms of its universal application), but forced her (or permitted her?) to write as a woman. In the autobiographies, she told the audience at one of her Japanese lectures, 'this "I" that I pronounce is the "I" of a woman'.[7] When she returns to fiction writing after the production of *Memoirs of a Dutiful Daughter*, *The Prime of Life*, *Force of Circumstance* and *A Very Easy Death*, with their use of the female 'I', the male narrative voice disappears.

Another factor which has to be considered is that of historical moment, and of Beauvoir's growing awareness of historical context. It is striking that the early self-deceived women characters of *When Things of the Spirit Come First* with their monologues, diaries and special use of words, are, like the women of the last two works of fiction, firmly embedded in a social context. The removal of this context in *She Came to Stay* – where characters seem to float free of family and social context – is clearly connected to the absolute sense of freedom which Beauvoir experienced in the period of her life when she had the feeling of living 'like Kant's dove, supported rather than hindered in flight by the resistant air' (*Prime of Life*, p.15).[8] Having fought free of the bourgeoisie in which she had been brought up, she failed, temporarily, to understand that she had simply exchanged one social status for another. She said in 1966:

> What we don't know has as much weight in a life as what we do know. I mean that for example between 1929 and 1938 I was apolitical; well! if I had to rewrite *The Prime of Life*, I would emphasise this indifference much more; it defines me as a French middle-class intellectual of the era, since most French intellectuals were at that time outside politics.[9]

I have suggested that *She Came to Stay* (written at the end of this apolitical period) can be read as above all an ostrich attempt precisely to avoid any discovery of politics, of the interrelation of the individual and the wider stage of history. However, with the approach of the Second World War came the eventual discovery of the individual's historicity and the elaboration of the structure of persuasion which the structure of preference and the double narrative organisation really is. Introduced for the first time in *The Blood of Others*, written during the German occupation of France, it permitted the inscription of the message of commitment into the structures of the text itself. The same can be said, in differing degrees, of *All Men Are Mortal* and *The Mandarins*, in which the same basic structure operates and in which Beauvoir is still caught up in the impact which the Second World War, and its aftermath in the Cold War, had on both her and her fiction. Of course it remains the case that even in these texts, in which the narrative structures are most strongly pressed into service to articulate a message, this official meaning is subverted or relegated to the sidelines by other elements of the text. The powerful narrators of these texts who articulate the concept of commitment and who are to be trusted by the reader are again curiously free of social constraints. Blomart has to shake off a wealthy background, but this is rapidly achieved – we know very little of the background of the characters of *The Mandarins*, and Fosca is inevitably a completely ahistorical figure. It is only after the 1954–66 gap that there is a return in *Les Belles Images* to a strong emphasis on social class, coupled with a new set of narrative structures.

We have already taken note of the writing of the autobiographies in this gap, but the period was also marked by the impact of the Algerian War on Beauvoir and her direct involvement in political action. 'The horror my class inspires in me has been brought to a white heat by the Algerian War' (*Force of Circumstance*, p.665);[10] the connection between class and history is made with the return of the focus on the sins of those who fail to act (instead of on the dilemmas of those who do act), no doubt also assisted by the greater sympathy for Marxism to which Beauvoir came round in the early 1950s. The Algerian War made the weight exercised on events by those who do not act clear to Beauvoir. The use of Riesman's theories in *Les Belles Images*, the implicit context of the socialisation of women in *The Woman Destroyed*, produce a much greater emphasis on the situation, on the weight of class, gender and upbringing on the individual. The return to the weight of the situation meant a return to the modes by which individuals try to hide from their situations; the creation of comfortable myths and the abuse of language analysed in *When Things of the Spirit Come First*, but pushed into the background in the middle novels, come full circle and return in *Les Belles Images* and *The Woman Destroyed*.

The narrative forms of bad faith (the monologue, the diary and a myth-making use of words) are effectively identified as those of a class as well as of a sex. Monologue, myth, the weight of the bourgeoisie are made to interlock on the one hand; dialogue (the double narrative), a proper use of words and a reliable narrator on the other. Femininity and the bourgeoisie seem here to be wrapped up with each other; the need to confirm her escape from these two forms of 'social character' learned in childhood is a powerful force in Beauvoir's texts, strongly marked in their narrative organisation.

'There are no arrivals anywhere, there are only points of departure,' writes Simone de Beauvoir in *Pyrrhus and Cinéas* (p.288).[11] The identification of narrative structures in a text is only a point of departure. It leads to the posing of new questions about meaning and not its foreclosure. I have tried to suggest relations between narrative structure and voice on the one hand, and Beauvoir's attitude as a woman to writing and to certain of her female characters on the other. I have also tried to look at changes in narrative organisation in terms of the impact which historical events had on Beauvoir's perception of the individual's relation to history, and on the growing weight given in the text to the constraints of gender, class and individual circumstances.

Other points of departure could be made, other links suggested. Beauvoir saw that narrative structure is a powerful means of persuasion at the author's disposal, but it is also a tool which can turn against its creator and allow rival meanings to spring up unbidden. One of the rival meanings which I have drawn attention to is the way in which the use of narrative voice betrays a fear that woman's voice, woman's writing is an abuse of words. In later life, Beauvoir came to admire the novels of Doris Lessing, but her work is situated at the antipodes of Lessing's admonition in *The Golden Notebook:* 'I tell you, there are a great line of women stretching out behind you into the past, and you have to seek them out and find them in yourself and be conscious of them.' Beauvoir sought to place her writing in a masculine intellectual tradition, and to respect the 'extraordinary power of words', but, almost despite herself, the treacherous woman's word creeps to the fore, and makes her writing part of the tradition of 'a literature of our own'.[12]

Notes

1 See S. Gilbert and S. Gubar, *The Madwoman in the Attic: The Woman Writer and the Nineteenth-Century Literary Imagination*, New Haven, Yale University Press, 1979, pp.77–8. T. Moi, *Sexual/Textual Politics. Feminist Literary Theory*, London and New York, Methuen, 1985.

2 In his analysis of the function of the epigraph in *Seuils*, Paris, Editions du Seuil, 1987, Genette describes the epigraph as a 'password of intellectualism' and as an attempt by writers 'to choose their equals, and thus their place in the Pantheon' (p.149).

3 Notably in 'Woman and Creativity', a lecture given in Japan in 1966 of which the French text is given in C. Francis and C. Gontier, *Les Ecrits de Simone de Beauvoir*, Paris, Gallimard, 1979, pp.458–74, and which appears in English in T. Moi's *French Feminist Thought*, Oxford, Blackwell, 1987, pp.17–32.

5 'My Experience as a Writer', in Francis and Gontier, *Les Ecrits*, pp.440–1.

5 Ibid., pp.449–50; and see A. Schwarzer, *Simone de Beauvoir Today*, London, Chatto and Windus, 1984.

6 Beauvoir, *The Mandarins*, translated by L. Friedman, London, Fontana, 1982. Cf. Laurence: 'What chance? She doesn't even know' (*Les Belles Images*, translated by P. O'Brian, London, Fontana, 1983, p.154, TA) and the woman of 'The Age of

Discretion': 'Will that make it bearable for us? Let us hope so. We have no choice in the matter' (*The Woman Destroyed*, translated by P. O'Brian, London, Fontana, 1985, p.71).

7 'My Experience as a Writer', p.450.

8 Beauvoir, *The Prime of Life*, translated by P. Green, Harmondsworth, Penguin, 1986.

9 'My Experience as a Writer', p.452.

10 Beauvoir, *Force of Circumstance*, translated by R. Howard, Harmondsworth, Penguin, 1985.

11 Beauvoir, *Pyrrhus et Cinéas*, Paris, Gallimard, 1944.

12 Quotation from Doris Lessing's *The Golden Notebook* borrowed from Elaine Showalter (p.298), to the title of whose book *A Literature of Their Own* (Princeton, Princeton University Press, 1977) I also refer in my last line.

FURTHER READING

Works of Simone de Beauvoir

The original French edition is given first, followed by the English translation where available.

L'Invitée, Paris, Gallimard, 1943. *She Came to Stay*, translated by Y. Moyse and R. Senhouse, Harmondsworth, Penguin, 1978.

Pyrrhus et Cinéas, Paris, Gallimard, 1944.

Le Sang des autres, Paris, Gallimard, 1945. *The Blood of Others*, translated by Y. Moyse and R. Senhouse, Harmondsworth, Penguin, 1978.

Les Bouches inutiles, Paris, Gallimard, 1945. *Who Shall Die?*, translated by C. Francis and F. Gontier, Florissant, Missouri, River Press, 1983.

Tous les hommes sont mortels, Paris, Gallimard, 1946. *All Men Are Mortal*, translated by L. Friedman, Cleveland, World Publishing, 1955.

Pour une morale de l'ambiguïté, Paris, Gallimard, 1947. *The Ethics of Ambiguity*, translated by B. Fretchman, New York, Citadel Press, 1976.

L'Existentialisme et la sagesse des nations, including 'Idéalisme moral et réalisme politique', 'Littérature et métaphysique' and 'Œil pour œil', Paris, Nagel, 1948.

L'Amérique au jour le jour, Paris, Morihien, 1948. *America Day by Day*, translated by P. Dudley, London, Duckworth, 1952.

Le Deuxième Sexe, 2 vols, Paris, Gallimard, 1949. *The Second Sex*, translated by H. Parshley, Harmondsworth, Penguin, 1986.

Les Mandarins, Paris, Gallimard, 1954. *The Mandarins*, translated by L. Friedman, London, Fontana, 1986.

Privilèges, including 'Faut il brûler Sade?', 'La Pensée de droite aujourd'hui', 'Merleau Ponty et le pseudo-sartrisme', Paris, Gallimard, 1955.

La Longue Marche, Paris, Gallimard, 1957. *The Long March*, translated by A. Wainhouse, London, Deutsch, 1958.

Mémoires d'une jeune fille rangée, Paris, Gallimard, 1958. *Memoirs of a Dutiful Daughter*, translated by James Kirkup, Harmondsworth, Penguin, 1987.

La Force de l'âge, Paris, Gallimard, 1960. *The Prime of Life*, translated by P. Green, Harmondsworth, Penguin, 1986.

Djamile Boupacha, Paris, Gallimard, 1962, with G. Hamili.

Brigitte Bardot and the Lolita Syndrome, translated by B. Fretchman, London, Four Square, 1962 [no published French edition].

La Force des choses, 2 vols, Paris, Gallimard, 1963. *Force of Circumstance*, translated by R. Howard, Harmondsworth, Penguin, 1985.

Une mort très douce, Paris, Gallimard, 1964. *A Very Easy Death*, translated by P. O'Brian, Harmondsworth, Penguin, 1983.

Les Belles Images, Paris, Gallimard, 1966. *Les Belles Images*, translated by P. O'Brian, London, Fontana, 1985.

La Femme rompue, Paris, Gallimard, 1967. *The Woman Destroyed*, translated by P. O'Brian, London, Fontana, 1987.

La Vieillesse, Paris, Gallimard, 1970. *Old Age*, translated by P. O'Brian, Harmondsworth, Penguin, 1986.

Tout compte fait, Paris, Gallimard, 1972. *All Said and Done*, translated by P. O'Brian, Harmondsworth, Penguin, 1987.

Quand prime le spirituel, Paris, Gallimard, 1979. *When Things of the Spirit Come First*, translated by P. O'Brian, London, Fontana, 1986.

La Cérémonie des adieux, Paris, Gallimard, 1981. *Adieux: A Farewell to Sartre*, translated by P. O'Brian, Harmondsworth, Penguin, 1986.

Lettres à Sartre, 2 vols: 1930–39 and 1940–63, Paris, Gallimard, 1990. *Letters to Sartre*, translated by Q. Hoare, New York, Arcade, 1991.

Journal de guerre. Septembre 1939–Janvier 1941, ed. Sylvie Le Bon de Beauvoir, Paris, Gallimard, 1990.

Lettres à Nelson Algren. Un amour transatlantique. 1947–1964, ed. Sylvie Le Bon de Beauvoir, Paris, Gallimard, 1997.

Further critical reading

Al-Hibri, A. and Simons, M., eds, *Hypatia Reborn: Essays in Feminist Philosophy*, Bloomington, Indiana University Press, 1990.

Bair, D., *Simone de Beauvoir. A Biography*, London, Jonathan Cape, 1990.

Barnes, H., 'Simone de Beauvoir's Journal and Letters: A Poisoned Gift?', *Simone de Beauvoir Studies*, 8, pp.13–29, 1991.

—— *The Literature of Possibility: A Study in Humanistic Existentialism*, London, Tavistock, 1961.

Bennett, J. and Hochmann, G., *Simone de Beauvoir. An Annotated Bibliography*, New York and London, Garland, 1988.

Bergoffen, D., *The Philosophy of Simone de Beauvoir: Gendered Phenomenologies, Erotic Generosities*, Albany, NY, SUNY Press, 1996.

Brosman, C., *Simone de Beauvoir Revisited*, Boston, Twayne, 1991.

Butler, J., 'Gendering the Body: Beauvoir's Philosophical Contribution', in *Women, Knowledge and Reality*, ed. A. Garry and M. Pearsall, Boston, Unwin Hyman, 1989, pp.253–62.

Card, C., 'Lesbian Attitudes and *The Second Sex*', *Women's Studies International Forum*, 8, 1985, pp.209–14 (reprinted in Al-Hibri and Simons).

Crosland, M., *Simone de Beauvoir: The Woman and Her Work*, London, Heinemann, 1992.

Dijkstra, S., 'Simone de Beauvoir and Betty Friedan: The Politics of Omission', *Feminist Studies*, 6, 1980, pp.283–90.

Eaubonne, F. de, *Une Femme nommée Castor. Mon amie Simone de Beauvoir*, Paris, Encre, 1986.

Fallaize, E., 'Resisting Romance: Simone de Beauvoir, "The Woman Destroyed" and the Romance Script', in *Contemporary French Fiction by Women. Feminist Perspectives*, ed. M. Atack and P. Powrie, Manchester and New York, Manchester University Press, 1990, pp.15–23.

—— *The Novels of Simone de Beauvoir*, London and New York, Routledge, 1988.

Forster, P. and Sutton, I., eds, *Daughters of de Beauvoir*, London, The Women's Press, 1989.

Francis, C. and Gontier, F., *Les Ecrits de Simone de Beauvoir*, Paris, Gallimard, 1979.

Fullbrook, K. and E., *Beauvoir: A Critical Introduction*, Cambridge, Polity Press, 1998.

—— *Simone de Beauvoir and Jean-Paul Sartre: The Remaking of a Twentieth-Century Legend*, Hemel Hempstead, Harvester Wheatsheaf, 1993.

Heath, J., *Simone de Beauvoir*, Brighton, Harvester, 1989.

Hewitt, L., *Autobiographical Tightropes*, Lincoln, University of Nebraska Press, 1990.

Hughes, A., *Beauvoir: Le Sang des autres*, Glasgow, University of Glasgow French and German Publications, 1995.

Idt, G., 'Simone de Beauvoir's Adieux: A Funeral Rite and a Literary Challenge', in *Sartre Alive*, ed. R. Aronson, Detroit, Wayne State University Press, 1991.

Jardine, A., 'Death Sentences: Writing Couples and Ideology', *Poetics Today*, 6, 1985, pp.119–31 (reprinted in Marks, 1987).

Jeanson, F., *Simone de Beauvoir ou l'entreprise de vivre*, Paris, Seuil, 1966.

Keefe, T., *Beauvoir: Les Belles Images/La Femme rompue*, Glasgow, University of Glasgow French and German Publications, 1991.

—— *Simone de Beauvoir. A Study of her Writings*, London, Harrap, 1983.

Kruks, S., 'Gender and Subjectivity: Simone de Beauvoir and Contemporary Feminism', *Signs*, 18, 1992, pp.89–110.

—— *Situation and Human Existence. Freedom, Subjectivity and Society*, London, Routledge, 1990.

Larsson, B., *La Réception des Mandarins*, Lund, 1988.

Lasocki, A.M., *Simone de Beauvoir ou l'entreprise d'écrire*, The Hague, Nijhoff, 1970.

Le Doeuff, M., *L'Etude et le rouet*, Paris, Seuil, 1989. Translated by T. Selous as *Hipparchia's Choice*, Oxford, Blackwell, 1991.

Lundgren-Gothlin, E., *Sex and Existence. Simone de Beauvoir's 'The Second Sex'*, translated by L. Schenck, London, Athlone, 1996.

McCall, D., 'Simone de Beauvoir, *The Second Sex*, and Jean-Paul Sartre', *Signs*, 5, 1979, pp.209–23.

Marks, E., ed., *Critical Essays on Simone de Beauvoir*, Boston, G.K. Hall, 1987.

—— *Simone de Beauvoir: Encounters with Death*, New Brunswick, Rutgers University Press, 1973.

Moi, T., *Simone de Beauvoir: The Making of an Intellectual Woman*, Oxford, Blackwell, 1994.

—— *Feminist Theory and Simone de Beauvoir*, Oxford, Blackwell, 1990.

—— *French Feminist Thought. A Reader*, Oxford, Blackwell, 1987.

Okely, J., *Simone de Beauvoir. A Re-Reading*, London, Virago, 1986.

Ophir, A., *Regards féminins: Beauvoir, Etcherelli, Rochefort*, Paris, Denoël, 1976.

Patterson, Y., *Simone de Beauvoir and the Demystification of Motherhood*, Ann Arbor, UMI Research Press, 1989.

Pilardi, J., 'Philosophy becomes Autobiography: The Development of the Self in the Writings of Simone de Beauvoir', in *Writing the Politics of Difference*, ed. H. Silverman, Albany, NY, SUNY Press, 1991, pp.145–62.

Roman 20–50, no. 13, 1992. Special issue on Beauvoir's fiction.

Sartre, J.P., *Lettres au Castor et à quelques autres*, ed. S. de Beauvoir, Paris, Gallimard, 1983.

Schwarzer, A., *Simone de Beauvoir Today. Conversations 1972–1982*, London, Chatto and Windus, 1984.

Simons, M., *Feminist Interpretations of Simone de Beauvoir*, University Park, PA, Penn State University Press, 1995.

—— 'Lesbian Connections: Simone de Beauvoir and Feminism', *Signs*, 18, 1992, pp.136–61.

—— The Silencing of Simone de Beauvoir: 'Guess What's Missing from *The Second Sex*', *Women's Studies International Forum*, 6, 1983, pp.559–64.

Tidd, U., *Simone de Beauvoir: Writing the Self, Writing the Life*, Cambridge, Cambridge University Press, forthcoming.

Vintges, K., *Philosophy as Passion*, Bloomington, Indiana University Press, 1996.

Wenzel, H., ed., *Simone de Beauvoir: Witness to a Century*. Special issue of *Yale French Studies* 72, 1986.

Wilson, E., 'Daughters and Desire: Simone de Beauvoir's *Journal de guerre*', in T. Keefe and E. Smythe, eds, *Autobiography and the Existential Self: Studies in Modern French Writing*, Liverpool, Liverpool University Press, 1994, pp.83–98.

INDEX